SEXUALITY AND TRANSSEXUALITY UNDER THE EUROPEAN CONVENTION ON HUMAN RIGHTS

This book undertakes a critical analysis of international human rights law through the lens of queer theory. It pursues two main aims: first, to make use of queer theory to illustrate that the field of human rights law is underpinned by several assumptions that determine a conception of the subject that is gendered and sexual in specific ways. This gives rise to multiple legal and social consequences, some of which challenge the very idea of universality of human rights. Second, the book proposes that human rights law can actually benefit from a better understanding of queer critiques, since queer insights can help it to overcome heteronormative beliefs currently held. In order to achieve these main aims, the book focuses on the case law of the European Court of Human Rights, the leading legal authority in the field of international human rights law. The use of queer theory as the theoretical approach for these tasks serves to deconstruct several aspects of the Court's jurisprudence dealing with gender, sexuality, and kinship, to later suggest potential paths to reconstruct such features in a queer(er) and more universal manner.

Sexuality and Transsexuality under the European Convention on Human Rights

A Queer Reading of Human Rights Law

Damian A Gonzalez-Salzberg

•HART•

OXFORD • LONDON • NEW YORK • NEW DELHI • SYDNEY

HART PUBLISHING

Bloomsbury Publishing Plc

Kemp House, Chawley Park, Cumnor Hill, Oxford, OX2 9PH, UK

HART PUBLISHING, the Hart/Stag logo, BLOOMSBURY and the Diana logo are trademarks of Bloomsbury Publishing Plc

First published in Great Britain 2019

Reprinted 2019

A catalogue record for this book is available from the British Library.

Library of Congress Cataloging-in-Publication data

Names: Salzberg, Damian A. Gonzalez, author.

Title: Sexuality and transsexuality under the European Convention on Human Rights : a queer reading of human rights law / Damian A Gonzalez-Salzberg.

Description: Portland : Hart Publishing, 2019.

Identifiers: LCCN 2018041452 (print) | LCCN 2018041584 (ebook) | ISBN 9781509914944 (Epub) | ISBN 9781509914937 (hardback)

Subjects: LCSH: Sexual rights—Europe. | Sexual minorities—Legal status, laws, etc.—Europe. | Transsexuals—Legal status, laws, etc.—Europe. | Convention for the Protection of Human Rights and Fundamental Freedoms (1950 November 5) | Human rights—Europe. | BISAC: LAW / Gender & the Law.

Classification: LCC KJC5144.G39 (ebook) | LCC KJC5144.G39 S25 2019 (print) | DDC 341.4/83—dc23

LC record available at https://lccn.loc.gov/2018041452

ISBN: HB: 978-1-50991-493-7
ePDF: 978-1-50991-492-0
ePub: 978-1-50991-494-4

Typeset by Compuscript Ltd, Shannon

To find out more about our authors and books visit www.hartpublishing.co.uk. Here you will find extracts, author information, details of forthcoming events and the option to sign up for our newsletters.

To my mum and Chris

CONTENTS

TABLE OF CASES, TREATIES AND LEGISLATION

Cases

European Court of Human Rights

International Treaties

Legislation

Canada

Germany

1

An Introduction to Queer(ing) Human Rights Law

Human rights can be defined as the rights held by all individuals, anywhere they are, for the mere fact of being human.[1] These rights are characterised by their particular aspiration to universality, which is apparent in three different levels: every right, for every person, and everywhere. As affirmed by Amartya Sen, it is certainly a deeply attractive idea that every person anywhere in the world, irrespective of citizenship or territorial legislation, has a number of fundamental rights, which others should respect.[2] This global aspiration allows human rights to act as a common language for victims of injustice to communicate their suffering in universally understandable terms. In fact, human rights have been used in contemporary struggles against oppression, cruelty and violence and can be seen as invaluable tools for improving people's lives.[3] Moreover, existing legal procedures for the redress of human rights violations offer a path for victims to seek a decision that can put an end to the violation and establish certain forms of reparation for their suffering.

Human rights have been proclaimed the only political-moral idea that has received universal acceptance,[4] and have been declared the greatest legal invention of our civilisation.[5] It can even be affirmed that human rights have become

[1] Micheline R Ishay, *The History of Human Rights: from Ancient Times to the Globalization Era* (University of California Press, 2004) 3; Lynn Hunt, *Inventing Human Rights: A History* (Norton and Company Press, 2007) 20.

[2] Amartya Sen, 'Elements of a Theory of Human Rights' (2004) 32 *Philosophy and Public Affairs* 315, at 315.

[3] V Spike Peterson and Laura Parisi, 'Are Women Human? It's Not an Academic Question' in Tony Evans (ed), *Human Rights Fifty Years On: A Reappraisal* (Manchester University Press, 1998) 132–60, at 154; David Kennedy, 'The International Human Rights Movement: Part of the Problem?' (2002) 15 *Harvard Human Rights Journal* 101, at 101; David Chandler (ed), *Rethinking Human Rights: Critical Approaches to International Politics* (Palgrave Macmillan, 2003) 6; Upendra Baxi, *The Future of Human Rights*, 2nd edn (Oxford University Press, 2008) 3; Navanethem Pillay, 'What are Human Rights For?' in Daniel Moeckli, Sangeeta Shah and Sandesh Sivakumaran (eds), *International Human Rights Law* (Oxford University Press, 2010) 3–11, at 4; Makau Mutua, *Human Rights Standards: Hegemony, Law and Politics* (State University of New York Press, 2016) vii; Anthony Tirado Chase, 'Human Rights Contestations: Sexual Orientation and Gender Identity' (2016) 20 *International Journal of Human Rights* 703, at 713.

[4] Louis Henkin, *The Age of Rights* (Columbia University Press, 1990) ix.

[5] Carlos S Nino, *The Ethics of Human Rights* (Clarendon Press, 1993) 1.

the ideology of our century.[6] They have acquired a central position in the fields of politics and law, as the notion of human rights appears to be present in every discussion on international themes.[7] The language of human rights has been accepted by policy-makers and governments, by NGOs and academics, by the media and wide sectors of the general population, and it is seen by many as providing a framework for a progressive transformation of international relations and international law.[8]

That being said, human rights are certainly not a perfect invention. This book undertakes a critical analysis of the notion of human rights from a theoretical perspective grounded in queer theory. The purpose of this work is to illustrate that the field of human rights law is underpinned by several assumptions that determine a certain conception of the subject of human rights. In particular, the individual entitled to these universal rights has been conceived as gendered and sexual in specific ways, giving rise to multiple legal and social consequences, some of which betray the very idea of universality of human rights.

To clarify, this is not a doctrinal legal study of the human rights of LGBT individuals,[9] by which I mean lesbians, gays, bisexuals and trans people.[10] Many pages have already been written on that topic.[11] This book is aimed at critically engaging with the construction of sexual and gender identities within human

[6] Costas Douzinas, *Human Rights and Empire: The Political Philosophy of Cosmopolitanism* (Routledge-Cavendish 2007) 12; Costas Douzinas, 'Humanity, Military Humanism and the New Moral Order' (2003) 32 *Economy and Society* 159, at 161.

[7] Chandler, *Rethinking Human Rights* (n 3) 4.

[8] ibid 1–2.

[9] Throughout the book I use the acronym LGBT due to its wide acceptance within the field of sexuality and gender identity, but without any intention of suggesting that all possible identities can be comprehended by those four initials. I agree with Carey Jean Sojka that even if we try adding other letters to include more people based on their identities (another 'T' or two, an extra 'Q' and an 'I', perhaps also a 'P' or an 'A'), we will still be leaving out some other groups. See Carey Jean Sojka, 'Partners of Transgender People' in Steven Seidman, Nancy Fischer and Chet Meeks (eds), *Introducing the New Sexuality Studies*, 2nd edn (Routledge, 2011) 236–41, at 236.

[10] I use the word 'trans' as an umbrella term to refer to every person who does not perceive their gender identity as the same as the one they were socially expected to fulfil as a result of their sex designation at birth.

[11] To mention only a few important academic works: Robert Wintemute, *Sexual Orientation and Human Rights: The United States Constitution, the European Convention, and the Canadian Charter* (Oxford University Press, 1995); Eric Heinze, *Sexual Orientation: A Human Right, An Essay on International Human Rights Law* (Martinus Nijhoff, 1995); Robert Wintemute, 'Strasbourg to the Rescue? Same-Sex Partners and Parents' in Robert Wintemute and Mads Andenæs (eds), *Legal Recognition of Same-Sex Partnerships: A Study of National, European and International Law* (Hart Publishing, 2001) 713–29; Eric Heinze, 'Sexual Orientation and International Law: A Study in the Manufacture of Cross-Cultural "Sensitivity"' (2001) 22 *Michigan Journal of International Law* 283; Robert Wintemute, 'From "Sex Rights" to "Love Rights": Partnership Rights as Human Rights' in Nicholas Bamforth (ed), *Sex Rights: The Oxford Amnesty Lectures 2002* (Oxford University Press, 2005) 186–224; Robert Wintemute, 'Sexual Orientation and Gender Identity' in Colin Harvey (ed), *Human Rights in the Community: Rights as Agents for Change* (Hart Publishing, 2005) 175–99; Michael O'Flaherty and John Fisher, 'Sexual Orientation, Gender Identity and International Human Rights Law: Contextualising the Yogyakarta Principles' (2008) 8 *Human Rights Law Review* 207; Paul Johnson, *Homosexuality and the European Court of Human Rights* (Routledge, 2012); Dominic McGoldrick, 'The Development and Status of Sexual Orientation Discrimination under International Human Rights Law' (2016) 16 *Human Rights Law Review* 613.

rights law and queer theory is the theoretical lens chosen to perform this task. Within the legal field, the use of queer theory as a theoretical tool for research remains largely unexplored,[12] but its use in closely related areas, such as political science, international relations and criminology, reveals an increasing academic interest in queer theory.[13] As to the use of queer theory to inform the interconnected study of sexual and gender identities in international human rights law, this is missing in the literature. In this specific area it is only possible to find shorter, more limited interventions.[14] Therefore, this book comes to fill an existing gap in the literature. One of the primary aims of this work is to demonstrate that human rights law can make use of insights from queer theory in order to further approach its ideal of universality.

I. The Method and the Methodology of the Book

I purposely distinguish between the method and the methodology of this book. While I give the term 'methodology' a strong theoretical connotation, by 'method'

[12] In fact, after Carl Stychin's seminal piece *Law's Desire*, there are only a few extensive works on queer theory and the law, such as Leslie Moran's *The Homosexual(ity) of Law* and Janet Halley's *Split Decisions*. Carl F Stychin, *Law's Desire: Sexuality and the Limits of Justice* (Routledge, 1995); Leslie Moran, *The Homosexual(ity) of Law* (Routledge, 1996); Janet Halley, *Split Decisions: How and Why to Take a Break from Feminism* (Princeton University Press, 2006).

[13] Nico J Beger, *Tensions in the Struggle for Sexual Minority Rights in Europe: Que(e)rying Political Practices* (Manchester University Press, 2009); Carrie Buist and Emily Lenning, *Queer Criminology* (Routledge, 2015); Cynthia Weber, *Queer International Relations: Sovereignty, Sexuality and the Will to Knowledge* (Oxford University Press, 2016).

[14] These include the work of Michele Grigolo, Aeyal Gross, Wayne Morgan, Diane Otto, as well as my own. Michele Grigolo, 'Sexualities and the ECHR: Introducing the Universal Sexual Legal Subject' (2003) 14 *European Journal of International Law* 1023; Aeyal Gross, 'Queer Theory and International Human Rights Law: Does Each Person Have a Sexual Orientation?' (2007) 101 *American Society of International Law Proceedings* 129; Aeyal M Gross, 'Sex, Love, and Marriage: Questioning Gender and Sexuality Rights in International Law' (2008) 21 *Leiden Journal of International Law* 235; Aeyal Gross, 'Gender Outlaws Before the Law: The Courts of the Borderland' (2009) 32 *Harvard Journal of Law and Gender* 165; Aeyal Gross 'The *Burden* of Conjugality' in Eva Brems (ed), *Diversity and European Human Rights: Rewriting Judgments of the ECHR* (Cambridge University Press, 2013) 265–92; Wayne Morgan, 'Law and Change: Identifying Evil for What It Is: Tasmania, Sexual Perversity and the United Nations' (1994) 19 *Melbourne University Law Review* 742; Wayne Morgan, 'Queering International Human Rights Law' in Carl Stychin and Didi Herman (eds), *Sexuality in the Legal Arena* (Athlone, 2000) 208–25; Dianne Otto, 'Queering Gender [Identity] in International Law' (2015) 33 *Nordic Journal of Human Rights* 299; Dianne Otto, 'Resisting the Heteronormative Imaginary of the Nation-State: Rethinking Kinship and Border Protection' in Dianne Otto (ed), *Queering International Law: Possibilities, Alliances, Complicities, Risks* (Routledge, 2017) 236–57; Damian A Gonzalez-Salzberg, 'The Making of the Court's Homosexual: A Queer Reading of the European Court of Human Rights' Case Law on Same-Sex Sexuality' (2014) 65 *Northern Ireland Legal Quarterly* 371; Damian A Gonzalez-Salzberg, 'The Accepted Transsexual and the Absent Transgender: A Queer Reading of the Regulation of Sex/Gender by the European Court of Human Rights' (2014) 29 *American University International Law Review* 797; Damian A Gonzalez-Salzberg, 'Confirming (The Illusion of) Heterosexual Marriage: *Hämäläinen v Finland*' (2015) 2 *Journal of International and Comparative Law* 173; Damian A Gonzalez-Salzberg, 'An Improved Protection for the (Mentally Ill) Trans Parent: A Queer Reading of *AP, Garçon and Nicot v France*' (2018) 81 *Modern Law Review* 526.

I refer to how the research has actually been conducted.[15] Hence, the methodology used in this work is queer theory. This is the approach that guides the interpretation of the analysis performed.[16] As a result, a very important number of the secondary sources drawn upon in this work are the writings of queer theorists. As to the method, I have read, analysed and engaged with the jurisprudence of the European Court of Human Rights ('the Court') on sexuality and transsexuality. The main primary sources of this research project are the judgments of that Court. In addition to this, another essential part of the secondary sources used in this project consists of the work produced by legal scholars concerning the rulings of the Court. An important clarification is needed, in that while I have read and examined every published ruling issued by this Court on matters of sexuality and transsexuality up to the end of the year 2017, not every judgment will appear in the book's discussion. The purpose of this work is not to analyse all the decisions adopted, but to use a selection of those decisions to illustrate how the Court has constructed the notions of sex, gender and sexuality through its case law.

The methodology adopted has several implications for the method. The analysis of the cases does not consist of a traditional doctrinal reading of legal sources, or even a general critical interpretation of them. This book performs a reading of the case law inspired by queer theory, and *deconstruction* is queer's technique *par excellence*.[17] I use the term deconstruction to mean a critical reading of texts that is specifically aimed at highlighting certain meanings that, while present in the text, do not appear as the obvious focus of attention.[18] This is of extreme importance for legal sources, since what becomes law is the text as read, rather than the text as written.[19] As affirmed by Jack Balkin, there are at least three very appealing reasons for making use of a deconstructive reading of legal texts:

> First, deconstruction provides a method for critiquing existing legal doctrines; in particular, a deconstructive reading can show how arguments offered to support a particular rule undermine themselves, and instead, support an opposite rule. Second, deconstructive techniques can show how doctrinal arguments are informed by and disguise ideological thinking … Third, deconstructive techniques offer both a new kind of interpretive strategy and a critique of conventional interpretations of legal texts.[20]

[15] See Robert Cryer, Tamara Hervey and Bal Sokhi-Bulley, *Research Methodologies in EU and International Law* (Hart Publishing, 2011) 5.

[16] For an analysis of the work of the European Court of Human Rights under different theoretical approaches, see Marie-Bénédicte Dembour, *Who Believes in Human Rights? Reflections on the European Convention* (Cambridge University Press, 2006).

[17] Carl F Stychin, 'Couplings: Civil Partnership in the United Kingdom' (2005) 8 *New York City Law Review* 543, at 544 and 545.

[18] JM Balkin, 'Deconstructive Practice and Legal Theory' (1987) 96 *Yale Law Journal* 743. Jacques Derrida has offered a more fluid definition of 'deconstruction' in the following terms: 'Deconstruction is inventive or it is nothing at all; it does not settle for methodical procedures, it opens up a passageway, it marches ahead and leaves a trail; its writing is not only performative, it produces rules – other conventions – for new performatives and never installs itself in the theoretical assurance of a simple opposition between performative and constative'. Jacques Derrida, *Psyche: Invention of Other* (Stanford University Press, 2007) 23.

[19] Balkin, 'Deconstructive Practice and Legal Theory' (n 18) 782.

[20] ibid 743.

I aim to demonstrate that a deconstructive reading of the Court's case law can shed new light on the meaning and scope of human rights law. This theoretically grounded method will allow me to engage with the following question: How has the European Court of Human Rights constructed the gendered and sexual subject of human rights?

II. The European Court of Human Rights

As I mentioned above, the method of the book consists of a specific type of critical analysis (one inspired by queer theory) of the case law of the European Court of Human Rights. The use of this Court in order to study the field of human rights can be justified for several reasons. The European Court of Human Rights is the longest standing monitoring body regarding the international protection of human rights, as its work started in February 1959, and it had delivered more than 20,000 judgments by the end of 2017.[21] In fact, many authors consider the Court as the world leading authority in human rights law, since its judgments are a source of reference not only for the domestic judicial bodies of the states of the Council of Europe, but also for many states worldwide and for other international courts.[22] This system of international protection of human rights has also been characterised as the most effective one in existence.[23] In addition to this, the Court is the human rights monitoring body that has decided the largest number of cases concerning sexual and gender identities.

Having stated the main reasons for selecting the jurisprudence of this Court as the object of study, I will briefly explain how this Court works.[24] The Court was conceived by the Convention for the Protection of Human Rights and Fundamental Freedoms (hereinafter, 'European Convention on Human Rights' or 'Convention'), adopted in 1950.[25] This is an international treaty aimed at the protection of human rights within the states of the Council of Europe. This Convention was actually the first international treaty by which states acquired an international obligation to

[21] European Court of Human Rights, *Overview 1959–2017* (March 2018).

[22] John B Attanasio, 'Rapporteur's Overview and Conclusions: Of Sovereignty, Globalization, and Courts' (1996) 28 *New York University Journal of International Law and Politics* 1, at 16; Anne-Marie Slaughter, 'Judicial Globalization' (2000) 40 *Virginia Journal of International Law* 1103, at 1109–11.

[23] Ed Bates, *The Evolution of the European Convention on Human Rights: From its Inception to the Creation of a Permanent Court of Human Rights* (Oxford University Press, 2010) 2.

[24] For in-depth studies on the work of the European Court of Human Rights, see Pieter van Dijk and others, *Theory and Practice of the European Convention on Human Rights*, 4th edn (Intersentia, 2006); David J. Harris and others, *Law of the European Convention on Human Rights*, 3rd edn (Oxford University Press, 2014); Bernadette Rainey, Elizabeth Wicks and Clare Ovey, *The European Convention on Human Rights*, 6th edn (Oxford University Press, 2014).

[25] Convention for the Protection of Human Rights and Fundamental Freedoms (adopted 4 November 1950, entered into force 3 September 1953) 213 UNTS 221 ('European Convention on Human Rights').

secure to every person within their jurisdiction a number of rights and freedoms.[26] As affirmed by Ed Bates:

> [B]y becoming a party to the Convention, a member State was assenting to the principle that matters that had hitherto been solely within their domestic jurisdiction were now subject to international law *and* a level of international control and censure by international bodies.[27]

This Convention established a Court (and back then, also a Commission),[28] with jurisdiction to decide whether the conduct of States Parties to the treaty amounted to violations of the protected rights.[29] That is to say, the international obligations assumed by the states concerning the protection of human rights were to be supervised by a judicial body with the ability to evaluate states' conduct towards individuals within their own jurisdiction and to impose legal sanctions upon states in case of violations of these norms. Nowadays, there are 47 States Parties subject to the jurisdiction of the Court,[30] and the role of the Court could be seen as having many similarities to that of a constitutional court of domestic jurisdiction, but with a focus on the interpretation and application of the European Convention on Human Rights.[31]

Furthermore, the European Court of Human Rights became the first international body with the ability to issue binding decisions concerning human rights when a violation of any of those rights was claimed by individuals.[32] This gave individuals the opportunity to challenge the laws and practices of particular states. However, it is worth highlighting that at the same time that the Convention granted the individual access to an international body, it was also giving an international court access to the individual. In other words, the existence of the Court granted individuals the possibility of requesting that an international body protect their rights, but this right to petition also conceded to this international body the ability to study the individuals that appear before it. The Court was given the authority to examine individuals' lives, in order to be able to decide the scope

[26] Bates, *The Evolution of the European Convention on Human Rights* (n 23) 108.

[27] ibid.

[28] For a study of the history of the European Convention on Human Rights and its monitoring organs see Bates, *The Evolution of the European Convention on Human Rights* (n 23).

[29] However, in the original text of the Convention, the jurisdiction of the Court was not compulsory, but states needed to express their consent to be subject to the Court according to the optional clause contemplated in Art 46 of the Treaty. See Art 46 of the original text of the Convention, available at www.echr.coe.int/Documents/Collection_Convention_1950_ENG.pdf (accessed 1 June 2018). See also Bates, *The Evolution of the European Convention on Human Rights* (n 23) 138–39; Dembour, *Who Believes in Human Rights?* (n 16) 22.

[30] See the European Court of Human Rights' website, www.echr.coe.int/Pages/home.aspx?p=press/factsheets&c=#n1347951547702_pointer (accessed 1 June 2018).

[31] David J Harris and others, *Law of the European Convention on Human Rights*, 2nd edn (Oxford University Press, 2009) 2.

[32] Nevertheless, in the original version of the Convention, individuals could not bring cases directly to the Court. Only the Commission and the states had legal standing before the Court. See Arts 44 and 48 of the original text of the Convention, available at www.echr.coe.int/Documents/Collection_Convention_1950_ENG.pdf (accessed 1 June 2018).

of those individuals' rights. After an individual's request, the Court has the ability to review the criminal conviction imposed upon them, as well as the reasons why the conviction was decided.[33] The Court has the capacity to examine individuals' religions and beliefs,[34] together with their right to manifest those convictions and the freedom to express their opinions.[35] The Court also has the power to inspect people's right to assembly in public,[36] and the activities that should be protected when performed in private.[37] The Court has jurisdiction to decide upon the right of individuals to marry, or the lack thereof,[38] and to rule on the scope of their family relationships.[39]

In particular, it is of extreme relevance to this book that the Court has shown its ability to decide about the protection of individuals' sexuality, as well as about the right of individuals to obtain the amendment of their legal sex and gender. In fact, a group of judges, sitting in Strasbourg, nationals of the different states of the Council of Europe, have exercised the power of the Court to examine, discuss, and decide upon the sexual and gender identities of over 200 individuals that have appeared before them. Moreover, the effect of these decisions extends much further than those individuals directly involved in the cases, since they have implications for the more than 800 million people living within the jurisdiction of the Court.[40] As affirmed by Paul Johnson, the jurisprudence of the European Court of Human Rights has become an extremely important site at which sexual (and, I would add, gender) identities have been constructed.[41]

[33] Article 6.1 of the Convention states: 'In the determination of his civil rights and obligations or of any criminal charge against him, everyone is entitled to a fair and public hearing within a reasonable time by an independent and impartial tribunal established by law'. See *Al-Khawaja and Tahery v United Kingdom* (GC), Application nos 26766/05 and 22228/06, ECHR 2011.

[34] Article 9.1 of the Convention establishes: 'Everyone has the right to freedom of thought, conscience and religion; this right includes freedom to change his religion or belief and freedom, either alone or in community with others and in public or private, to manifest his religion or belief, in worship, teaching, practice and observance'. See *Bayatyan v Armenia* (GC), Application no 23459/03, ECHR 2011.

[35] Article 10.1 of the Convention reads: 'Everyone has the right to freedom of expression. This right shall include freedom to hold opinions and to receive and impart information and ideas without interference by public authority and regardless of frontiers. This Article shall not prevent States from requiring the licensing of broadcasting, television or cinema enterprises'. See *Mladina dd Ljubljana v Slovenia*, Application no 20981/10, 17 April 2014.

[36] Article 11.1 of the Convention says: 'Everyone has the right to freedom of peaceful assembly and to freedom of association with others, including the right to form and to join trade unions for the protection of his interests'. See *Alekseyev v Russia*, Application nos 4916/07, 25924/08 and 14599/09, 21 October 2010.

[37] Article 8 of the Convention prescribes: 'Everyone has the right to respect for his private and family life, his home and his correspondence'. See *Dudgeon v United Kingdom*, Series A no 45, 22 October 1981.

[38] Article 12 of the Convention establishes: 'Men and women of marriageable age have the right to marry and to found a family, according to the national laws governing the exercise of this right'. See *Schalk and Kopf v Austria*, Application no 30141/04, ECHR 2010.

[39] See n 37 above. See also *X, Y and Z v United Kingdom*, Reports of Judgments and Decisions 1997-II, 22 April 1997.

[40] Paul Johnson, 'An Essentially Private Manifestation of Human Personality: Constructions of Homosexuality in the European Court of Human Rights' (2010) 10 *Human Rights Law Review* 67, at 68.

[41] Johnson, *Homosexuality and the European Court of Human Rights* (n 11) 41 and 43; Paul Johnson, 'Sociology and the European Court of Human Rights' (2014) 62 *Sociological Review* 547, at 558.

III. Homosexuality and Transsexuality before the Court

By the end of 2017, the Court had decided over 100 cases concerning homosexuality and transsexuality.[42] A brief outline of this case law allows us to see that the Court began discussing the criminalisation of same-sex sexuality between

[42] *Van Oosterwijck v Belgium*, Series A no 40, 6 November 1980; *Dudgeon v United Kingdom* (n 37); *Rees v United Kingdom*, Series A no 106, 17 October 1986; *Norris v Ireland*, Series A no 142, 26 October 1988; *Cossey v United Kingdom*, Series A no 184, 27 September 1990; *B v France*, Series A no 232-C, 25 March 1992; *Modinos v. Cyprus*, Series A no 259, 22 April 1993; *Scherer v Switzerland*, Series A no 287, 25 March 1994; *Laskey, Jaggard and Brown v United Kingdom*, Reports of Judgments and Decisions 1997-I, 19 February 1997; *X, Y and Z v United Kingdom* (n 39); *Sheffield and Horsham v United Kingdom*, Reports of Judgments and Decisions 1998-V, 30 July 1998; *Smith and Grady v United Kingdom*, Application nos 33985/96 and 33986/96, ECHR 1999-VI; *Lustig-Prean and Beckett v United Kingdom*, Application nos 31417/96 and 32377/96, September 1999; *Salgueiro da Silva Mouta v Portugal*, Application no 33290/96, ECHR 1999-IX; *Craig v United Kingdom* (Dec) no 45396/99, 21 March 2000; *ADT v United Kingdom*, Application no 35765/97, ECHR 2000-IX; *Cardoso and Johansen v United Kingdom* (striking out), Application no 47061/99, 5 September 2000; *Sutherland v United Kingdom* (striking out) (GC), Application no 25186/94, 22 March 2001; *Mata Estevez v Spain* (Dec), Application no 56501/00, ECHR 2001-VI; *Morris v United Kingdom* (striking out), Application no 31701/96, 27 November 2001; *Connell and others v United Kingdom* (striking out), Application no 43495/98, 8 January 2002; *Goddard v United Kingdom* (striking out), Application no 57821/00, 15 January 2002; *Fretté v France*, Application no 36515/97, ECHR 2002-I; *I v United Kingdom* (GC), Application no 25680/94, 11 July 2002; *Christine Goodwin v United Kingdom* (GC), Application no 28957/95, ECHR 2002-VI; *Tosto v Italy* (striking out), Application no 49821/99, 15 October 2002; *Crescimone v Italy* (striking out), Application no 49824/99, 15 October 2002; *Faranda v Italy* (striking out), Application no 51467/99, 15 October 2002; *Beck, Copp and Bazeley v United Kingdom*, Application nos 48535/99, 48536/99 and 48537/00, 22 October 2002; *Perkins and R v United Kingdom*, Application nos 43208/98 and 44875/98, 22 October 2002; *Waite v United Kingdom*, Application no. 53236/99, 10 December 2002; *L and V v Austria*, Application nos 39392/98 and 39829/98, ECHR 2003-I; *SL v Austria*, Application no 45330/99, ECHR 2003-I; *Karner v Austria*, Application no 40016/98, ECHR 2003-IX; *Brown v United Kingdom* (friendly settlement), Application no 52770/99, 29 July 2003; *Van Kück v Germany*, Application no 35968/97, ECHR 2003-VII; *BB v United Kingdom*, Application no 53760/00, 10 February 2004; *F v United Kingdom* (Dec), Application no 17341/03, 22 June 2004; *Woditschka and Wilfling v Austria*, Application nos 69756/01 and 6306/02, 21 October 2004; *INN v The Netherlands* (Dec.), Application no 2035/04, 9 December 2004; *Enhorn v Sweden*, Application no 56529/00, ECHR 2005-I; *Ladner v Austria*, Application no 18297/03, 3 February 2005; *Fairfield v United Kingdom* (Dec), Application no 24790/04, ECHR 2005-VI; *Wolfmeyer v Austria*, Application no 5263/03, 26 May 2005; *HG and GB v Austria*, Application nos 11084/02 and 15306/02, 2 June 2005; *Love and others v United Kingdom* (Dec), Application nos 4103/04, 5498/04, 10617/04, 14557/04 and 27313/04, 13 December 2005; *RH v Austria*, Application no 7336/03, 19 January 2006; *Grant v United Kingdom*, Application no 32570/03, ECHR 2006-VII; *Kobenter and Standard Verlags GmbH v Austria*, Application no 60899/00, 2 November 2006; *Ayegh v Sweden* (Dec), Application no 4701/05, 7 November 2006; *R and F v United Kingdom* (Dec), Application no 35748/05, 28 November 2006; *Parry v United Kingdom* (Dec), Application no 42971/05, ECHR 2006-XV; *Bączkowski and others v Poland*, Application no 1543/06, 3 May 2007; *Guerrero Castillo v Italy* (Dec), Application no 39432/06, 12 June 2007; *L v Lithuania*, Application no 27527/03, ECHR 2007-IV; *EB v France* (GC), Application no 43546/02, 22 January 2008; *NN and TA v Belgium*, Application no 65097/01, 13 May 2008; *Nunez v France* (Dec), Application no 18367/06, 27 May 2008; *Courten v United Kingdom* (Dec), Application no 4479/06, 4 November 2008; *Marangos v Cyprus*, Application no 12846/05, 4 December 2008; *Schlumpf v Switzerland*, Application no 29002/06, 8 January 2009; *Korelc v Slovenia*, Application no 28456/03, 12 May 2009; *Small v United Kingdom* (striking out), Application no 7330/06, 2 June 2009; *MW v United Kingdom* (Dec), Application no 11313/02, 23 June 2009; *Hunt and Miller v United Kingdom* (friendly settlement), Application nos 10578/05 and 10605/05, 23 June 2009; *Porubova v Russia*, Application no 8237/03, 8 October 2009; *Kozak v Poland*, Application no 13102/02, 2 March 2010; *Schalk and Kopf v Austria* (n 38); *PB and JS v Austria*, Application no 18984/02, 22 July 2010; *Manenc v France* (Dec.), Application no 66686/09, 21 September 2010; *Santos Couto v Portugal*, Application

men, originally in Northern Ireland, in the *Dudgeon v United Kingdom* case,[43] and later in the Republic of Ireland (*Norris v Ireland*),[44] and Cyprus (*Modinos v Cyprus*),[45] ruling that it amounted to a violation of human rights. It later examined the criminalisation of group homosexual sex (*ADT v United Kingdom*)[46]

no 31874/07, 21 September 2010; *JM v United Kingdom*, Application no 37060/06, 28 September 2010; *Alekseyev v Russia* (n 36); *PV v Spain*, Application no 35159/09, 30 November 2010; *Wasmuth v Germany*, Application no 12884/03, 17 February 2011; *DBN v United Kingdom* (striking out), Application no 26550/10, 31 May 2011; *P v Portugal* (striking out), Application no 56027/09, 6 September 2011; *Stasi v France*, Application no 25001/07, 20 October 2011; *Zontul v Greece*, Application no 12294/07, 17 January 2012; *Vejdeland v Sweden*, Application no 1813/07, 9 February 2012; *Gas and Dubois v France*, Application no 25951/07, ECHR 2012; *Genderdoc-M v Moldova*, Application no 9106/06, 12 June 2012; *KN v France* (striking out), Application no 47129/09, 19 June 2012; *ASB v The Netherlands* (striking out), Application no 4854/12, 10 July 2012; *X v Turkey*, Application no 24626/09, 9 October 2012; *Molnar v Romania* (Dec) Application no 16637/06, 23 October 2012; *Verlagsgruppe News GmbH and Bobi v Austria*, Application no 59631/09, 4 December 2012; *Rothe v Austria*, Application no 6490/07, 4 December 2012; *Küchl v Austria*, Application no 51151/06, 4 December 2012; *X and others v Austria* (GC), Application no 19010/07, 19 February 2013; *Eweida and others v United Kingdom*, Application nos 48420/10 and 3 others 15 March 2013; *Boeckel and Gessner-Boeckel v Germany* (Dec), Application no 8017/11, 7 May 2013; *MKN v Sweden*, Application no 72413/10, 27 June 2013; *Cassar v Malta* (striking out), Application no 36982/11, 9 July 2013; *Georgescu v Romania* (Dec), Application no 4867/03, 22 October 2013; *EB and others v Austria*, Application nos 31913/07 and 4 others 7 November 2013; *Vallianatos and others v Greece* (GC), Application nos 29381/09 and 32684/09, 7 November 2013; *Mladina dd Ljubljana v Slovenia* (n 35); *FJ and EB v Austria* (Dec), Application nos 2362/08 and 26271/08, 25 March 2014; *HÇ v Turkey* (striking out), Application no 6428/12, 3 June 2014; *EB v Austria* (Dec), Application no 27783/09, 24 June 2014; *Hämäläinen v Finland* (GC), Application no 37359/09, 16 July 2014; *YY v Turkey*, Application no 14793/08, 10 March 2015; *ME v Sweden* (GC) (striking out), Application no 71398/12, 8 April 2015; *Identoba and others v Georgia*, Application no 73235/12, 12 May 2015; *Oliari and others v Italy*, Application nos 18766/11 and 36030/11, 21 July 2015; *AE v Finland* (striking out), Application no 30953/11, 22 September 2015; *Pshenkina v Sweden* (Dec), Application no 7528/15, 8 December 2015; *Kostadinov v Bulgaria*, Application no 61701/11, 21 January 2016; *Pajić v Croatia*, Application no 68453/13, 23 February 2016; *Sousa Goucha v Portugal*, Application no 70434/12, 22 March 2016; *MC and AC v Romania*, Application no 12060/12, 12 April 2016; *AN v France* (Dec), Application no 12956/15, 19 April 2016; *'Accept' v Romania* (Dec), Application no 48301/08, 24 May 2016; *Chapin and Charpentier v France*, Application no 40183/07, 9 June 2016; *Aldeguer Tomás v Spain*, Application no 35214/09, 14 June 2016; *Taddeucci and McCall v Italy*, Application no 51362/09, 30 June 2016; *OM v Hungary*, Application no 9912/15, 5 July 2016; *Kaos GL v Turkey*, Application no 4982/07, 22 November 2016; *MB v Spain* (Dec), Application no 15109/15, 13 December 2016; *Đorđević v Serbia* (Dec), Application no 5591/10, 17 January 2017; *DÇ v Turkey* (Dec), Application no 10684/13, 7 February 2017; *Lashmankin and others v Russia*, Application nos 57818/09 and 14 others, 7 February 2017; *Rubio Dosamantes v Spain*, Application no 20996/10, 21 February 2017; *Hörmann and others* (striking out), Application nos 31176/11 and 31185/13, 7 March 2017; *AP, Garçon and Nicot v France*, Application nos 79885/12 and 2 others 6 April 2017; *Bayev and others v Russia*, Application nos 67667/09 and 2 others 20 June 2017; *ES v Spain* (Dec), Application no 13273/16, 26 September 2017; *Ratzenböck and Seydl v Austria*, Application no 28475/12, 26 October 2017; *D and B v Austria* (Dec), Application no 40597/12, 31 October 2017; *MB v The Netherlands* (Dec), Application no 63890/16, 28 November 2017; *Orlandi and others v Italy*, Application nos 26431/12 and three others, 14 December 2017; *Karine Hallier and others v France* (Dec), Application no 43386/10, 12 December 2017; *IK. v Switzerland* (Dec), Application no 21417/17, 19 December 2017.

[43] *Dudgeon v United Kingdom* (n 37).

[44] *Norris v Ireland* (n 42). For a short case comment on *Norris*, see Ann Sherlock, 'Article 8, Privacy and the Rights of Homosexuals' (1989) 14 *European Law Review* 112.

[45] *Modinos v Cyprus* (n 42). For a case comment on *Modinos*, see Ann Sherlock, 'Prohibition of Homosexual Relations in Private and the Convention' (1994) 19 *European Law Review* 112.

[46] *ADT v United Kingdom* (n 42). For a short case comment on *ADT*, see Steve Foster, 'Gross Indecency and the Right to Private Sexual Life' (2000) 5 *Coventry Law Journal* 77.

and of sadomasochism (*Laskey, Jaggard and Brown v United Kingdom*),[47] giving its approval to the first, but not to the second. The Court also analysed the existence of differential age for sexual consent for male homosexual sex, compared to heterosexual intercourse or lesbian sex (*L and V v Austria* and *SL v Austria*),[48] and it found that establishing different ages for sexual consent was discriminatory.

Another group of cases decided by the Court concerned the state policy prohibiting homosexual individuals to serve in the armed forces (*Smith and Grady v United Kingdom* and *Lustig-Prean and Beckett v United Kingdom*),[49] which was found to constitute a breach of human rights. The Court also ruled on the prohibition of public assembly based on the sexuality of those aiming to exercise this right (*Bączkowski and others v Poland* and *Alekseyev v Russia*),[50] and found the imposed restrictions to be discriminatory in character. Regarding discrimination, another topic examined by the Court was the legislation that refused the right to succeed to a partner's tenancy based on sexual orientation (*Karner v Austria* and *Kozak v Poland*),[51] ruling that the legislation amounted to discriminatory treatment.

The topic of parenting and adoption has also been central to the Court's jurisprudence on sexuality. The Court studied a case in which the parental custody of a child had been refused based on the sexuality of the father (*Salgueiro da Silva Mouta v Portugal*),[52] as well as a case in which the quantum of child support ordered to be paid by a mother took into consideration her sexuality (*JM v United Kingdom*).[53] On both occasions, it found violations of the Convention. Regarding adoption, the Court has overturned its original decision, which allowed states to refuse the possibility of applying for adoption based on the sexuality of the

[47] *Laskey, Jaggard and Brown v United Kingdom* (n 42). For a legal discussion of *Laskey, Jaggard and Brown*, see Nicholas Bamforth, 'Sexual Privacy and the European Convention on Human Rights' (1997) 56 *Cambridge Law Journal* 480. For a critical analysis of *Laskey, Jaggard and Brown*, see Leslie Moran, 'Laskey v The United Kingdom: Learning the Limits of Privacy' (1998) 61 *Modern Law Review* 77.

[48] *L and V v Austria* (n 42); *SL v Austria* (n 42).

[49] *Smith and Grady v United Kingdom* (n 42); *Lustig-Prean and Beckett v United Kingdom* (n 42). For a short case comment of these judgments, see Ivan Hare, 'Privacy and the Gay Right to Fight' (2000) 59 *Cambridge Law Journal* 6. For a critical analysis of *Lustig-Prean and Beckett*, see Derek McGhee, *Homosexuality, Law and Resistance* (Routledge, 2001) 54–61. See also Michael Kavey, 'The Public Faces of Privacy: Rewriting Lustig-Prean and Beckett v. United Kingdom' in Eva Brems (ed), *Diversity and European Human Rights: Rewriting Judgments of the ECHR* (Cambridge University Press, 2012) 293–325.

[50] *Bączkowski and others v Poland* (n 42); *Alekseyev v Russia* (n 36). For a discussion of *Bączkowski and others*, see Sina Van den Bogaert, 'ECHR Rules on Illegal Ban of Warsaw Equality Parade: The Case of Bączkowski and Others v Poland' (2007) 8 *German Law Journal* 890. For a critical analysis of *Alekseyev*, see Paul Johnson 'Homosexuality, Freedom of Assembly and the Margin of Appreciation Doctrine of the European Court of Human Rights: Alekseyev v Russia' (2011) 11 *Human Rights Law Review* 578.

[51] *Karner v Austria* (n 42); *Kozak v Poland* (n 42).

[52] *Salgueiro da Silva Mouta v Portugal* (n 42). For a legal analysis of *Salgueiro*, see Jonathan Herring, 'Gay Rights Come Quietly' (2002) 118 *Law Quarterly Review* 31.

[53] *JM v United Kingdom* (n 42). For a short comment on *JM v United Kingdom* see Desmond Rutledge, 'Child Support: Discrimination Based on Sexual Orientation – Justification' (2011) 18 *Journal of Social Security Law* 15.

adopter (*Fretté v France*),[54] and now holds that restricting individual adoption based on sexual orientation is discriminatory (*EB v France*).[55] Nonetheless, the Court continues to have a very restrictive view regarding the right to second-parent adoption for same-sex couples and their children (*Gas and Dubois v France* and *X and others v Austria*).[56]

Another important part of the Court's jurisprudence has dealt with the right to marry (*Schalk and Kopf v Austria*)[57] and to enter into a registered partnership (*Vallianatos and others v Greece* and *Oliari and others v Italy*),[58] and with certain benefits which those couples are entitled to receive. The Court decided in favour of the applicants in the cases concerning registered partnerships, as well as in the ones regarding the extension of medical insurance to a same-sex partner and access to a residence permit for family reasons (*PB and JS v Austria* and *Taddeucci and McCall v Italy*).[59] By contrast, the Court continues to allow states to ban same-sex marriage, and to refuse survivors' pensions and tax exemptions to same-sex couples in situations where these are granted to heterosexual married couples (*Manenc v France* and *Courten v United Kingdom*).[60]

As to trans rights, the Court has dramatically changed its early jurisprudence regarding the right of transsexual individuals to obtain an amendment of their legal gender. Initially, the Court considered that states were not obliged to fully recognise the gender transition of transsexual people (*Rees v United Kingdom* and

[54] *Fretté v France* (n 42).

[55] *EB v France* (n 42). For critical discussions on the jurisprudential change from *Fretté* to *EB*, see Kathleen Doty, 'From *Fretté* to *E.B.*: The European Court of Human Rights on Gay and Lesbian Adoption' (2009) 18 *Law and Sexuality: A Review of Lesbian, Gay, Bisexual, and Transgender Legal Issues* 121. See also Linda Hart, 'Individual Adoption by Non-Heterosexuals and the Order of Family Life in the European Court of Human Rights' (2009) 36 *Journal of Law and Society* 536.

[56] *Gas and Dubois v France* (n 42); *X and others v. Austria* (n 42). For a critical comment on *Gas and Dubois*, see Paul Johnson, 'Adoption, Homosexuality and the European Convention on Human Rights: Gas and Dubois v France' (2012) 75 *Modern Law Review* 1123. For a discussion of the topic of adoption within the Court's case law, see Francesco Crisafulli, 'Same-Sex Couples' Rights (Other than the Right to Marry) Before the ECtHR' in Daniele Gallo, Luca Paladini and Pietro Pustorini (eds), *Same-Sex Couples before National, Supranational and International Jurisdictions* (Springer, 2013) 409–36, 425–33.

[57] *Schalk and Kopf v Austria* (n 38). For a critical comment on *Schalk and Kopf*, see Loveday Hodson, 'A Marriage by Any Other Name? Schalk and Kopf v Austria' (2011) 11 *Human Rights Law Review* 170. See also Holning Lau, 'Rewriting Schalk and Kopf: Shifting the Locus of Deference' in Eva Brems (ed), *Diversity and European Human Rights: Rewriting Judgments of the ECHR* (Cambridge University Press, 2012) 243–64.

[58] *Vallianatos and others v Greece* (n 42); *Oliari and others v Italy* (n 42). For a legal analysis of *Vallianatos and others*, see Ilias Trispiotis, 'Discrimination and Civil Partnerships: Taking "Legal" Out of Legal Recognition' (2014) 14 *Human Rights Law Review* 343. For a critical discussion of this case and its potential consequences see Sabrina Ragone and Valentina Volpe, 'An Emerging Right to a "Gay" Family Life? The Case *Oliari v. Italy* in a Comparative Perspective' (2016) 17 *German Law Journal* 451.

[59] *PB and JS v Austria* (n 42); *Taddeucci and McCall v Italy* (n 42). For a discussion of *PB and JS*, see Nicholas Bamforth, 'Families Not (Yet) Marriages? Same-Sex Partners and the Developing Convention "Margin of Appreciation"' (2011) 23 *Child and Family Law Quarterly* 128.

[60] *Manenc v France* (n 42); *Courten v United Kingdom* (n 42). For a comment on the *Courten* decision, see Crisafulli, 'Same-Sex Couples' Rights (Other than the Right to Marry) Before the ECtHR' (n 56) 423–25.

Cossey v United Kingdom).[61] From 2002 onwards, the Court has modified its case law, and now transsexual individuals have a right to obtain full legal recognition of their gender, as long as they had complied with the requirements established by Contracting States (*Goodwin v United Kingdom* and *I v United Kingdom*).[62] Until 2017, the Court had been of the opinion that a trans person had no right to obtain full recognition of their gender without previously undergoing sex affirming surgery (*Nunez v France*),[63] while at the same time it did not impose upon the states the obligation to provide access to this procedure (*L v Lithuania*).[64] Nonetheless, the Court has most recently ruled that genital surgery can no longer be made a requirement for gender recognition (*AP, Garçon and Nicot v France*).[65]

Regarding the right to marry of trans individuals, the Court's position on this topic has also seen important changes. Currently, trans individuals have the right to marry a person of the opposite sex to that attained through gender transition (*Goodwin v United Kingdom* and *I v United Kingdom*).[66] However, there is no right to marry (or to remain married to) someone of the same sex to that recognised after the gender affirming process (*Hämäläinen v Finland*).[67]

This summary of some of the most important areas of the jurisprudence of the European Court of Human Rights on sexuality and transsexuality maps the legal context in which this study is to be situated. Nevertheless, it is worth reiterating that the aim of this book is not to conduct a comprehensive doctrinal legal study of these cases, but rather to make use of these judgments in order to examine how sexual and gender identities have been constructed by the Court. This analysis will be performed through the methodological lens provided by queer theory.

IV. A (Working) Definition of Queer Theory

Queer theory is the methodology of this book. Nonetheless, defining queer theory is a particularly difficult task.[68] What I will offer is a working definition of queer

[61] *Rees v United Kingdom* (n 42); *Cossey v United Kingdom* (n 42). For a discussion of the Court's earlier cases on transsexuality, see Marie-Bénédicte Dembour, 'Why Should Biological Sex be Decisive? Transsexualism Before the European Court of Human Rights' in Alison Shaw and Shirley Ardener (eds), *Changing Sex and Bending Gender* (Berghahn, 2005) 39–59. For a critical analysis of the Court's case law on transsexuality, see Gonzalez-Salzberg, 'The Accepted Transsexual and the Absent Transgender' (n 14).

[62] *Christine Goodwin v United Kingdom* (n 42); *I v United Kingdom* (n 42). For a critical analysis of *Goodwin*, see Ralph Sandland, 'Crossing and Not Crossing: Gender, Sexuality and Melancholy in the European Court of Human Rights' (2003) 11 *Feminist Legal Studies* 191.

[63] *Nunez v France* (n 42).

[64] *L v Lithuania* (n 42).

[65] *AP, Garçon and Nicot v France* (n 42). For a critical analysis of this case see Gonzalez-Salzberg, 'An Improved Protection for the (Mentally Ill) Trans Parent' (n 14).

[66] *Christine Goodwin v United Kingdom* (n 42); *I v United Kingdom* (n 42).

[67] *Hämäläinen v Finland* (n 42). For a critical analysis of this case see Gonzalez-Salzberg, 'Confirming (The Illusion of) Heterosexual Marriage' (n 14).

[68] Stychin, *Law's Desire* (n 12) 140; Morgan, 'Queering International Human Rights Law' (n 14) 217; Janet Halley, 'Queer Theory by Men' in Martha Albertson Fineman, Jack E Jackson and Adam

theory, to explain how to understand this theoretical framework for the purpose of this book. The emergence of queer theory as a school of thought took place in the late 1980s.[69] David Halperin has explained that it was actually a joke that led to the birth of queer theory. The expression was coined by Teresa de Lauretis to serve as the title of a conference to be held in 1990.[70] During the opening remarks of the event, de Lauretis acknowledged that she meant to use the title 'queer theory' as a provocation in the hope to 'make theory queer', challenging heterosexists assumptions underpinning what passed for theory in academic circles, as well as to 'queer theory', calling attention to what was perverse about theorising sexual desire and sexual pleasure.[71]

In fact, it would be de Lauretis who provided the earliest definition of queer theory to be found, when a collection of essays generated in the mentioned conference were published in 1991. She wrote: '"Queer Theory" conveys a double emphasis – on the conceptual and speculative work involved in discourse production, and on the necessary critical work of deconstructing our own discourses and their constructed silences'.[72] This definition highlights two essential elements of queer theory. The first is the heavy influence of Michel Foucault in the field. This can be seen by the use of the expression 'discourse production' to refer to the idea that the notions and the language used to discuss specific aspects of reality should not be seen as merely descriptive tools, but as sites in which truth(s) is (are) constructed. The second element can be found in the reference to deconstruction, which is the technique of queer theory, as discussed above.

A more recent definition given by Eve Kosofsky Sedgwick, one the founding mothers of queer theory, states that queer refers to

> the open mesh of possibilities, gaps, overlaps, dissonances and resonances, lapses and excesses of meaning when the constituent elements of anyone's gender, of anyone's sexuality aren't made (or can't be made) to signify monolithically.[73]

This explanation clearly emphasises gender and sexuality as the two main concerns of queer theory. Indeed, it is possible to argue that queer theory was cemented as a theoretical standpoint by Judith Butler's ground-breaking book *Gender Trouble*,[74] which undertook an appealing postmodern critique of the notions of gender and

P Romero (eds), *Feminist and Queer Legal Theory: Intimate Encounters, Uncomfortable Conversations* (Ashgate, 2009) 9–28, 26; Aleardo Zanghellini, 'Queer, Antinormativity, Counter-normativity and Abjection' (2009) 18 *Griffith Law Review* 1, at 2; Neil Cobb, '"Gay Couple's Break Like Fawlty Towers": Dangerous Representations of Lesbian and Gay Oppression in an Era of "Progressive" Law Reform' (2009) 18 *Social and Legal Studies* 333, at 336.

[69] Arlene Stein and Ken Plummer, '"I Can't Even Think Straight" "Queer" Theory and the Missing Sexual Revolution in Sociology' (1994) 12 *Sociological Theory* 178, at 181; Steven Epstein, 'A Queer Encounter: Sociology and the Study of Sexuality' (1994) 12 *Sociological Theory* 188, at 194.

[70] David M Halperin, 'The Normalization of Queer Theory' (2003) 45 *Journal of Homosexuality* 339, at 339.

[71] ibid 340.

[72] Teresa de Lauretis, 'Queer Theory: Lesbian and Gays Sexualities, An Introduction' (1991) 3 *Differences: A Journal of Feminist Cultural Studies* iii, at iv.

[73] Eve Kosofsky Sedgwick, *Tendencies* (Routledge, 1994) 7.

[74] Judith Butler, *Gender Trouble: Feminism and the Subversion of Identity* (Routledge, 1990).

sexuality. An exploration of these two concepts is indispensable for a better understanding of queer theory.

A. Queer Theory and the Binary Sex/Gender System

Gender norms that divide individuals into men and women can be considered as the oldest normative system for the classification of people. Nonetheless, as with all other regulatory orders, one can argue that these norms are not timeless, but a historical creation.[75] The distinction between men and women, and the subordination of the latter group to the former, are the central issues of analysis of feminist theories. In order to theorise and challenge the subordination of women, since the 1970s, it has become usual within feminism(s) to distinguish between the categories of *sex* and *gender*. While sex has been understood as the biological differences between males and females, regarding genitalia and procreative functions, gender has been considered to be a cultural creation that refers to the social classification of men being masculine and women being feminine.[76] Consequently, gender began to be understood as a person's responsive role to their expected behaviour in society, according to their attributed sex.[77] In particular, gender was considered to be *done* in interaction with others as an unavoidable response to the normative conceptions of attitudes imposed as appropriate for belonging to a previously attributed sex.[78]

To repeat, the distinction between the sex and gender of individuals has usually been drawn in order to support the idea of gender as a cultural construction founded on the anatomical reality of sex. However, a different understanding is certainly possible. Christine Delphy's materialist analysis of gender allowed her to propose that gender, as the hierarchical division of humanity, is what transformed an anatomical difference, which in itself lacks any social implications, into a relevant distinction for social practice, making it an actual category of thought.[79] According to Delphy, the social relevance acquired by individuals' genitalia is not only as socially constructed as gender, but it is actually a consequence of an already gendered conception of human kind. In other words, sex is far from a biological notion, but a clear cultural construct.

[75] Gerda Lerner, *The Creation of Patriarchy* (Oxford University Press, 1986) 212 and 239.

[76] Ann Oakley, *Sex, Gender and Society* (Temple Smith, 1972) 16. Oakley was among the first to propose the cultural/biological dynamic between gender and sex. See Stevi Jackson, 'Theorising Gender and Sexuality' in Stevi Jackson and Jackie Jones (eds), *Contemporary Feminist Theories* (Edinburgh University Press, 1998) 131–45, 132–33.

[77] Suzanne J Kessler and Wendy McKenna, *Gender: An Ethnomethodological Approach* (University of Chicago Press, 1978) 11.

[78] Candace West and Don H Zimmerman, 'Doing Gender' (1987) 1 *Gender and Society* 125, at 126–27, 140 and 147.

[79] Christine Delphy, *Close to Home: A Materialist Analysis of Women's Oppression* (Hutchinson, 1984) 144; Christine Delphy, 'Rethinking Sex and Gender' in Stevi Jackson and Sue Scott (eds), *Gender: A Sociological Reader* (Routledge, 2001) 51–58, at 54.

Further foundations to the understanding of sex as a cultural construction have been provided by Thomas Laqueur, who explained that sex also has a history. Laqueur proposed that it was not until the eighteenth century that the 'fact' that men and women have different genitalia was 'discovered', creating sex as an ontological category.[80] Before that time, the distinction between the genitalia of men and women was considered to be not of kind but merely of degree.[81] Nevertheless, the socio-political distinctions between the two groups existed already, as different roles were assigned to individuals based on them being either men or women.[82] This allowed Laqueur to conclude that while gendered differences between individuals were already in place, it was not until the eighteenth century that the idea of two different and opposite sexes was created.[83]

Judith Butler made use of the works of Laqueur, and of materialist feminists,[84] and added a postmodern twist to the understanding of sex and gender as artificial constructs. She affirmed that the assumed distinction between the categories of men and women as a consequence of the existence of two biological sexes (male/female) was unsustainable, since there is no causal relation between sex and gender.[85] Butler's proposal adopted Delphy's thesis that gender is not a cultural construction founded on a biological fact, but sex is already the artificial creation of a gendered culture. Nevertheless, Butler took this idea even further. She proposed that the cultural character of gender and sex, coupled with the absence of a needed causal relation between those concepts, shows that the binary conceptions of gender and sex are actually unnecessary. Following Butler, what might prove to be the case is that the distinction between sex and gender is no distinction at all.[86] Sex can be understood to be the same as gender, since the sex/gender attributed to the human person is always culturally created. Neither sex nor gender is a pre-discursive notion that is fixed on individuals. Sex and gender could both be re-conceived outside the limited categorical binary manner in which they exist.[87] In particular, Butler developed the idea of gender as a *performative* construction. According to her, gender is performative in the sense that it is not an internal essence of the body, but its construction takes place through the repetition of acts, and it achieves its effect through its materialisation in the context of a body.[88] However, this gender *performativity* is far from being a free choice

[80] Thomas Laqueur, 'Orgasm, Generation, and the Politics of Reproductive Biology' (1986) 14 *Representations* 1, at 17–18; Thomas Laqueur, *Making Sex: Body and Gender from the Greeks to Freud* (Harvard University Press, 1990) 149.

[81] Laqueur, *Making Sex* (n 80) 25.

[82] ibid 8 and 149.

[83] ibid 6.

[84] Stevi Jackson suggested that the connection between the work of Delphy and that of Butler is given by Butler's use of the work of another materialist feminist, Monique Wittig. Jackson, 'Theorising Gender and Sexuality' (n 76) 137.

[85] Butler, *Gender Trouble* (n 74) 10–11 and 43–44.

[86] ibid 6–7.

[87] ibid 10–11.

[88] ibid 33; Judith Butler, *Gender Trouble: Feminism and the Subversion of Identity*, 2nd edn (Routledge, 1999) xv.

of the individual, but it is the actual effect of a constraining regulatory regime based on hierarchical differences, taboos and prohibitions.[89] As Butler clarified, performativity is a compulsory repetition of prior *subjectivating* norms.[90] This understanding of sex and gender as cultural notions and performative constructions is a foundational notion of queer theory. In fact, from this point forward, this book will use indistinguishably the concepts sex and gender, adopting Butler's idea that the distinction between them is no distinction at all. This understanding of sex/gender can allow us to re-think this concept outside the binary in which it is still mostly conceived.

B. A Queer Approach to Sexuality

Queer theorists, mostly following the work of Michel Foucault,[91] have embraced the idea of human sexuality as a cultural construction.[92] In the first volume of the *History of Sexuality*, Foucault argued that homosexuality as an identity has a relatively short history. According to him, the notion of homosexuality did not come into existence until the nineteenth century, when the regulation and administration of both individual and social bodies transformed the practice of sodomy, a legally punishable religious sin, into a deviant form of life.[93] In a paradigmatic sentence, Foucault affirmed: 'The sodomite had been a temporary aberration; the homosexual was now a species.'[94] Moreover, the construction of *homosexuality* as an identity also implied the constitution of the *heterosexual* category.[95] Both concepts (homosexuality and heterosexuality) have been conceived within a binary opposition, in which the meaning of one cannot be understood without the knowledge of the other, since their meaning actually derives from such a contrast.[96] However, the binary pair was constructed asymmetrically, as one of the

[89] Judith Butler, *Bodies that Matter: On the Discursive Limits of Sex* (Routledge, 1993) 59–60; Judith Butler, 'Critically Queer' in Shane Phelan (ed), *Playing with Fire: Queer Politics, Queer Theories* (Routledge, 1997) 11–29, at 16.

[90] Butler, 'Critically Queer' (n 89) 17.

[91] Michel Foucault, *The History of Sexuality: An Introduction* (Penguin, 1978) 105 and 157. Nonetheless, the work of Mary McIntosh has been one of the earliest ones regarding social constructionism and homosexuality. See Mary McIntosh, 'The Homosexual Role' (1968) 16 *Social Problems* 182.

[92] Jeffrey Weeks, *Sexuality* (Tavistock Publications, 1986) 15; David Halperin, *One Hundred Years of Homosexuality, And Other Essays on Greek Love* (Routledge, 1990) 25; Mary McIntosh, 'Queer Theory and the War of the Sexes' in Joseph Bristow and Angelia R Wilson (eds), *Activating Theory: Lesbian, Gay, Bisexual Politics* (Lawrence & Wishart, 1993) 30–52, 34; Gayle Rubin, 'Thinking Sex: Notes for a Radical Theory of the Politics of Sexuality' in Richard Parker and Peter Aggleton (eds), *Culture, Society and Sexuality: A Reader* (Routledge, 2007) 150–87, at 150 and 157.

[93] Foucault, *The History of Sexuality* (n 91) 43 and 139–46.

[94] ibid 43.

[95] Jonathan Katz, *The Invention of Heterosexuality* (Dutton, 1995) 12; Annamarie Jagose, *Queer Theory: An Introduction* (Melbourne University Press, 1996) 16–17; Nikki Sullivan, *A Critical Introduction to Queer Theory* (New York University Press, 2003) 120.

[96] See Joan W Scott, 'Deconstructing Equality-Versus-Difference: Or, the Uses of Post-structuralist Theory for Feminism' (1988) 14 *Feminist Studies* 33, at 36–37.

terms is considered to be normal (heterosexuality), while the other is understood to be deviant.[97]

Queer theory highlights that all identities are constructed through the dynamic interaction with and against overlapping cultural rules.[98] In order to be intelligible, every identity is constructed upon the notion of difference, with both concepts existing in a dialectic pair of identity/difference. Difference is constructed as the absence of identity and, necessarily, identity is understood as the absence of difference.[99] As explained by Butler, intelligible subjects are created through this exclusionary process that has, as a logical need, the simultaneous creation of the non-subject, the *other*.[100] Therefore, for an identity to emerge and prevail, the subsistence of the other is also required.[101]

The cultural and ideological construction of sexual identities caused the categorisation of every individual according to the heterosexual/homosexual binary and established particular consequences for those positioned in the 'wrong' category.[102] On the one hand, the regulation of the erotic desires of the human created a comprehensive set of laws establishing accepted and forbidden conduct.[103] On the other hand, these consequences exceeded the field of legal sanctions that already existed for the sin of sodomy. Next to them a new regulatory framework aimed at disciplining individuals was developed.[104] Since the homosexual subject performed acts that were not only criminal, but perverted,[105] homosexuality was the object of criminal and medical policies aimed at its control and treatment for the protection of society as a whole.[106] Homosexuality was observed, studied, problematised, pathologised, regulated, forced into confession and censored into secrecy. At the same time, the homosexual's existence was preserved, as it was needed for the very coherence of heterosexuality as an identity category.

Making use of the Foucauldian understanding of the (relatively) recent emergence of homosexual and heterosexual identities, queer theorist Kosofsky Sedgwick questioned the construction of sexuality in terms of gender.[107] She

97 Eve Kosofsky Sedgwick, *Epistemology of the Closet* (California University Press, 1990) 9–10; Diana Fuss (ed), *Inside/Out: Lesbian Theories, Gay Theories* (Routledge, 1991) 2; Katz, *The Invention of Heterosexuality* (n 95) 187; David Halperin, *Saint Foucault: Towards a Gay Hagiography* (Oxford University Press, 1997) 44–45.

98 Gloria Filax and others, 'Queer Theory / Lesbian and Gay Approaches' in Bridget Somekh and Cathy Lewin (eds), *Research Methods in the Social Sciences* (Sage, 2004) 81–88, at 81–82.

99 Balkin, 'Deconstructive Practice and Legal Theory' (n 18) 748.

100 Butler, *Bodies that Matter* (n 89) xi.

101 William Connolly, *Identity/Difference: Democratic Negotiations of Political Paradox* (Cornell University Press, 1991) 64.

102 Sedgwick, *Epistemology of the Closet* (n 97) 2; Halperin, *One Hundred Years of Homosexuality* (n 92) 26.

103 Rubin, 'Thinking Sex' (n 92) 180.

104 Foucault, *The History of Sexuality* (n 91) 43–44.

105 ibid 44–45.

106 David F Greenberg, *The Construction of Homosexuality* (University of Chicago Press, 1990) 403–33.

107 Sedgwick, *Epistemology of the Closet* (n 97) 8–9; According to Nikki Sullivan, this issue has been raised before by Pat Califia. Sullivan, *A Critical Introduction to Queer Theory* (n 95) 38.

highlighted that the accepted Western model of sexual identities privileged the conception of sexualities in binary heterosexual/homosexual terms, overshadowing (if not excluding) other possible dimensions along which sexualities extend, such as the types of preferred practices or the number of participants involved.[108] Kosofsky Sedgwick further proposed that the Western belief in a binary sexuality based on the gender of the desired sexual partner is underpinned by a number of different assumptions that can be questioned, such as the presumption that every person has a sexuality; that this sexuality is oriented towards another person; and that this sexuality is fixed and will not change over time.[109]

C. The Hallmarks of Queer Theory

Following the previous discussion, queer theory can be defined as a critique of identity.[110] It can be located in the realm of the postmodern,[111] given its rejection of objective, absolute, and naturalised views on identities. Butler's notion of performative identities is at the centre of queer theory and acts as a fundamental reason for questioning the understanding of identities as natural. Therefore, it can be affirmed that queer theory aims at stressing the arbitrary and fictional nature of identities,[112] and that denaturalising categories through deconstruction is one of its main elements.[113] It is at the core of queer thinking to continuously question the identities constructed through binary oppositions that result in the system of two mandatory sexes, two consequential genders, and one normal sexuality.[114]

Arlene Stein and Ken Plummer have identified four characteristics as the hallmarks of queer theory.[115] One of these characteristics is the problematisation of sexual and gender categories, and of identities in general, given that identities are

[108] Sedgwick, *Epistemology of the Closet* (n 97) 8–9 and 25–26.

[109] Sedgwick, *Tendencies* (n 73) 7.

[110] Beger, *Tensions in the Struggle for Sexual Minority Rights in Europe* (n 13) 41.

[111] Janice M Irvine, 'A Place in the Rainbow: Theorizing Lesbian and Gay Culture' (1994) 12 *Sociological Theory* 232, at 243; Laurie Rose Kepros, 'Queer Theory: Weed or Seed in the Garden of Legal Theory' (2000) 9 *Law and Sexuality: A Review of Lesbian, Gay, Bisexual, and Transgender Legal Issues* 279, at 282; Beger, *Tensions in the Struggle for Sexual Minority Rights in Europe* (n 13) 41. I choose to locate queer theory within postmodernism, although it is also commonly referred to as grounded on post-structuralism. While queer theory might be either postmodern or post-structural, both, or neither, it certainly shares postmodernism's incredulity towards metanarratives; its distrust of the existence of universal 'truths'; as well as its disbelief in history as a gradual journey of humanity towards a more developed end point. See Jean-François Lyotard, *The Postmodern Condition: A Report on Knowledge* (Geoff Bennington and Brian Massumi tr, University of Minnesota Press, 1984) xxiv; Jill Steans, Lloyd Pettiford, Thomas Diez and Imad El-Anis, *An Introduction to International Relations Theory*, 3rd edn (Pearson, 2010) 134–35 and 141.

[112] Jeffrey Weeks, *The Languages of Sexuality* (Routledge, 2011) 146.

[113] Lisa Duggan, 'Queering the State' (1994) 39 *Social Text* 1, at 4; Adam Isaiah Green, 'Queer Theory and Sociology: Locating the Subject and the Self in Sexuality Studies' (2007) 25 *Sociological Theory* 26, at 28.

[114] Filax and others, 'Queer Theory / Lesbian and Gay Approaches' (n 98) 81.

[115] Stein and Plummer, '"I Can't Even Think Straight"' (n 69) 181–82.

always considered to be on uncertain grounds.[116] As argued above, the categories of sexuality and gender are the main concerns of queer theory. Queer theory questions both the understanding of identities as stable categories, as well as their construction through binary divisions. The traditional understanding of individuals as either men or women and either heterosexual or homosexual is challenged by queer's postmodern view of these identities as cultural constructions that are fraught with incoherence and instability.[117] Current queer politics suggest going beyond the more traditional LGBT identities, arguing that what truly matters is the fluidity of desire.[118] As Kate Bornstein claimed:

> [I]f we buy into categories of sexual orientation based solely on gender – heterosexual, homosexual, or bisexual – we're cheating ourselves of a searching examination of our real sexual preferences. In the same fashion, by subscribing to the categories of gender based solely on the male/female binary, we cheat ourselves of a searching examination of our real gender identity.[119]

Indeed, queer theory focuses on the 'deviant' cases, on identities that cannot be comprehended by fixed binaries, and celebrates those identities that disrupt the normative alignment of gender and sexuality.[120] Queer strategies demand recognition of either border or mixed identities, or even of the lack of identity.[121] As Wilchins has proposed:

> In fact, why do any gender at all? What is the cultural demand that we answer to any gendered norm? Why can't Mariette simply feel like a woman when she does, feel like nothing at all when she doesn't, and have her little moments of masculinity if and when they emerge? Why can't she let all that be whatever it is?[122]

An additional hallmark mentioned by Stein and Plummer is: 'A conceptualization of sexuality which sees sexual power embodied in different levels of social life, expressed discursively and enforced through boundaries and binary divides'.[123] This characteristic shows queer's further reliance on the work of Foucault. As discussed above, Foucault proposed that Western sexual categories are a product of the social regulation that transformed the religious sin of sodomy into a deviant form of life. This idea fits within a broader conception of power he developed in the first volume of the *History of Sexuality*. Foucault argued that in the West, since the seventeenth century, sovereign power over life has

[116] ibid 182.
[117] Stephen Valocchi, 'Not Yet Queer Enough: The Lessons of Queer Theory for the Sociology of Gender and Sexuality' (2005) 19 *Gender and Society* 750, at 752–53.
[118] Carol Johnson, 'Heteronormative Citizenship and the Politics of Passing' (2002) 5 *Sexualities* 317, at 329.
[119] Kate Bornstein, *Gender Outlaw: On Men, Women, and the Rest of Us* (Vintage Books, 1995) 38.
[120] Halperin, 'The Normalization of Queer Theory' (n 70) 341; Valocchi, 'Not Yet Queer Enough' (n 117) 753.
[121] Gross, 'Sex, Love, and Marriage' (n 14) 252.
[122] Riki Wilchins, *Queer Theory, Gender Theory: An Instant Primer* (Alyson Books, 2004) 132.
[123] Stein and Plummer, '"I Can't Even Think Straight"' (n 69) 181–82.

experienced a drastic transformation. Power over the life and death of the subject increasingly became a life-administrating power, a power that rather than threatening life was involved in its reinforcement, its control, and its administration.[124] This power over life (which he called bio-power) manifested itself in two different but interlinked forms: an anatomo-politics of the human body and a biopolitics of the population.[125] The anatomo-politics was aimed at disciplining the individual body, a disciplinary power that was directed at optimising both the capabilities of the subject and its docility.[126] On the other hand, the biopolitics was concerned with the regulation of the body of the species, focused on controlling populations through the processes of birth, mortality, health and longevity.[127] This bio-power, aimed at taking charge of life, was not based on bringing death into play; rather what it needed were continuous regulatory and corrective mechanisms.[128]

A third highlighted hallmark is queer theory's 'willingness to interrogate areas which normally would not be seen as the terrain of sexuality, and to conduct queer "readings" of ostensibly heterosexual or nonsexualized texts'.[129] The deconstructive method of queer theory aims at demonstrating that even those seemingly neutral aspects of everyday life are underpinned by *heteronormative* assumptions. The term *heteronormativity* has been defined by Michael Warner and Lauren Berlant as: 'the institutions, structures of understanding, and practical orientations that make heterosexuality seem not only coherent – that is, organized as a sexuality – but also privileged'.[130] However, heteronormativity should be understood in a rather broader sense, to unveil that it has been built upon and comprehends other *normativities*. Examples of normalising regimes that underpin and support heteronormativity are: the idea of a *sexual imperative*, which assumes that every person conceives sexuality as an essential part of their lives;[131] a *mononormativity* that reifies the couple form as the ideal type of intimate relationship;[132] a *repronormativity* that presents reproduction as an irresistible natural drive;[133] and, certainly,

[124] Foucault, *The History of Sexuality* (n 91) 136.
[125] ibid 139.
[126] ibid.
[127] ibid.
[128] ibid 144.
[129] Stein and Plummer, '"I Can't Even Think Straight"' (n 69) 182.
[130] Lauren Berlant and Michael Warner, 'Sex in Public' (1998) 24 *Critical Inquiry* 547, at 548. Similarly, Ingraham has defined 'heteronormativity' as: 'the view that institutionalized heterosexuality constitutes the standard for legitimate and prescriptive sociosexual arrangement'. Chrys Ingraham, 'The Heterosexual Imaginary: Feminist Sociology and the Theories of Gender' (1994) 12 *Sociological Theory* 203, at 204.
[131] Sedgwick, *Tendencies* (n 73) 7; Ela Przybylo, 'Masculine Doubt and Sexual Wonder' in Karli June Cerankowski and Megan Milks (eds), *Asexualities: Feminist and Queer Perspectives* (Routledge, 2014) 442–81, at 448.
[132] ibid 453 and 473; Robin Bauer, 'Non-Monogamy in Queer BDSM Communities: Putting the Sex Back into Alternative Relationship Practices and Discourse' in Meg Barker and Darren Langdridge (eds), *Understanding Non-Monogamies* (Routledge, 2010) 142–53, at 145.
[133] Katherine M Franke, 'Theorizing Yes: An Essay on Feminism, Law, and Desire' in Martha Albertson Fineman, Jack E Jackson and Adam P Romero (eds), *Feminist and Queer Legal Theory: Intimate Encounters, Uncomfortable Conversations* (Ashgate, 2009) 29–44, 30–31. See also Michael Warner (ed), *Fear of a Queer Planet: Queer Politics and Social Theory* (University of Minnesota Press, 1993) ix.

cisnormativity,[134] which reveals that a heterosexual culture also assumes all people to be cissexual,[135] problematising and rendering invisible trans individuals. In fact, this book aims at performing a deconstructive analysis that will search for heteronormative assumption underpinning the field of human rights law, which tends to be assumed by many (on all sides of the political spectrum) to be a privileged site of gender and sexual neutrality open to the claims of LGBT individuals.

The remaining hallmark of queer theory, as discussed by Stein and Plummer, is its distrust of strategies based on rights, which goes to the core of this monograph. Queer theory is characterised by 'a rejection of civil rights strategies in favor of a politics of carnival, transgression, and parody which leads to deconstruction, decentering, revisionist readings, and an antiassimilationist politics'.[136] This highlights the clear tension between liberal rights and postmodern queer theory.[137] Indeed, the rationale for this book is to engage with this tension. At this point, it becomes easier to understand my previous statement that this project is not about LGBT rights. Human rights are a clear product of liberalism,[138] and queer theory is certainly not concerned with the incorporation of LGBT individuals into the realm of liberal rights, given that it offers a critique of rights and strategies for achieving them.[139] As claimed by Warner, queer aims not just at toleration or equal status, but at challenging institutions.[140] Queer theory places special emphasis on resisting these types of regimes, which are perceived as regulatory in Foucauldian terms of bio-power.[141] The interest of queer theory would be in critiquing such regimes, unveiling their hidden heteronormative conception of the notions of gender and sexuality.[142]

Nevertheless, the normative claim of this book is that the tension between queer theory and human rights discourse needs not to lead to unsolvable antagonism.

[134] Greta R Bauer, Rebecca Hammond, Robb Travers, Matthias Kaay, Karin M Hohenadel and Michelle Boyce, '"I Don't Think This is Theoretical; This is Our Lives": How Erasure Impacts Health Care for Transgender People' (2009) 20 *Journal of the Association of Nurses in AIDS Care* 348, at 356; Cristina Richie, 'Lessons from Queer Bioethics: A Response to Timothy F. Murphy' (2016) 30 *Bioethics* 365, at 366.

[135] I use the term 'cissexual' in binary opposition to 'transsexual'. See Jessica Cadwallader, 'Diseased States: The Role of Pathology in the (Re)Production of the Body Politic' in Nikki Sullivan and Samantha Murray (eds), *Somatechnics: Queering the Technologisation of Bodies* (Ashgate, 2009) 17.

[136] Stein and Plummer, '"I Can't Even Think Straight"' (n 69) 182.

[137] Graeme W Austin, 'Queering Family Law' (1999) 8 *Australasian Gay and Lesbian Law Journal* 39, at 42; Carlos A Ball, 'Sexual Ethics and Postmodernism in Gay Rights Philosophy' (2002) 80 *North Carolina Law Review* 371, at 457; Zanghellini, 'Queer, Antinormativity, Counter-normativity and Abjection' (n 68) 8.

[138] Dembour, *Who Believes in Human Rights?* (n 16) 6; Beger, *Tensions in the Struggle for Sexual Minority Rights in Europe* (n 13) 92.

[139] Morgan, 'Queering International Human Rights Law' (n 14) 224; Zanghellini, 'Queer, Antinormativity, Counter-normativity and Abjection' (n 68) 1; Cobb 'Gay Couple's Break Like Fawlty Towers' (n 68) 335; Jena McGill and Amy Salyzyn, 'Queer Insights on Women in the Legal Profession' (2014) 17 *Legal Ethics* 231, at 238.

[140] Warner, *Fear of a Queer Planet* (n 133) xiii.

[141] ibid xxvi; Carl F Stychin, 'Being Gay' (2005) 40 *Government and Opposition* 90, at 96.

[142] Beger, *Tensions in the Struggle for Sexual Minority Rights in Europe* (n 13) 99.

On the one hand, I propose that human rights can actually benefit from a better understanding of queer critiques, taking some of them on board, as various queer insights can help its aim of universality. On the other hand, I believe queer activism can also take advantage of human rights law. It is possible to explore different ways to *queer* human rights law while retaining a critical awareness of the regulatory power of legal rights.

To summarise, queer theory can be described as a deconstructive strategy that aims at denaturalising heteronormative understandings of genders and sexualities.[143] It can be a very important tool for challenging the definition, stability, and dynamic articulation of identity categories based on gender and sexuality. Central to queer thinking is the continuous interrogation of discourses that reinforce the system of two mandatory genders and one normal sexuality. The use of this powerful theoretical framework has made some important appearance within legal analyses, in an approach to legal studies that can be labelled *queer legal theory*.

V. Queer Legal Theory

There is no general agreement within the scholarship as to what constitutes queer legal theory. In fact, it is possible to find different definitions of this concept. For instance, Francisco Valdes has offered the following definition:

> *Queer* legal theory therefore is the name employed … to signify a self-conscious, self-defined, and self-sustaining body of liberational *legal* scholarship that voices and pursues the interests of sexual minorities as its particular contribution toward the end of sex/gender subordination.[144]

Adam Romero has argued that: 'The concept of queer legal theory is something of a paradox given the tension between 'queer' and 'legal'',[145] and offered the definition that follows:

> [L]egal theory that is queer is legal scholarship that is oppositional or at odds with – and thus in relation to – that which is normal or dominant. The term 'queer', then, refers to relational scholarship that postures itself somehow against or at variance with the normative. Though much queer legal scholarship concerns itself with sexual and gendered minorities, the general term 'queer', as I have suggested, is not prefigured to refer to any issue or set of issues in particular.[146]

[143] Sullivan, *A Critical Introduction to Queer Theory* (n 95) 81.
[144] Francisco Valdes, 'Queers, Sissies, Dykes, and Tomboys: Deconstructing the Conflation of "Sex", "Gender", and "Sexual Orientation" in Euro-American Law and Society' (1995) 83 *California Law Review* 1, at 349.
[145] Adam P Romero, 'Methodological Descriptions: "Feminist" and "Queer" Legal Theories' (2007) 19 *Yale Journal of Law and Feminism* 227, at 247.
[146] ibid 254.

Nonetheless, it was Carl Stychin's *Law's Desire*,[147] which acted as the seminal text that established queer legal theory as a disciplinary field.[148] As affirmed by Aleardo Zanghellini, in that book, Stychin has sketched the foundations of what can be considered queer legal theory.[149] A first element that characterises queer legal theory is an understanding that the power of law is not only repressive, but also disciplinary.[150] In particular, the law can be seen as one of the sources of the regulatory power over individuals' identities, which includes individuals' gender and sexuality.[151] A further component is the awareness that the law conceives its regulated universe through categories, which becomes particularly evident in the regulation of gender and sexuality through a binary conception (man/woman, heterosexual/homosexual).[152] Faced with this regulatory system, queer legal theory would make use of a deconstructive analysis in order to unveil the lack of coherence and stability of these categories.[153] In addition to this, queer legal theory holds an anti-essentialist view, grounded in the queer notion of the performative construction of identities, which offers a possible space for questioning the assumed natural character of identity categories that are used by the law.[154]

Having established the main elements of queer legal theory, a question that remains is whether queer legal theory can have a normative goal, or if it can only constitute a critical approach to the law. A number of academics working in the field of sexuality and the law have expressed their scepticism as to the possibility of *queering* the law, considering that queer's concern with being critical forecloses its possibility of also being normative.[155] Nevertheless, I remain convinced that the law can be queered.[156] I actually share Zanghellini's perplexity as to why queer legal theory has not yet managed to articulate serious inputs into how to change the law. As he asserted: 'we must unleash Queer's full potential for making original and distinctive contributions to jurisprudential knowledge',[157] including normative jurisprudence.

[147] Stychin, *Law's Desire* (n 12).
[148] Zanghellini, 'Queer, Antinormativity, Counter-normativity and Abjection' (n 68) 5.
[149] ibid 3, 4 and 5.
[150] Carl F Stychin, *Governing Sexuality: The Changing Politics of Citizenship and Law Reform* (Hart Publishing, 2003) 3.
[151] Stychin, *Law's Desire* (n 12) 156.
[152] ibid 148.
[153] ibid 143.
[154] ibid 146.
[155] Nicholas Bamforth, *Sexuality, Morals and Justice: A Theory of Lesbian and Gay Rights Law* (Cassell, 1997) 229; Romero, 'Methodological Descriptions' (n 145) 248.
[156] Valdes, 'Queers, Sissies, Dykes, and Tomboys' (n 144) 342 and 356; Francisco Valdes, 'Sex and Race in Queer Legal Culture: Ruminations on Identities and Inter-connectivities' (1996) 5 *California Review of Law and Women's Studies* 25, at 70; Austin, 'Queering Family Law' (n 137) 51; Lisa Gotell, 'Queering Law: Not by Vriend' (2002) 17 *Canadian Journal of Law and Society* 89, at 92; Zanghellini, 'Queer, Antinormativity, Counter-normativity and Abjection' (n 68) 2; Otto, 'Queering Gender [Identity] in International Law' (n 14) 318.
[157] Zanghellini, 'Queer, Antinormativity, Counter-normativity and Abjection' (n 68) 14.

This book is aimed at elaborating ideas that can be useful for queering the field of international human rights law. It is worth highlighting that given the fluid character of the notion of queer itself, the outcome of queering the law can have many different possible manifestations. For instance, Stychin has elaborated on the possibility of a legal framework that acknowledges the lack of categorical value of its own categories.[158] Elsewhere, I have suggested that emphasis on legal indifference towards identity categories could actually favour the diversity of sexualities.[159] However, these are just two of the multiple possible paths that might (or might not) lead to a queer(er) law.

VI. Queering Human Rights Law

As I mentioned above, the ultimate goal of this book is to engage with the complex relationship between human rights law and queer theory, with the conviction that a constructive dialogue between the two can lead to a fruitful outcome. While there is an obvious tension between liberal human rights and postmodern queer theory, there is also some shared common ground. The most evident example of a shared value between both theoretical frameworks is their positive view on the idea of freedom,[160] but this is not the only coincidence between queer thought and human rights. As Zanghellini has pointed out, queer theory does have a commitment to liberal values such as respect, pluralism, and personal autonomy.[161] He has argued that

> the failure of Queer and liberal theory to seriously converse with each other is perplexing, given that many of the presuppositions, assumptions and normative commitments of Queer look very much like those one finds in the best strands of the liberal tradition.[162]

Michael Warner, one of the most influential queer theorists, has offered an enumeration of the different principles that act as the foundations of queer thought.[163] It is not my intention to discuss them all, but to emphasise that a number of these principles are shared by human rights and, therefore, can be deployed in the service of its proclaimed aim of universal enjoyment of rights. These are four of Warner's principles of queer theory:

- It recognize[s] the diversity of sexual and intimate relations as worthy of respect and protection.
- …

[158] Stychin, *Law's Desire* (n 12) 155–56.
[159] Gonzalez-Salzberg, 'The Making of the Court's Homosexual' (n 14) 371.
[160] Ball, 'Sexual Ethics and Postmodernism in Gay Rights Philosophy' (n 137) 457.
[161] Zanghellini, 'Queer, Antinormativity, Counter-normativity and Abjection' (n 68) 8.
[162] ibid 14.
[163] Michael Warner, *The Trouble with Normal: Sex, Politics, and the Ethics of Queer Life* (Harvard University Press, 2000) 88–89.

- It resist[s] any attempt to make the norms of straight culture into the standards by which queer life should be measured.
- It especially resist[s] the notion that the state should be allowed to accord legitimacy to some kinds of consensual sex but not others …
- …
- It [makes] itself alert to the invidiousness of any institution, like marriage, that is designed both to reward those inside it and to discipline those outside it.[164]

I fail to see how human rights theory could actually oppose any of these principles. On the contrary, human rights law, properly understood, is bound to respect and protect consensual sexualities and diverse intimate relationships, without discrimination. Similarly, the universal character of human rights stands at odds with the imposition of any lifestyle as the standard by which all lives should be lived. Lastly, human rights should not validate any institution that is aimed at delegitimising those who do not take part in it, since the value of personal autonomy is one of the main principles upon which human rights are based.

My main claim in this book is that given this existent common ground between human rights and queer theory, a deconstructive reading of human rights discourse on gender identity and sexuality can help to envision the reconstruction of the subject of human rights beyond strict categories. Both my confidence in the value of human rights as a strategy for improving people's lives, as well as my conviction in the need to overcome the current shortcomings of human rights in relation to sexual and gender identities,[165] allow me to believe that human rights law can take advantage of queer's technique of continuous interrogation in order to test and improve the actual scope of the purported universality of rights. Similarly, a more queer human rights regime will be beneficial to the lives of queer individuals. Queer theory can help us imagine a normative system in which the subject would not need to fit within strict sexed and sexual binaries, since the humanity of individuals would not depend on their ability to conform to rigid categories. It can help us re-think human rights law in a more universal way. To this end, in the following chapters, I will make use of insights from queer theory to critically analyse the legal regulation of the gendered and sexual subject of human rights through the work of the highest legal authority within the European context of human rights law: the European Court of Human Rights.

VII. Outline of the Book

This first chapter has provided the framework within which this project will be conducted. Chapters 2 and 3 will offer the central analysis of this book, directly

[164] ibid.

[165] Sonia Corrêa, Rosalind Petchesky and Richard Parker, *Sexuality, Health and Human Rights* (Routledge, 2008) 152, 161 and 223–24; Anthony J Langlois, 'Human Rights in Crisis? A Critical Polemic Against Polemical Critics' (2012) 11 *Journal of Human Rights* 558, at 568.

interrogating the notions of gender and sexual identities within the case law of the European Court of Human Rights. Chapter 2 will focus on the sex/gender of the subject of human rights law, discussing how the Court has constructed the conception of gender within its jurisprudence. Moreover, the tension between the human rights approach to gender identity and queer views on the topic will be exposed and put into a productive relationship. This chapter will end with a queer claim for resistance against the human rights constructed universe of two strict genders. It will point out the potential for making use of the Court's unstable discourse on transsexuality in order to reach a possible queer existence within human rights law.

Chapter 3 will focus on the notion of sexuality, with special emphasis on the Court's construction of homosexuality. While the topic of homosexuality has been discussed by a number of scholars in different studies, the chapter will offer an original approach to the topic. It will propose an understanding of the Court's protection of the homosexual subject that is focused on the regulatory power exercised by the law over identities. The Chapter will explore how the case law has constructed homosexuality as a stable identity worthy of protection, which helps to explain why homosexual individuals have been successful when claiming certain rights before the Court. However, I will argue that the Court's understanding of sexuality can be (queerly) reshaped.

While Chapters 2 and 3 are about the construction of gender and sexuality through the case law, Chapters 4 and 5 will focus on how these constructions have had a clear impact on the enjoyment of human rights by LGBT individuals. Chapter 4 will deal with the Court's case law concerning LGBT family rights, presenting a legal analysis informed by insights from queer theory of the construction of the family within human rights law. It will also engage with the Court's method for deciding cases under Article 14 (the prohibition of discrimination), as this provision has been the one most frequently used by claimants bringing cases to Strasbourg concerning LGBT family rights. Chapter 5 will continue the examination of LGBT families and their protection under the Convention, focusing on the familial bonds of marriage and parenthood. It will analyse the Court's jurisprudence on marriage, examining how the idea of heterosexuality in marriage has been constructed through the case law in a relatively unstable way. This will allow an understanding of marriage as an institution that is less heterosexual in practice than in theory. The last part of the chapter will be devoted to the analysis of parenting by LGBT individuals, focusing on the created tension between the best interests of the children and parents' sexualities.

Chapter 6 will provide a shift in method: it will be the only chapter that is not about deconstructing judgments. Rather, it will be concerned with reconstructing some of the decisions examined in Chapters 4 and 5. In Chapter 6, I will undertake the task of re-writing four of the most contentious rulings of the Court concerning sexual and gender identities. I will use some of the insights from queer theory discussed throughout the book in order to show how the Court could have made use of them. This will highlight how the decisions the Court adopted were, by no means, the only possible solutions to the cases. The other main goal of the chapter will be to illustrate that queer theory is not just a methodology limited to performing a critique, but it can also be normative and constructive. The chapter will conclude by arguing that the Court should overcome the heteronormative assumptions that underpin its jurisprudence and will put across the idea that queer theory can offer a path to achieve this goal.

Lastly, the Conclusion will provide a summary of the most important arguments developed in each chapter. I will also highlight different queer insights that have been (maybe inadvertently) held by the Court and which can be unveiled when the case law is read through the use of queer's deconstructive technique. Then, I will set out future challenges that can be addressed in the ambit of the Court's jurisprudence on sexuality and trans rights.

2

The Court's Conception of Gender*

I. Introduction

This chapter will make use of insights from queer theory to analyse how the European Court of Human Rights ('the Court') has constructed (and re-constructed) the notion of individuals' gender through its case law. As discussed in Chapter 1, queer theory works within a postmodern understanding of identities that contests their stability, challenging not only the fixity of categories such as sex/gender and sexuality,[1] but also the traditional construction of these characteristics as opposed binaries.[2] Queer theory also highlights the role played by the law in the regulation of individuals' identities in general, and regarding individuals' genders in particular.[3] Actually, the law can be seen as one of the sources of the gender regulatory system that discursively transforms observed genitalia into sex.[4] Every person is constructed by the law as a legal woman or a legal man,[5] and this legally imposed gender is the first assumption of the identity of a person.[6] Almost automatically after birth, every newly born person is gendered. In fact, the sex of the newborn appears as a prerequisite for their recognition as a human being. As argued by Judith Butler, the sex of a person acts as the ontological basis for their body to become intelligibly human.[7] In turn, individuals who do not appear

* An earlier version of this chapter has been awarded the 2013 Human Rights Essay Award by the American University, Washington College of Law. That earlier version has been published in the *American University International Law Review*. See Damian A Gonzalez-Salzberg, 'The Accepted Transsexual and the Absent Transgender: A Queer Reading of the Regulation of Sex/Gender by the European Court of Human Rights' (2014) 29 *American University International Law Review* 797.

[1] As explained in Chapter 1, I use the terms 'sex' and 'gender' interchangeably, in order to highlight both notions as social constructions.

[2] Annamarie Jagose, *Queer Theory: An Introduction* (Melbourne University Press, 1996) 3; Carl Stychin, *Law's Desire: Sexuality and the Limits of Justice* (Routledge, 1995) 141 and 145; Jeffrey Weeks, *The Language of Sexuality* (Routledge, 2011) 146.

[3] Stychin, *Law's Desire* (n 2) 156.

[4] Carol Smart, *Feminism and the Power of Law* (Routledge, 1989) 6 and 162; Carol Smart, 'Law's Power, the Sexed Body, and Feminist Discourse' (1990) 17 *Journal of Law and Society* 194, at 204.

[5] Smart, *Feminism and the Power of Law* (n 4) 93; Katherine O'Donovan, *Sexual Divisions in Law* (Weidenfeld and Nicolson, 1985) 59.

[6] The fact that the law does not usually offer a definition of male and female sexes can be understood as a reproduction of the belief in biological sexes as obvious characteristics, which would make it redundant to legally define them. See Julie A Greenberg, 'Intersexuality and the Collision Between Law and Biology' (1999) 41 *Arizona Law Review* 270.

[7] Judith Butler, *Gender Trouble: Feminism and the Subversion of Identity* (Routledge, 1999) xxiii.

to be 'properly' gendered have their own humanity put into question.[8] The legal attribution of a sex to a person has the value of a truth that is, at the same time, read and imposed on the body. As asked and answered by Michel Foucault in his Introduction to *Herculine Barbin*:

> Do we truly need a true sex? With a persistence that borders on stubbornness, modern Western societies have answered in the affirmative. They have obstinately brought into play this question of a 'true sex' in an order of things where one might have imagined that all that counted was the reality of the body and the intensity of its pleasures.[9]

The gender system adopted by the law is not only mandatory, but is also conceived in terms of an oppositional man/woman binary. These two genders are constructed as ontologically opposite; therefore, belonging to one of the sexes implies being excluded from the other. The law can only comprehend its subjects as legally gendered in a binary manner, problematising every individual who does not fit properly within the binary understanding of these categories. This chapter will focus on the problematisation of the bodies that do not fit the normalising gender model. In particular, I will centre my attention on existing challenges to the binary understanding of legally gendered bodies. The categorical model of fixed dualistic genders is challenged by the existence of those who do not neatly fit on one side of the binary: the intersex, the transsexual, and the transgender subjects appear as the paradigmatic examples.

The terminology I use follows the definitions offered by Stephen Whittle.[10] The term *trans* is used as an umbrella concept, to refer to every person who does not perceive their gender identity as the same as the one they were socially expected to fulfil as a result of their sex designation at birth. The term *transgender* refers to those individuals who live, or desire to live, a part of their life performing a gender role that does not follow the socially expected one that is allegedly correlative to the sex assigned to them at birth. Lastly, the term *transsexual* is used to refer to those individuals who intend to undergo, are undergoing, or have undergone a gender affirming process.

On the other hand, by *intersex* I refer to any subject whose body is understood by medical science as not fitting the rigid binary of the sexes and is, therefore, pathologised.[11] Intersex subjects highlight the incapacity of the female/male sex model to comprehend every individual. However, it is the intersex body that is

[8] Judith Butler, *Bodies that Matter: on the Discursive Limits of Sex* (Routledge, 1993) 7–8.

[9] Michel Foucault, *Herculine Barbin: Being the Recently Discovered Memoirs of a Nineteenth-Century French Hermaphrodite* (Harvester Press, 1980) vii.

[10] Stephen Whittle, *Respect and Equality: Transsexual and Transgender Rights* (Routledge, 2002) xxii–xxiii. These definitions do not intend to be anything else than a useful clarification to establish a common understanding of terms, limited to this work. In fact, I believe that any given definition would be arbitrary and, most likely, insufficient to describe all possibilities people can have to construct their own identities.

[11] Anne Fausto-Sterling, *Sexing the Body: Gender Politics and the Construction of Sexuality* (Basic Books, 2000) 257.

pathologised through its alleged inability to fit into the culturally constructed idea of binary opposed genitalia.[12] The legally accepted medical reaction to this challenge is to perform surgery to adapt the reality of the body into the constructed understanding of binary sexes.[13] The belief in a true sex is so legally unquestionable that it is the intersex body that needs correction to fit the binary system.

Nevertheless, the intersex subject is almost absent from the case law of the Court. Only a brief mention of the intersex body can be seen in a handful of rulings of the Court, which dealt with transsexuality.[14] The Court has stated that:

> It is known however that chromosomal anomalies may arise naturally (for example, in cases of intersex conditions where the biological criteria at birth are not congruent) and in those cases, some persons have to be assigned to one sex or the other as seems most appropriate in the circumstances of the individual case.[15]

The absence of the intersex subject can be explained by the validation of the systematic practice of 'normalising' surgery. As Anne Fausto-Sterling has argued, the existence of intersex bodies is usually only a matter of hours.[16] The law continues to allow medical discourse to produce the intersex as an anomaly that needs fixing according to the 'true' sex of the intersex body.[17] In turn, the surgical construction of a neatly sexed body reinforces the validity of the two-sex system.[18] This surgical erasure of the intersex subject can help to explain their absence from the Court's case law.

While the absent intersex individual shows the artificial nature of the (surgically maintained) two-sex model, transsexual subjects prove the lack of rigidity of the man/woman categories. Transsexual individuals who undergo a transition process to adapt their bodies to their gender identity show that the rigid separation of sex categories is nothing but an illusory rule. Moreover, while intersex individuals have been almost absent from the Court's rulings, transsexual bodies have been the main focus of the case law on gender. Hence, the current chapter will have the transsexual individual as its main subject.

[12] Jessica Knouse, 'Intersexuality and the Social Construction of Anatomical Sex' (2006) 12 *Cardozo Journal of Law and Gender* 135, at 146.

[13] Suzanne Kessler, 'The Medical Construction of Gender: Case Management of Intersexed Infants' (1990) 16 *Signs* 3, at 4; Greenberg, 'Intersexuality and the Collision Between Law and Biology' (n 6) 271–72.

[14] The term 'intersex' appeared in *Rees* and *Cossey* when stating the criteria that allowed amending birth certificates. Also, in 2015 an intersex applicant had a case dismissed by the Court on procedural grounds. See *Rees v United Kingdom*, Series A no 106, 17 October 1986, para 23; *Cossey v United Kingdom*, Series A no 184, 27 September 1990, para 20; *Klaedes v Cyprus* (Dec), Application no. 72491/12, 22 September 2015.

[15] *Christine Goodwin v United Kingdom* (GC), no 28957/95, ECHR 2002-VI, para 82; *I v United Kingdom* (GC), no 25680/94, 11 July 2002, para 62.

[16] Fausto-Sterling, *Sexing the Body* (n 11) 44.

[17] ibid 56.

[18] ibid 31.

This chapter will also be concerned with those trans identities that are made non-existent through the binary understanding of gender. The categorical ambition of sex classification fails when trying to contain within a limited man/woman binary individuals who identify as transgender, bi-gender, or non-binary,[19] amongst other possible gender non-conforming identities. In fact, the existence of subjects who refuse to neatly fit within the men and women classifications helps prove the possibility of transcending the categorical understanding of sex.[20] Nonetheless, as I will discuss towards the end of the chapter, these trans identities have not (yet) been central in the Court's case law.[21]

This chapter will be divided into nine sections. Section II will focus on the gendered subject conceived by the European Convention on Human Rights. Sections III and IV will analyse how sex has been defined and re-defined by the Court's case law through the years and its consequences concerning trans individuals. Section V will discuss the value of surgery in the re-definition of sex and section VI will focus on the current limitations of accessing sex affirming surgery as a human right. Section VII will then engage with the most recent advances in the Court's case law and section VIII will evaluate the potentially *queer* consequences of such jurisprudence. Lastly, conclusions will be drawn in section IX.

[19] The term 'non-binary' (as well as 'genderqueer') has been used by individuals who identify themselves as falling outside the currently dominant binary gender system. See Dylan Vade, 'Expanding Gender and Expanding the Law: Toward a Social and Legal Conceptualization of Gender that Is More Inclusive of Transgender People' (2005) 11 *Michigan Journal of Gender and Law* 253, at 266; Nancy Knauer, 'Gender Matters: Making the Case for Trans Inclusion' (2008) 6 *Pierce Law Review* 1, at 22–23; Alison Rooke, 'Telling Trans Stories: (Un)doing the Science of Sex' in Sally Hines and Tam Sanger (eds), *Transgender Identities: Towards a Social Analysis of Gender Identity* (Routledge, 2010) 64–83, at 79; Tam Sanger, 'Beyond Gender and Sexuality Binaries in Sociological Theory: The Case for Transgender Inclusion' in Sally Hines and Tam Sanger (eds), *Transgender Identities: Towards a Social Analysis of Gender Identity* (Routledge, 2010) 259–76, at 272; Rob Clucas and Stephen Whittle, 'Law' in Christina Richards, Walter Pierre Bouman and Meg-John Barker (eds), *Genderqueer and Non-Binary Genders* (Palgrave Macmillan, 2017) 73–99, at 73–74; Alex Iantaffi, 'Future Directions' in Christina Richards, Walter Pierre Bouman and Meg-John Barker (eds), *Genderqueer and Non-Binary Genders* (Palgrave Macmillan, 2017) 283–96, at 283.

[20] While the law has mostly refused recognition of gender beyond the binary, the existence of third gender options has started to appear in different jurisdictions, such as Australia, Germany and India. See *NSW Registrar of Births, Deaths and Marriages v Norrie* [2014] HCA 11 (2 April 2014); German Civil Status Act (Personenstandsgesetz), s 22 para 3 (amended on 7 May 2013) and German Federal Constitutional Court, Decision of 10 October 2017, Application no. 1 BvR 2019/16; *National Legal Service Authority v Union of India* (Writ Petition (Civil) No 400 of 2012) (15 April 2014).

[21] The use of the term 'transgender' to identify the applicants in trans cases has appeared in *Hämäläinen v Finland* and in the English translation of *YY v Turkey*. However, in those cases, 'transgender' has been given a similar meaning to 'transsexual' in the previous case law, and has not been used in the sense given to the term within this chapter. A transgender identity in which gender recognition appears detached from sex affirming surgery has only appeared in the Court's case law in 2017 in *AP, Garçon and Nicot v France*. See *H v Finland*, Application no 37359/09, 13 November 2012; *Hämäläinen v Finland* (GC), Application no 37359/09, 16 July 2014; *YY v Turkey*, Application no 14793/08, 10 March 2015; *AP, Garçon and Nicot v France*, Application nos 79885/12, 52471/13 and 52596/13, 6 April 2017.

II. The Sexed/Gendered Subject of Human Rights

The text of the European Convention on Human Rights portrays the subject of human rights as a gendered person. The concept of sex is present in the original text as the first prohibited ground for discrimination in the enjoyment of the human rights protected by the treaty. The Convention states:

> The enjoyment of the rights and freedoms set forth in this Convention shall be secured without discrimination on any ground such as *sex*, race, colour, language, religion, political or other opinion, national or social origin, association with a national minority, property, birth or other status.[22]

Furthermore, within the context of the Convention, the division of individuals based on their sex results in two opposite sexed individuals: man and woman. In the provision that recognises the human right to marry and to found a family, the treaty grants such rights to both men and women of marriageable age. The Convention reads: 'Men and women of marriageable age have the right to marry and to found a family, according to the national laws governing the exercise of this right'.[23] It seems implausible to maintain that the purpose of that article is deliberately to exclude from the right to marry those human beings of 'marriageable age' who can be classified neither as 'men' nor 'women'. Thus, it is only logical to infer from the article the belief that every individual must fit, or be made to fit, the binary classification of either man or woman. Therefore, the Convention understands its subject, the human entitled to the detailed rights, as a binary gendered person. Conversely, people who do not conform to this strict classification can face problems when turning to the Convention in search of protection of their human rights.

While the Convention conceives the subject of human rights as a binary sexed person, it does not offer a definition of the notion of sex, or the characteristics needed for a person to be considered a man or a woman. Nor has the Court given a straightforward definition of sex, but its understanding can be inferred from the case law. In particular, it has been the cases concerning trans individuals that have offered the understanding of the concepts of gender and man/woman within the legal system of the Convention. In these cases, it was the challenge posed by trans bodies to the assumed understanding of sex which forced the Court to define these concepts. Nevertheless, the Court performed an exclusionary use of

[22] Convention for the Protection of Human Rights and Fundamental Freedoms (adopted 4 November 1950, entered into force 3 September 1953) 213 UNTS 221 ('European Convention on Human Rights') (emphasis added). A similar use of the notion of sex is reiterated in Protocol No 12, which also prohibits discrimination on the grounds of sex, but this time in the enjoyment of any right granted by national laws. See Protocol No 12 to the European Convention on Human Rights and Fundamental Freedoms on the Prohibition of Discrimination (adopted 4 November 2000, entered into force 1 April 2005) ETS 177.

[23] European Convention on Human Rights, Art 12.

the transsexual person to produce the truth about sex. As will be discussed in section III, the Court originally defined sex in opposition to the transsexual body: sex was that which transsexual individuals could not change about themselves.

III. The Legal Meaning of Sex

Three specific cases established the understanding of sex held by the Court during the first two decades of dealing with the transsexual body. These cases, all against the United Kingdom, were *Rees*, *Cossey*, and *Sheffield and Horsham*.[24] In the *Rees* case, the applicant was a transsexual man who had undergone a gender affirming process, which was paid for by the National Health Service.[25] Following his transition, the applicant got his name changed and his sex recognised in his passport. However, his request for the amendment of his birth certificate was refused. He continued to be considered a legal woman for multiple purposes, such as marriage, pension and employment.[26]

The context of the *Cossey* decision was very similar to the *Rees* case.[27] The applicant was a transsexual woman who had undergone a gender affirming process on the National Health Service. After this process, the applicant also legally changed her name and her new sex was recognised in her passport, but her request for the amendment of her birth certificate was refused. She continued to be considered a man for the purposes of marriage, which was confirmed by the annulment obtained of her marriage to a man. Similarly, in the *Sheffield and Horsham* case, the applicants were two transsexual women, who had both undergone gender affirming processes.[28] Once again, they both changed their names, which were recognised in their passports and drivers' licences. Nonetheless, they continued to be considered legally men in multiple aspects, such as marriage, employment, social security, and pension.

The judgments of the Court in the three cases were almost identical. The Court rejected the applicants' claims that their birth certificates should be amended to reflect their self-determined sex, and that they should be considered as members of this sex category for all legal purposes. The *Rees* judgment affirmed that the limited level of consensus between the States Parties to the Convention concerning the legal recognition of the sex of transsexual individuals allowed

[24] The Court lacked an opportunity to decide a case concerning transsexuals' rights until the 1980s. In 1980, the Court issued its first judgment on the subject, but this consisted of a rejection of the claim solely based on procedural reasons. *Van Oosterwijck v Belgium*, Series A no 40, 6 November 1980.

[25] *Rees v United Kingdom* (n 14) paras 12–17.

[26] ibid para 40.

[27] *Cossey v United Kingdom* (n 14) paras 10–14.

[28] *Sheffield and Horsham v United Kingdom*, Reports of Judgments and Decisions 1998-V, 30 July 1998, paras 27–32.

the United Kingdom a wide margin of appreciation. Consequently, the state was considered to be free to decide the extension of the legal recognition offered to the gender of transsexual people.[29] The following two judgments, *Cossey* and *Sheffield and Horsham*, adopted a similar reasoning, and the Court stated that there were no reasons to justify a departure from its decision in *Rees*.[30]

A. Inferring the Definition of Sex

In none of the mentioned cases did the Court offer its own definition of gender, but it validated the criteria used in the United Kingdom to establish the sex of a person.[31] The adopted criteria consisted of the 'biological' determination of sex at the time of birth, as it was legally established in the 1970 English case *Corbett v Corbett*.[32] According to Alex Sharpe, these 'biological' criteria are based on the conception that birth is the true moment for the legal determination of a person's sex. This determination takes place by the alleged congruence of chromosomes, gonads and genitals.[33] However, in the potential case of incongruence between those factors, the observable genitals of the newborn act as the decisive factor.[34] In brief, the sex of a person is to be found in their body at the moment of birth.

The adoption of the definition of sex established by Justice Ormrod in 1970 can be observed in the three discussed cases,[35] and its use by the Court was also confirmed by the dissenting opinion of Judge Martens in the *Cossey* case.[36] The biological character of the criteria adopted is easy to observe in the description the Court made of the applicants' complaints in the *Sheffield and Horsham* case:

> [T]he essence of their complaints concerns the continuing insistence by the authorities on the determination of gender according to biological criteria alone and the immutability of the gender information once it is entered on the register of births.[37]

[29] *Rees v United Kingdom* (n 14) para 47.

[30] Nevertheless, it is worth noting that the level of consensus between the judges of the Court changed greatly through the decisions. While *Rees* was adopted by a 12 to 3 clear majority, *Cossey* and *Sheffield and Horsham* were decided by a 10 to 8 and 11 to 9 majority, respectively.

[31] The European Court of Human Rights has used the terms 'sex' and 'gender' interchangeably. While discussing how the legal sex/gender of individuals was established in domestic law, the Court has referred to the 'legal definition of sex' in the *Rees* and *Cossey* cases, and the 'definition of gender in domestic law' in the *Sheffield and Horsham* case. *Rees v United Kingdom* (n 14); *Cossey v United Kingdom* (n 14); *Sheffield and Horsham v United Kingdom* (n 29).

[32] *Corbett v Corbett* [1970] 2 All ER 33.

[33] A Sharpe, *Transgender Jurisprudence: Dysphoric Bodies of Law* (Cavendish, 2002) 41–42.

[34] ibid 42.

[35] *Rees v United Kingdom* (n 14) paras 23 and 29; *Cossey v United Kingdom* (n 14) paras 20 and 26; *Sheffield and Horsham v United Kingdom* (n 28) para 29.

[36] *Cossey v United Kingdom* (n 14), dissenting opinion of Judge Martens, para 4.3.2.

[37] *Sheffield and Horsham v United Kingdom* (n 28) para 53.

This understanding of sex as biological also means that it is immutable. Indeed, the Court insisted on the impossibility of changing sex. In the *Cossey* case, the Court affirmed that:

> The Court has been informed of no significant scientific developments that have occurred in the meantime; in particular, it remains the case – as was not contested by the applicant – that gender reassignment surgery does not result in the acquisition of all the biological characteristics of the other sex.[38]

In other words, the Court upheld the belief in a biological foundation of sex, which was accepted as the reason for the impossibility of abandoning the assigned gender. Even if genitalia had changed through surgery, that would still not be real enough. The truth about sex seemed to lie beyond human modification.

This belief in an immutable biological reality of sex was reiterated in the *Sheffield and Horsham* case, in which the Court stated:

> [I]t still remains established that gender reassignment surgery does not result in the acquisition of all the biological characteristics of the other sex despite the increased scientific advances in the handling of gender reassignment procedures.[39]

The Court's denial of full legal recognition of the sex of transsexual individuals, during the first twenty years of case law, was certainly consistent with the biological criteria already mentioned. It was impossible to modify one's sex, since sex was conceived as a biological truth.

The Court's case law suffered from the unquestionable Western belief in a true sex, as denounced by Foucault.[40] The Court seemed to believe in the existence of a true sex of the body and this conviction brings together the idea of its immutability, since if sex could actually be modified, it would no longer be an undeniable truth. Consequently, the Court seemed convinced that sex was a unique biological reality inscribed within the individual, and which the law simply recognised on a birth certificate. However, this understanding of a law that simply acknowledges a pre-existing reality has itself got consequences. It is worth emphasising that the law is not just a discourse that describes reality, but a source of production of truth.[41] Therefore, the legal discourse recognising the seeming reality of the biologic foundation of sex was itself a source of consolidation of the belief in sex as biology. Only one Judge has actually put in evidence that the legal notion of sex did not need to be grounded in biological determinism. In the opinion of Judge van Dijk:

> I cannot see any reason why legal recognition of reassignment of sex requires that biologically there has also been a (complete) reassignment; the law can give an autonomous meaning to the concept of 'sex', as it does to concepts like 'person', 'family', 'home', 'property', etc.[42]

[38] *Cossey v United Kingdom* (n 14) para 40.
[39] *Sheffield and Horsham v United Kingdom* (n 28) para 56.
[40] Foucault, *Herculine Barbin* (n 9) vii.
[41] Sharpe, *Transgender Jurisprudence* (n 33) 80.
[42] *Sheffield and Horsham v United Kingdom* (n 28), dissenting opinion of Judge van Dijk, para 8.

In other words, the law has always been free to define and re-define the legal concept of sex, since sex within the law is nothing more than a legal category. In fact, the concept of sex itself, even outside the law, could be argued to be nothing more than a cultural construction, hence subject to re-definition.

B. Who is the Court's Transsexual?

To repeat, the legal foundation of the Court's definition of sex was the transsexual body, since the Court did not elaborate on a definition of sex until it was confronted with a transsexual person. As mentioned above, the Court understood sex in an oppositional relation to the transsexual body: sex was what transsexuals could not change about themselves. While the Court has never offered an explicit definition of sex, the contrary is true for transsexual. In the *Rees* case, the Court said that the term 'transsexual' is

> usually applied to those who, whilst belonging physically to one sex, feel convinced that they belong to the other; they often seek to achieve a more integrated, unambiguous identity by undergoing medical treatment and surgical operations to adapt their physical characteristics to their psychological nature.[43]

That is to say, a transsexual individual was considered to be a person whose body and mind were positioned on the opposite side of the binary understanding of sex. Since sex was understood in an oppositional manner, transsexuals were conceived as persons who feel the need to cross to the opposite side of the sex binary. However, during the period in which the Court understood sex as an immutable biological category, transsexuality ended up being a legal impossibility. Paraphrasing, while sex remained fixed at birth, and unalterable on the birth certificate, transsexual individuals were not permitted to cross the limit of the sex binary. The Court observed the transsexual's attempt to achieve an 'unambiguous identity', but refused its legal recognition.

The Court produced its truth about transsexuality through the combined use of the powerful discourses of medicine and law.[44] The reason for the transsexual's desire to cross the rigid boundary of the sex binary was considered by the Court to be a medical condition.[45] The Court resorted to medical discourse in order to affirm that medical and surgical treatments were offered to 'alleviate' the transsexual 'condition', but they were unable to grant the biological characteristics of the 'opposite' sex.[46] The biological reality of the transsexual body could not be modified. In other words, the Court positioned itself as a mere spectator to the

[43] *Rees v United Kingdom* (n 14) para 38.

[44] See Sharpe, *Transgender Jurisprudence* (n 33) 8; Smart, *Feminism and the Power of Law* (n 4) 11.

[45] *Rees v United Kingdom* (n 14) para 38; *Sheffield and Horsham v United Kingdom* (n 28) para 56.

[46] *Rees v United Kingdom* (n 14) para 38; *Cossey v United Kingdom* (n 14) para 39; *Sheffield and Horsham v United Kingdom* (n 28) para 56.

failure of transsexual individuals to cross the limit of binary sex. Medical and legal discourses constructed the truth towards which transsexuals' expectations crashed. Instead of daring to question the legal system that imposed on individuals the need to comply with a gender role that was forced upon them, the Court opted for identifying transsexuality as the problem. The system appeared as unquestionable and it was the transsexual individual who failed to fit in and, therefore, could not obtain the recognition of their sex.

Nevertheless, if the gender affirming process did not allow the applicants to change the sex imposed on their birth certificates, one last question remained: What legal significance was attributed to the gender transition? The applicants who saw their claims refused by the Court remained transsexual individuals who found certain human rights recognised and others rejected. These transsexual individuals were recognised by domestic law as men in certain legal aspects, and as women in others. Consequently, a law that established that individuals could only be either men or women compelled the transsexual person to be both, depending on the legal subject. The law refused to recognise that a person who had undergone a gender affirming process has definitely crossed the limit of the dichotomy, but forced the person to intermittently cross that frontier depending on the area of their legal life they were living.

In the *Cossey* case, a dissenting group of judges who actually supported the claim of Miss Cossey to have her sex legally recognised, referred to her as follows: 'biologically she is considered not to be a woman. But neither is she a man, after the medical treatment and surgery. She falls somewhere between the sexes'.[47] This statement was partially true. However, it was not that Miss Cossey fell between the sexes, since she was asking to cross the sex boundary, but it was the Court who made her legally exist between the sexes. It was the Court's refusal to acknowledge her right to have her gender recognised which did not allow the transsexual person to cross to the other side of the sex binary. I certainly agree with Sharpe when she affirmed that, while the law portrays the transsexual body as ambiguous, contradictory and dissonant, it has been the transsexual body that has shown that what is ambiguous and contradictory is the law.[48]

Nonetheless, it is possible to extract some positive elements from this refusal. There certainly is an inadvertent queer twist in the Court's rulings. Indeed, the Court recognised that the binary sexes are not as neat as they are supposed to be and that not everyone can be clearly fitted on one of the sides. That is to say, the Court acknowledged and validated a queer existence, a denial of neatly belonging to the man/woman binary, in favour of the existence in-between the gender categories. Unfortunately, this was done in cases in which transsexual applicants were requesting recognition of their belonging to a neat sex category.

[47] *Cossey v United Kingdom* (n 14), joint dissenting opinion of Judges Palm, Foighel and Pekkanen, para 5.
[48] Sharpe, *Transgender Jurisprudence* (n 33) 4.

Consequently, the transsexual person appeared in the Court's case law as someone who unsuccessfully requested recognition of having crossed the boundary between the sexes. In turn, the Court's refusal to grant the transsexual individual's claim opened up a queer path of legal identity, allowing the possibility of actually transcending the fixed binary categories of men and women. Because the transsexual bodies were calling into question the assumed stability of the binary division of sex, the law would feel the need to re-incorporate them into the normalising sex binary.[49] Nevertheless, before the Court proceeded to reconstruct the meaning of both sex and transsexuality, a group of judges would raise the question of who is a 'true' (and a false) transsexual.

C. The True and the False Transsexual

During the first twenty years of transsexuality in the Court's case law only on one occasion was a transsexual individual partially successful in her claim: it was the case of *B v France*.[50] In that case, the applicant was a transsexual woman who had undergone gender transition, including genital surgery, which took place outside her country of residence. However, when she returned to France, she could not obtain the amendment of either her name or her sex on any official document. The Court accepted her claim and ruled that the state was infringing the applicant's right to respect for private life.[51] In order to reach this decision, the Court affirmed that the situation was different from the one in the *Rees* and *Cossey* cases, since Miss B found herself in daily situations that were not compatible with due respect for her private life as none of her documents disclosed her current gender.

Within the *B v France* judgment, the debate was not whether Miss B should be entitled to cross the limit of the sex binary in all legal aspects, as it was in the previous cases. On this occasion, the disagreement between the majority ruling and the dissenting judges was about whether the applicant could even be considered to be transsexual. In other words, the decision of the Court in favour of the applicant did not impose upon the state the obligation to fully recognise transsexual individuals as having transitioned gender in every legal aspect. Conversely, the Court actually ruled against France for not granting Miss B the queer intermediate gender existence the United Kingdom had imposed on Mr Rees and Miss Cossey. At the same time, the dissenting judges opposed upholding the applicant's claim, raising their concern about the truthful character of her transsexuality.

[49] See A Sharpe, *Foucault's Monsters and the Challenge of the Law* (Routledge, 2010) 14 and 88.

[50] This case has actually been labelled a 'false positive', since it did not grant the recognition of more rights than prior judgments, but the recognition of certain basic rights that were already ensured by the state in previous cases. See Marie-Bénédicte Dembour, 'Why Should Biological Sex be Decisive? Transsexualism Before the European Court of Human Rights' in Alison Shaw and Shirley Ardener (eds), *Changing Sex and Bending Gender* (Berghahn, 2005) 39–59, at 49.

[51] *B v France*, Series A no 232-C, 25 March 1992, para 63.

In different dissenting opinions, prefaced by a joint introduction, six judges (Matscher, Pinheiro Farinha, Pettiti, Valticos, Loizou and Morenilla) questioned the majority of the Court for failing to distinguish between what they labelled 'true' and 'false' transsexuals. The actual reason for uncovering false transsexuals remains a mystery, as these six judges have ruled against trans rights in every case they sat on, regardless of how 'truthful' the transsexual applicants were in those cases.[52] Nonetheless, the truth (and the untruth) about transsexuality was explicitly questioned in the Court's case law for the first time.

The dissenting judges highlighted that it should be medical doctors (if psychiatrists, even better) who diagnose and decide whether Miss B should have had access to gender transition (which had occurred already), since medicine was considered to hold the recipe for recognising true transsexuals and uncovering false ones. Even so, these judges were not afraid to offer their own medical opinions for evaluating the human rights of the applicant. In his dissenting opinion, Judge Pettiti affirmed:

> Many cases of true or false transsexual applicants correspond to psychiatric states which should be treated by psychiatry only, so as not to risk disaster, and for this reason a medical report is essential. Furthermore, cases of double personality and schizophrenia are known to medicine. If one were to be guided solely by the wish to make the individual will of the patient coincide with his social life, one would then have to accept change of civil status even in such deviant cases.[53]

That is to say, Judge Pettiti took it upon himself to propose that Miss B could be a case of double personality or schizophrenia. Consequently, his judicial opinion was that treatment might have been better with psychiatry only, rather than hormones and surgery.[54]

Judge Pinheiro Farinha concurred with Judge Pettiti in that psychiatric treatment was his suggested cure, instead of irreversible surgical operations.[55] In fact, he manifested his disagreement with the surgery undergone by the applicant/patient by affirming that the operation was performed 'voluntarily and intentionally'.[56] This double confirmation of the unnecessary character of the followed treatment highlighted the capricious nature of the surgery. Even more, Judge

[52] Besides *B v France*, Judge Matscher opposed the claims of transsexual applicants in the cases *Rees*, *Cossey*, *X, Y and Z*, and *Sheffield and Horsham*; Judge Pinheiro Farinha also voted against transsexual applicants in the *Rees* case; Judge Pettiti did the same in *Rees*, *Cossey*, and *X, Y and Z*; Judge Loizou rejected transsexuals' claims in *Sheffield and Horsham*; Judge Morenilla ruled against the applicants in *Cossey*, and *Sheffield and Horsham*; and Judge Valticos did the same in *X, Y, and Z*, and *Sheffield and Horsham*. See *Rees v United Kingdom* (n 14); *Cossey v United Kingdom* (n 14); *B v France* (n 51); *X, Y and Z v United Kingdom*, Reports of Judgments and Decisions 1997-II, 22 April 1997; *Sheffield and Horsham v United Kingdom* (n 28).

[53] *B v France* (n 51), dissenting opinion of Judge Pettiti, at 34.

[54] ibid.

[55] *B v France* (n 51), dissenting opinion of Judge Pinheiro Farinha, para 1.

[56] ibid para 6.

Pinheiro Farinha considered that the Court's decision in favour of the applicant's claim was paving the way for the 'trivialisation of irreversible surgical operations'.[57]

Nonetheless, the most concise diagnosis was the one made by Judge Valticos, joined by Judge Loizou. Judge Valticos explained:

> [T]here are, as we know, numerous types of transsexual. Thus there is considerable variation from one case to another in the psychological or physiological factor and the natural or acquired character (acquired to a greater or lesser extent as a result of surgical operations, themselves very diverse as to motivation and scope).[58]

Clearly, prognosis would differ according to the type of transsexuality. Therefore, after having considered the psychological and physiological aspects of the case and classified the character (natural or acquired) of the applicant's transsexuality, Judge Valticos asked himself: 'Why does it seem to me that in this case the facts of the case do not justify the decision which has been taken?'[59] And he replied:

> Because in *reality*, while the applicant, who professes to be a woman, asks for the alleged change of sex to be legally recognised, the situation here is one where the change in question is in *reality* incomplete, artificial and voluntary.[60]

Judge Valticos diagnosis was persuasive, since it was based on 'reality' (twice) and it coincided with the opinion of Judge Pinheiro Farinha: the gender transition of the applicant was voluntary, in addition to 'artificial'.

Moreover, Judge Valticos, who referred to Miss B using male pronouns, claimed to have found the proof of Miss B's maleness and, arguably, the source of her untruthful transsexuality. In his own words: 'he was originally of male sex, at least in essence, and had performed his military service'.[61] In Judge Valticos' diagnosis, Miss B's maleness was found 'in essence' and confirmed in praxis. Not only she was essentially a man, but she has also been in the military. The fact that Miss B had been in the military seemed to override her sex affirming surgery and came to confirm the sex essence of the applicant. Judge Valticos' diagnosis was developed even further when he offered his understanding of 'change of sex'. He affirmed that one should not restrict this definition to psychological or social factors alone, but that it was also necessary to take into consideration the psychological point of view, since: 'One cannot accept dubious hermaphrodites and ambiguous situations'.[62] However, at the same time that he argued that ambiguous situations could not be accepted, he was ambiguously gendering the applicant. He refused to recognise Miss B as a woman (her claim before the Court) and, while referring to her as a man, Judge Valticos stated that: 'he found himself in a position where he was no

[57] ibid para 1.
[58] *B v France* (n 51), dissenting opinion of Judge Valticos, joined by Judge Loizou, at 36.
[59] ibid.
[60] ibid (emphasis added).
[61] ibid.
[62] ibid.

longer completely a man, nor indeed truly a woman, but to a certain extent had some of the characteristics of both sexes'.[63]

As I stated in section III.B, while there are many reasons to praise the queer twist on gender flowing from the Court's earlier jurisprudence, this was also problematic when used to deny a transsexual's claim of belonging to one specific sex. Furthermore, in order to impose on Miss B this queer belonging, Judge Valticos supported the idea of the existence of two idealised binary genders. Judge Valticos' binary model was based on the assumption that there is a 'complete man', binary opposed to a 'true woman', since he affirmed that Miss B 'was no longer completely a man, nor indeed truly a woman'. However, Miss B was excluded from Judge Valticos' binary model, as she 'had some of the characteristics of both sexes'.

Judith Butler has explained that binary conceptions of identity categories, such as gender, not only allow understanding those individuals belonging to each side of the binary (men/women), but also produce a domain of those excluded from the binary.[64] These excluded bodies are plainly unintelligible, since they cannot be conceived within the constructed binary. In his dissenting judgment, Judge Valticos constructed Miss B as an excluded body, and it was because she could not be comprehended within the gender binary that she could not find her claim (to be recognised as a woman) accepted. Nonetheless, Judge Valticos' allegations did not clarify what were the characteristics of the 'complete man' and of the 'true woman' that Miss B did not fulfil, in order to justify her exclusion from the gendered universe. It is uncertain who Judge Valticos did have in mind as the 'complete' man, who acted as the grounds for excluding Miss B from the universe of binary genders because she was neither recognised as his idealised opposite, nor as a reflection of the self. In fact, do we not all show characteristics that different views attribute to the realm of one gender or the other? Whichever the case, Miss B was portrayed as alien to the strict binary sexes; she was not a man and she had failed to become a woman. She was clearly a false transsexual.

Miss B's failure to qualify as a true transsexual in the eyes of the dissenting judges left the question as to an alleged 'truth' of transsexuality for the Court to answer in the future. Even though all the dissenting judges expressed their opinions around the true/false transsexual, only Judge Pettiti ventured to clarify who was a true transsexual. According to him, the true transsexual was the individual 'operated on in public hospitals with medical supervision and documentation'.[65] Nevertheless, in an ironic twist, considering the abundant medical vocabulary of the judgments, he affirmed that states remained free to define the criteria for recognising true transsexuals, 'dependent upon undisputed scientific knowledge'.[66]

[63] ibid 37.

[64] Butler, *Bodies that Matter* (n 8) xi. Ralph Sandland also utilises this idea in his analysis of the UK Gender Recognition Act 2004. See Ralph Sandland, 'Feminism and the Gender Recognition Act 2004' (2005) 13 *Feminist Legal Studies* 43, at 50.

[65] *B v France* (n 51), dissenting opinion of Judge Pettiti, 32–33.

[66] ibid 33.

It took the Court almost ten years to give an answer to the question of the truth of transsexuality, as I will discuss in the next section. On the one hand, the Court rejected as unfounded the claims made by the dissenting judges about the voluntary and almost arbitrary decision made by transsexual individuals to undergo a sex affirming process. On the other hand, the Court embraced even further the path of medicalisation proposed by the dissenting judges and the idea of the existence of a truth about sex and transsexuality. As argued by Susan Stryker and Aren Aizura, when trans people become intelligible they also come to be the subject of further biopolitical regulation, which includes specific criteria establishing if, how, and when gender transition could happen.[67] Section IV will show how the Court reconstructed the meaning of both sex and the transsexual subject in order to regulate transsexual bodies. The Court's case law acted as a clear example of the normalising power of the law,[68] regulating and re-defining the sex of the applicants. Through the Court's judgments, the law established a new 'truth' about the sex of transsexual subjects.[69]

IV. Reconstructing the Legal Meaning of Gender

The Court's case law concerning legal sex and the rights of transsexual individuals underwent an important change in 2002 with the *Goodwin* and *I* cases, both against the United Kingdom. These cases were about two transsexual women who had undergone gender affirming processes on the National Health Service. They both argued that the lack of full legal recognition of their sex, after undergoing gender transition, was a violation of their human rights. In these cases the Court unanimously decided to abandon its previous case law. The Court affirmed that the applicants were right and that they should enjoy full legal recognition of their sex, which included considering them as women for the purposes of pension, retirement and marriage, as well as amending their birth certificates to show their attained gender.[70] The victory of *Goodwin* and *I* showed that the Court decided to re-define its understanding of legal sex in a manner that allowed this concept to incorporate transsexual individuals who have moved across the binary as members of the sex group on the other side of the boundary.[71] As foreshadowed by Judge van Dijk in the *Sheffield and Horsham* case,[72] the law was always capable of reconstructing the legal concept of sex; rather it was the Court itself that had refused to take this step until 2002.

[67] Susan Stryker and Aren Aizura (eds), *The Transgender Studies Reader 2* (Routledge, 2013) 7.
[68] See Smart, *Feminism and the Power of Law* (n 4) 6 and 162; Stychin, *Law's Desire* (n 2) 156.
[69] See Sharpe, *Transgender Jurisprudence* (n 33) 80.
[70] *Goodwin v United Kingdom* (n 15) paras 93 and 104; *I v United Kingdom* (n 15) paras 73 and 84.
[71] Ralph Sandland, 'Crossing and Not Crossing: Gender, Sexuality and Melancholy in the European Court of Human Rights' (2003) 11 *Feminist Legal Studies* 191, at 201.
[72] *Sheffield and Horsham v United Kingdom* (n 28), dissenting opinion of Judge van Dijk.

Nevertheless, the Court missed another opportunity to fully recognise that the definition of legal sex is a matter of legal, rather than medical, science. The Court decided to modify the legal understanding of gender because medical science did not provide any conclusive criteria. In its own words:

> The Court is not persuaded therefore that the state of medical science or scientific knowledge provides any determining argument as regards the legal recognition of transsexuals.[73]

Consequently, the Court reserved for itself the right to re-define its understanding of legal sex in the future. However, it was unclear whether this move was an acknowledgment of its own ability to re-define the meaning of gender within the law, or if it was only because medicine could not (yet) provide the 'truth' about gender.

Not surprisingly then, the judgments in *Goodwin* and *I* have relied more heavily on medical discourse than its predecessors. These cases could be read as a step further in the medical *pathologisation* of transsexuality, where the gender affirming process is justified as the medically endorsed formula for 'relief'.[74] In fact, one of the main reasons for abandoning the 'biological' criteria to establish gender was found in medical discourse:

> [A] test of congruent biological factors can no longer be decisive in denying legal recognition to the change of gender of a post-operative transsexual. There are other important factors – the acceptance of the condition of gender identity disorder by the medical professions and health authorities within Contracting States, the provision of treatment including surgery to assimilate the individual as closely as possible to the gender in which they perceive that they properly belong and the assumption by the transsexual of the social role of the assigned gender.[75]

Nonetheless, biology was not fully abandoned, and the belief in the existence of a true biological sex kept appearing in the judgment:

> It remains the case that a transsexual cannot acquire all the biological characteristics of the assigned sex; the principal unchanging biological aspect of gender identity is the chromosomal element. However, it is not apparent to the Court that the chromosomal element must inevitably take on decisive significance for the purposes of legal attribution of gender identity for transsexuals.[76]

Accordingly, it was the preference of the Court to give privilege to another factor in the determination of legal sex, but this was done despite the acknowledgment of a truth of sex that is located in biology. For the Court, the gender affirming process did not truly allow the person to acquire their gender. It only provided 'assimilation' to this acquired gender.[77] In other words, transsexual people could

[73] *Goodwin v United Kingdom* (n 15) para 83; *I v United Kingdom* (n 15) para 63.
[74] *Goodwin v United Kingdom* (n 15) paras 78 and 81; *I v United Kingdom* (n 15) paras 58 and 61.
[75] *Goodwin v United Kingdom* (n 15) para 100; *I v United Kingdom* (n 15) para 80.
[76] *Goodwin v United Kingdom* (n 15) para 82; *I v United Kingdom* (n 15) para 62.
[77] *Goodwin v United Kingdom* (n 15) paras 78 and 100; *I v United Kingdom* (n 15) paras 58 and 80.

never cross the 'true' limit of the sex binary. They could only get very close to the limit. Close enough that the law would ignore the 'biological truth' and concede a change of sex.

Moreover, one of the defining elements for recognising that Goodwin and I had changed their gender was the legal limbo in which the applicants had been living, due to the partial recognition of their acquired sex. The Court affirmed that: 'The unsatisfactory situation in which post-operative transsexuals live in an intermediate zone as not quite one gender or the other is no longer sustainable'.[78] Therefore, the Court seemed to timidly recognise its contribution to the legal ambiguity imposed upon Mr Rees, Miss Cossey, Ms Sheffield, and Ms Horsham with its previous judgments, and decided not to do the same with Ms Goodwin and Ms I.

The consequences flowing from the *Goodwin* and *I* rulings were multiple. On the one hand, by neatly incorporating the transsexual bodies of Goodwin and I into the gender system, allowing them to cross the sex frontier, the Court normalised their bodies.[79] These naturalised bodies no longer posed a threat to the coherence of law and its rigid gender system. On the contrary, the Court's suppression of the ambiguity represented by the un-recognised transsexual bodies helped to reinforce the binary character of the gender system. In fact, the queer path opened by the early cases seemed to be getting closed by the Court.

On the other hand, the decision adopted by the Court in *Goodwin* and *I* demonstrated the performative character of legal and anatomical sex. Sex was no longer conceived as a permanent characteristic.[80] With the help of surgery, the Court proved that the sex of the applicants could be different to that originally stated on their birth certificates. Even though the Court continued to believe in the existence of an undeniable biological truth,[81] the determination of gender no longer needed to follow strict biological criteria.[82] Gender was to be found in the surgically modified genitalia of transsexual individuals.

However, requiring sex affirming surgery for gender recognition did not only establish a time limitation. It also meant that only trans individuals who desire to undergo genital surgery were entitled to have their sex legally amended. When a tribunal normalises the body of the post-operative transsexual, trans bodies that refuse normalisation remain in the domain of the abnormal.[83] This abnormality is not conceived as an external imposition, but as voluntarily decided by trans individuals, in a clear display of their refusal to belong to the strict system of binary sexes. Following *Goodwin* and *I*, trans individuals who have not had their genitalia surgically modified could be refused their rights, since they had rejected the invitation granted by the Court to belong to the gender system. It could be said that the

[78] *Goodwin v United Kingdom* (n 15) para 90; *I v United Kingdom* (n 1) para 70.
[79] See Sharpe, *Foucault's Monsters and the Challenge of the Law* (n 49) 14 and 109.
[80] Sharpe, *Transgender Jurisprudence* (n 33) 80 and 194.
[81] *Goodwin v United Kingdom* (n 15) para 82; *I v United Kingdom* (n 15) para 62.
[82] *Goodwin v United Kingdom* (n 15) para 100; *I v United Kingdom* (n 15) para 80.
[83] Sharpe, *Foucault's Monsters and the Challenge of the Law* (n 49) 101 and 103.

'capriciousness' and the 'arbitrariness' the Court found lacking in the behaviour of the normalised transsexual,[84] appear in the rejection of trans identities who refuse to neatly fit within the binary sexes.

While the Court granted transsexual individuals who have transitioned the recognition they claimed, it remained silent regarding the legal limbo to which it was still condemning other trans identities. The path to a queer legal identity was not completely closed, then. As will be discussed towards the end of the chapter, the Court made queerly remain in-between the sexes those trans identities who did not embrace the medically prescribed solution to transsexuality.

A. *Goodwin* and *I* as the Moment of the Reconstruction of Sex

The significance of the *Goodwin* and *I* cases for the re-definition of sex has been acknowledged by the Court itself. In the subsequent *Grant* case, the Court implicitly recognised these cases as the genesis of a new conception of legal sex. In *Grant v United Kingdom*,[85] the applicant was a transsexual woman who had undergone gender affirming surgery. When she reached the pensionable age for women, she applied to start receiving her pension, but her application was refused, since the law did not recognise her as a woman for pension purposes. The Court considered that the lack of full recognition of her sex was a violation of her rights, but subjected the violation to temporal limitations. That is, the Court did not believe the violation to have started at the time she applied for her pension. On the contrary, the Court understood the beginning of the violation of rights to have occurred the day the Court issued its judgments in the *Goodwin* and *I* cases, in which the gender of transsexual individuals was finally recognised. Moreover, the violation of rights was considered to have finished when the Gender Recognition Act of the United Kingdom came into force in 2004, providing the applicant the means to obtain the legal recognition of her gender.[86]

It is interesting to analyse the reasons behind the temporal limitation established by the Court for the beginning of the obligation to recognise the applicant's claim. If the lack of recognition of Grant's gender did not begin with the denial of her pension rights, but with the *Goodwin* and *I* cases, then these judgments did more than to decide a violation of a right. *Goodwin* and *I* did not just impose a legal obligation upon the state to respect transsexuals' genders, but these judgments have actually redefined the meaning of legal sex. It was only since the *Goodwin* and *I* rulings that legal gender was no longer a 'biological fact' acknowledged by the law. From that moment, legal sex became a performative characteristic

[84] *Goodwin v United Kingdom* (n 15) para 81; *I v United Kingdom* (n 15) para 61.
[85] *Grant v United Kingdom*, Application no. 32570/03, ECHR 2006-VII.
[86] ibid para 41.

(re)constructed by the law and surgery. That is to say, the judgments were not simply a new interpretation of sex based on mutability. If that were the case, the decision could be applied retroactively, since it would have been a discovery made by the Court of a pre-existing situation. The fact that it was only from that day that sex was considered to be legally and surgically amendable means that a brand new conception of gender was constructed. This conception could not be applied retroactively, because it did not exist prior to the judgments.

Consequently, with its ruling in *Grant*, the Court implicitly recognised that the re-definition of legal sex was its own creation in the *Goodwin* and *I* judgments. This acknowledgment opened the door to the possibility of the further re-conception of legal gender. The Court's fascination with biology, only partially overcome in *Goodwin* and *I*, could be abandoned in the future. This ability of the Court to define and re-define gender could be of great relevance for dealing with the queer existence of other gender non-conforming identities.

B. When Does the Sex Binary Frontier Get Crossed?

Through its *Goodwin* and *I* judgments, the Court recognised that the limit between the binary sexes could be legally crossed. Gender was no longer a biological fact fixed at birth, but an amendable human characteristic. However, the Court stated that while the gender affirming process was the manner by which to move across the gender binary, it was left for the states to decide when that process has been 'properly effected'.[87]

Disregarding the open-ended criteria for determining when gender transition has taken place, in *Goodwin* and *I* the Court established certain basic requisites. There are three specific elements that the Court identified as essential for crossing the boundary of the gender binary: medical diagnosis, surgery and sacrifice. The medical diagnosis of being 'pathologically' transsexual was stated as the first essential element.[88] In the Court's judgments, the diagnosis of 'gender dysphoria' appeared as the needed condition for starting the gender transition process:

> In this case, as in many others, the applicant's gender re-assignment was carried out by the national health service, which recognises the condition of gender dysphoria and provides, inter alia, re-assignment by surgery.[89]

[87] *Goodwin v United Kingdom* (n 15) para 103; *I v United Kingdom* (n 16) para 83.

[88] It should be highlighted that the understanding of transsexuality as a mental disorder has been criticised by other human rights monitoring bodies, such as the Committee on Economic, Social and Cultural Rights, the Commissioner for Human Rights of the Council of Europe, and the Inter-American Commission on Human Rights. See Committee on Economic, Social and Cultural Rights, Concluding Observations of the Committee on Economic, Social and Cultural Rights on Germany, E/C.12/DEU/CO/5 (20 May 2011) para 26; Commissioner for Human Rights of the Council of Europe, *Issue Paper on Human Rights and Gender Identity*, CommDH/IssuePaper(2009)2 (29 July 2009) para 3.3; Inter-American Commission on Human Rights, *Violence Against LGBTI Persons in the Americas*, OAS/Ser.L/V/II.rev.1 (12 November 2015) para 419 and recommendations at 26.

[89] *Goodwin v United Kingdom* (n 15) para 78; *I v United Kingdom* (n 15) para 58.

The second element was surgery, including genital surgery.[90] This appeared as the medical treatment to 'alleviate' the 'disease'. In the Court's words, it was the medical and surgical procedures which actually allow transitioning gender: 'The medical and surgical acts which in this case rendered the gender re-assignment possible'.[91] In the eyes of the Court, surgery became the most essential element for transitioning, as will be discussed in sections V and VI.

Finally, the process of transition needed to have a clear element of sacrifice, as the undeniable proof of the authenticity of transsexuality. As affirmed by Sharpe, the law has decided to measure the authenticity of transsexuality through the sacrifices made by the transsexual. In the judgments in *Goodwin* and *I*, the sacrifice of the genitalia was constructed as the final and definitive proof.[92] The Court stated that:

> [G]iven the numerous and painful interventions involved in such surgery and the level of commitment and conviction required to achieve a change in social gender role, can it be suggested that there is anything arbitrary or capricious in the decision taken by a person to undergo gender re-assignment.[93]

The centrality of surgery and the sacrifice of the genitalia for crossing the limit between the binary sexes appeared unequivocally in the Court's jurisprudence for a decade and a half.[94] The following two sections will focus on genital surgery as a key element for gender transition, examining what has been labelled as the *genitocentrism* of the law.[95] The remaining element, that of medical diagnosis, will be discussed in section VII.

V. The Transsexual Creation of Surgery and the Law

To reiterate, following the *Goodwin* and *I* judgments, gender was no longer determined by an immutable 'biological truth' of the body, but rather it was found in the surgically modified anatomy of the transsexual individual's genitalia. It was this surgery that unveiled the truth of sex as the Court clearly stated in the

[90] It should be mentioned that having sterilising surgery as a requisite for recognising a gender transition has been opposed by different human rights monitoring organs, such as the High Commissioner for Human Rights and the Commissioner for Human Rights of the Council of Europe. In 2017, the Court joined this position when deciding *AP, Garçon and Nicot v France*. See High Commissioner for Human Rights, *Discriminatory Laws and Practices and Acts of Violence Against Individuals Based on their Sexual Orientation and Gender Identity* A/HRC/19/41 (17 November 2011) paras 72 and 84(h); Council of Europe, *Discrimination on Grounds of Sexual Orientation and Gender Identity in Europe*, 2nd edn (September 2011) 13; *AP, Garçon and Nicot v France* (n 21).

[91] *Goodwin v United Kingdom* (n 15) para 81; *I v United Kingdom* (n 15) para 61.

[92] Sharpe, *Foucault's Monsters and the Challenge of the Law* (n 49) 108.

[93] *Goodwin v United Kingdom* (n 15) para 81; *I v United Kingdom* (n 15) para 61.

[94] The Court has amended this interpretation in 2017, when adopting its judgment on *AP, Garçon and Nicot v France*, as will be discussed in section VII below.

[95] Sharpe, *Transgender Jurisprudence* (n 33) 39.

Court highlighted the heterosexuality of the applicants.[107] The Court emphasised that: 'The applicant in this case lives as a woman, is in a relationship with a man and would only wish to marry a man'.[108] This narrative acted as the foundation onto which heterosexuality was re-created. In fact, genital surgery was granted the ability to *heterosexualise* the transsexual subject, since only through acquiring the 'appropriate' genitalia can the transsexual become heterosexual. As Sharpe has explained: 'Sex reassignment surgery proceeds on the basis of a reimagined heterosexuality, a heterosexuality uncoupled from its biological referent'.[109] Consequently, the same surgery that produced sex also produced heterosexual desire. That is to say, the Court allowed the combination of law and surgery the power to produce heterosexuality.[110]

This legal ability to heterosexualise transsexual individuals revealed the secret fear of the law of the homosexual body, the *homophobia of law* in the words of Sharpe.[111] It was the legal rejection of the homosexual body which acted as the basis for recognising the transsexual crossing to the other side of the sex binary. Therefore, the legal and surgical construction of transsexuality showed the relevance of sexuality, especially homosexuality, for establishing the sex of transsexual individuals. Given that the recognition of transsexuals' sex was based on their heterosexuality, in turn, homosexuality was what became the grounds of sex. It was the impulse to deny homosexuality which motivated the law to recognise the lack of stability of the limit between binary sexes. The transsexual's crossing of the binary limit allowed their sexual desire to become (truly) heterosexual. At the same time, this recognition was a clear attempt to erase from the legal imaginary (although not from reality) the possibility of sexually diverse transsexuals,[112] since only straight transsexuals are 'true' transsexuals.

To summarise, the surgical heterosexualisation of the transsexual person, validated by the law, helped to prove the performative character of both sex and sexuality.[113] Nonetheless, the reality of sex and sexuality was still located in the body. In the case of transsexual people, surgery was legally required for the change of gender and sexuality. In other words, all these notions were founded on the belief in the (now) anatomical truth of the sexed body.[114]

[107] ibid 201.

[108] *Goodwin v United Kingdom* (n 15) para 101; *I v United Kingdom* (n 15) para 81.

[109] Sharpe, *Transgender Jurisprudence* (n 33) 34.

[110] ibid 129.

[111] ibid 5; A Sharpe, 'From Functionality to Aesthetics: The Architecture of Transgender Jurisprudence' in Susan Stryker and Stephen Whittle (eds), *The Transgender Studies Reader* (Routledge, 2006) 621–31, at 628.

[112] As affirmed by Vade, trans people have all sorts of sexual orientations, some are straight, others are gay, some are bisexual and others are queer. Dylan Vade, 'Expanding Gender and Expanding the Law: Toward a Social and Legal Conceptualization of Gender that is More Inclusive of Transgender People' (2005) 11 *Michigan Journal of Gender and Law* 253, at 270.

[113] Sharpe, *Transgender Jurisprudence* (n 33) 81 and 194.

[114] Foucault, *Herculine Barbin* (n 9) vii.

VI. A Human Right to Gender Affirming Surgery?

Since the surgical affirming process appeared to be decisive for the recognition of the transsexual's gender, it becomes important to question whether transsexual people have the right to be provided with such a process. The Court has dealt with access and financing of the gender affirming process in three cases: *Van Kück v Germany*, *Schlumpf v Switzerland*, and the already mentioned *L v Lithuania*.[115]

In the *Van Kück* case, the applicant was a transsexual woman who had undergone a sex affirming process, which she paid for herself. She claimed in court that her private insurance should partially reimburse the cost of treatment. However, the domestic courts rejected her claim, affirming that she had not proved the necessity of the treatment. The decision of the Court was based on the analysis of the compatibility of the ruling of the domestic courts with the rights of the applicant. The Court objected to the domestic decisions, affirming that it was disproportionate to require a transsexual person to prove the necessity of gender affirming surgery.[116]

In the *Schlumpf* case, the applicant was a transsexual woman who had undergone a gender affirming process and claimed reimbursement from her health insurance company. The company refused the claim and the refusal was confirmed by the domestic courts. The reason for the refusal was the existence of a jurisprudentially established two-year waiting period for cases of transsexuality before surgery was allowed.[117] This surveillance period allegedly enabled proving the authenticity of transsexuality. The Court found a violation of the applicant's rights, since the mechanical application of a waiting period was given preference over the possibility of providing expert medical opinion.[118]

Finally, the previously discussed *L v Lithuania* judgment concerned a transsexual man whose gender affirming process was discontinued. In this case, the Court did not order the state to provide the applicant with the remaining surgical and medical procedures needed for the transition to be completed. Nevertheless, it did accept that: 'As a short-term solution, it may be possible for the applicant to have the remaining operation abroad, financed in whole or in part by the State'.[119] Therefore, the Court only imposed upon the state the obligation to finance, at least partially, the gender affirming process.

Consequently, the Court has only established very basic standards regarding the accessibility of gender transition. In the cases against Germany and Switzerland, the Court only analysed the denial by health insurance companies to reimburse medical expenses of the gender affirming process, arguing that certain conditions imposed by the domestic authorities were detrimental to the possibility of accessing gender transition.[120] Specifically, the burden imposed on the transsexual

[115] The factual basis of *L v Lithuania* has been already discussed in section V.
[116] *Van Kück v Germany*, Application no 35968/97, ECHR 2003-VII, para 56.
[117] *Schlumpf v Switzerland*, Application no 29002/06, 8 January 2009, paras 11 and 28.
[118] ibid paras 56–57.
[119] *L v Lithuania* (n 96) para 58.
[120] *Van Kück v Germany* (n 116); *Schlumpf v Switzerland* (n 117).

to prove the necessity of the medical treatment was disproportionate.[121] Likewise, it was unreasonable to impose a rigidly fixed two-year period that every person had to mandatorily wait before undergoing a gender affirming process.[122] While in those cases the Court affirmed that the health insurance should cover the expenses of the gender affirming process, it was only in *L v Lithuania* that the Court recognised certain positive obligations upon states towards facilitating access to this process.[123]

Furthermore, while these judgments have only offered limited access for transsexual individuals to the gender affirming process, they have been quite clear in the reinforcement of the medicalisation of transsexuality. Perhaps because the cases dealt with the transsexual need to access medical and surgical technology, they have heavily relied on the medical understanding of transsexuality as a pathology in need of surgical alleviation. In fact, the rejection of the domestic decisions that have hindered access to surgery or the reimbursement of its costs was founded on their opposition to medical expertise.[124] As affirmed in the *Van Kück* case:

> The Court, bearing in mind the complexity of assessing the applicant's transsexuality and the need for medical treatment, finds that the Regional Court rightly decided to obtain an expert medical opinion on these questions.[125]

In the *Schlumpf* case, the assertion was that

> the federal Court of insurance took the place of the medical doctors and psychiatrics, while the Court had already established in the past that determining the medical necessity of gender reassignment measures is not a matter of legal definition.[126]

To summarise, during the many years in which the Court maintained the need for undergoing full gender transition in order to obtain the legal recognition of the attained gender, it actually refused to grant transsexual individuals the right to access such an essential requisite. Moreover, this refusal has not been based on economic concerns, since the Court affirmed that given the few individuals that desire to undergo a gender affirming process, the budgetary burden on the state would not be expected to be unduly heavy.[127] Therefore, the Court found no obstacles in demanding the transsexual applicants to make extreme sacrifices (such as the sacrifice of their genitalia), while at the same time did not grant them

[121] *Van Kück v Germany* (n 116) paras 56–57.

[122] *Schlumpf v Switzerland* (n 117) para 115.

[123] On the contrary, the Commissioner for Human Rights of the Council of Europe seemed to understand that the Court had already established upon the states the obligation to provide sex-reassignment surgery for transsexual individuals since the *Van Kück* case. See Commissioner for Human Rights of the Council of Europe, *Issue Paper on Human Rights and Gender Identity*, CommDH/IssuePaper(2009)2 (29 July 2009) para 3.3.

[124] *Van Kück v Germany* (n 116) para 54; *Schlumpf v Switzerland* (n 117) para 57.

[125] *Van Kück v Germany* (n 116) para 54.

[126] *Schlumpf v Switzerland* (n 117) para 57. Author's own translation from the original paragraph in French: 'le Tribunal fédéral des assurances s'est substitué aux médecins et aux psychiatriques, alors que la Cour avait déjà précisé par le passé que la détermination de la nécessité de mesures de conversion sexuelle n'est pas une affaire d'appréciation juridique'.

[127] *L v Lithuania* (n 96) para 59.

a right to access surgery. Nonetheless, maybe asking the Court to order states to finance gender transition is not the right question to ask. It might be that the most appropriate question is: Why does gender transition need to be subjected to genital surgery at all? And, indeed, the Court revised its position on this topic in 2017, when it decided the *AP, Garçon and Nicot v France* case, as will be discussed in the following section.

VII. Overcoming a Genitocentric Case Law

It took the Court one and a half decades to partially overcome the fixation with transsexuals' genitalia that started with the *Goodwin* and *I* judgments. The Court adopted a first (timid) step in this direction in 2015, when it decided a case regarding the requirement of sterilisation for gender transition. In the case *YY v Turkey*, the Court examined whether the legislation that established infertility as a prerequisite for obtaining a judicial authorisation to undergo a gender affirming process was consistent with the Convention.[128] It ruled that such a requirement amounted to a breach of the right to respect for private life.

However, while the Court was clear that sterilisation could not be a prerequisite for authorising a gender transition process, it avoided offering a straightforward opinion as to whether sterilisation could ever be a requirement for the legal recognition of gender. In fact, the judgment can be read as implicitly validating the requirement of sterilisation that exists in many states' legislations,[129] provided that sterility was not a condition for undergoing a gender affirming process, but a consequence of the transition. There are different elements in the judgment that certainly pointed in that direction.[130] In particular, there was a cryptic paragraph in the judgment, which should have been more clear if the Court aimed to object to the requirement of infertility altogether. The paragraph reads:

> However, the Court cannot understand why the inability to procreate of a person wishing to undergo a sex-reassignment surgery should be established *even before* the person has undergone the gender reassignment procedures.[131]

[128] *YY v Turkey* (n 21).

[129] ibid paras 42–43.

[130] In fact, the concurring opinion of Judge Lemmens, joined by Judge Kūris, specifically stated that: 'the present judgment cannot be interpreted as definitely excluding as a requirement for individuals to be permanently unable to procreate in the context of gender transition', clarifying that the judgment was not concerned with infertility as a requisite for gender recognition, but only with sterility as a prior requirement for accessing surgery. Ibid, concurring opinion of Judge Lemmens, joined by Judge Kūris, para 3. Author's own translation from the French original: 'le présent arrêt ne saurait être interprété comme excluant définitivement l'exigence de l'incapacité définitive de procréer du contexte de la conversion sexuelle'.

[131] *YY v Turkey* (n 21) para 116 (emphasis added). Author's own translation from the French original: 'Or, la Cour ne s'explique pas pourquoi l'incapacité de procréer d'une personne souhaitant se soumettre à une opération de changement de sexe devrait être établie avant même que ne soit engagé le processus physique de changement de sexe'.

Thus, while the Court was unequivocal that making sterilisation a prerequisite to undergo transition amounted to a violation of the Convention, it opted to remain silent as to whether infertility can be required in order to obtain gender recognition. Therefore, this ruling did not offer sufficient reasons for celebrating a (queer) advancement of the Court's jurisprudence on gender identity, as the requirement of sterility for gender recognition seemed to have been left in place.

A. Changing Focus: From Genitalia to Mental Health

If the Court's decision in *YY v Turkey* did not provide a clear answer as to whether sterility can be made a requirement for gender recognition, this answer can be found in the ruling adopted in *AP, Garçon and Nicot* in 2017.[132] Even more, in this case, the Court also revised its position concerning genital surgery. The case involved three trans women who had been denied recognition of their gender, as they had not fulfilled different requirements imposed by the domestic legislation. While the situation of each applicant was different, across the three claims the Court had to decide on the compatibility with the Convention of legislation that made gender recognition subject to fulfilling the following requirements: undergoing intrusive physical and psychological examinations by an inter-disciplinary medical team; being medically diagnosed with suffering from the mental disorder of 'transsexualism'; and having undergone a gender transition process that could be considered to be 'irreversible'.[133]

The most important change that spread out of this judgment had to do with the examination of the third of these requirements. The Court had to decipher the meaning of the 'irreversible character of the transformation of the appearance'[134] demanded by the legislation as a condition for obtaining gender recognition. It affirmed that this requirement had to mean that either sterilising surgery or a medical treatment very likely to cause sterilisation was requested by the authorities.[135] The Court ruled that by imposing such a requirement, the state had overstepped its margin of appreciation. It concluded that the irreversibility of the transition requested by the legislation was a violation of the applicants' right to respect for private life, stating that neither sterilising surgery, nor medical treatments likely to lead to sterility, could be made conditions for obtaining gender recognition under the Convention.[136]

[132] *AP, Garçon and Nicot v France* (n 21). For a critical discussion of this case see Damian A Gonzalez-Salzberg, 'An Improved Protection for the (Mentally Ill) Trans Parent: A Queer Reading of *AP, Garçon and Nicot v France*' (2018) 81 *Modern Law Review* 526.

[133] *AP, Garçon and Nicot v France* (n 21) paras 83–85.

[134] Author's own translation from the original French: 'caractère irréversible de la transformation de [l']apparence'. *AP, Garçon and Nicot v France* (n 21) para 83.

[135] ibid para 120.

[136] ibid para 135.

A significant consequence of this finding regarding sterilisation is that the Court implicitly overcame the genitocentrism of its case law.[137] Given that genital surgery can be considered a sterilising procedure, it follows that it cannot be used anymore as a requirement for obtaining gender recognition.[138] In fact, the Court explicitly acknowledged that not every trans person can – or even wishes to – go through a gender transition process that entails genital surgery.[139] This means that one's position towards genitalia should not be determinant of one's gender and, as a consequence, gender can no longer be naturalised by the case law as the evident expression of an anatomical feature.[140] Therefore, in the *AP, Garçon and Nicot* judgment it is possible to find reasons for queer activism to celebrate. The traditionally expected congruence between gender and genitalia can no longer be demanded for gender recognition by States Parties. The belonging to a specific gender despite of genitalia has returned to the Court's case law, but not as a consequence of the denial of gender recognition as in the past. Now, it can actually be requested by applicants who so desire.[141]

Conversely, the Court found that the other two requirements under examination – the need for a medical diagnosis and of undergoing intrusive medical evaluations – did not amount to breaches of the Convention. Consequently, this judgment can be understood as a confirmation that medicine will continue to play a central role in determining the legal recognition of gender. The Court seems to have abandoned the anatomical criteria for gender recognition in favour of a purely psychiatric model.[142]

The next section will focus on those trans identities who either fail or refuse to comply with the evolving requirements for gender recognition validated by the Court through the years: biological characteristics, genital surgery, or medical certification. It will explore the gender 'in-between' created by the jurisprudence for those who 'fail' to completely cross the frontier between genders, as well as its potential use to (continue to) *queer* the Court's conception of gender.

VIII. Revisiting the Gender In-Between

As discussed in section III.B, from its early case law on transsexuality the Court (inadvertently) validated the existence of a space in-between binary genders. Originally, this took place through the Court's denial to find a violation of the Convention rights of transsexual individuals when states refused to recognise their

[137] Gonzalez-Salzberg, 'An Improved Protection for the (Mentally Ill) Trans Parent' (n 132) 532.
[138] ibid.
[139] *AP, Garçon and Nicot v France* (n 21) para 126.
[140] Gonzalez-Salzberg, 'An Improved Protection for the (Mentally Ill) Trans Parent' (n 132) 532–33.
[141] ibid 537.
[142] ibid 533.

gender. The Court allowed states to treat trans individuals as belonging to different genders in different legal areas. Since the *Goodwin* and *I* cases in 2002, (straight) transsexual individuals could have their gender recognised by the Court. Nonetheless, only those who have completed the prescribed gender affirming process were considered to have acquired a new legal sex. The Court's early fascination with biology was substituted for its discovered passion for genital surgery. Through the validation of genital surgery as a requirement for moving across the binary, the Court continued to allow the legal existence of persons that live in an in-between position, being sometimes man and sometimes woman, depending on the subject. If until 2002 the Court constructed the post-operative transsexual as the 'intermediate' sex,[143] after *Goodwin* and *I*, the Court placed the pre-operative transsexual in that same 'intermediate position',[144] 'between two sexes'.[145]

Following *AP, Garçon and Nicot*, the in-between space continues to exist. Now it is no longer inhabited by trans individuals who refused genital surgery, but by those who object to being pathologised through the medical diagnosis of suffering a mental disorder. In fact, the gender in-between will subsist as long as the Court continues to validate the existence of strict requirements for obtaining gender recognition. However, as mentioned above, while a legal space between genders is problematic when imposed upon individuals who desire the recognition of their gender, it can actually be of interest for those who oppose conforming to binary genders.

The possibility of an in-between existence is an obvious subject of queer fascination because it challenges the imperative of neatly fixed identity categories. In particular, Gloria Anzaldúa's work explored the idea of living in the borderland, which she called the *neplanta*; a Nahuatl word meaning 'in-between space'.[146] She claimed that borders are set up to define a place, to distinguish one side from the other (and the *self* from the *other*) and, therefore, the in-between space opens up possibilities of ambivalence and indeterminacy.[147] The in-between becomes a place of belonging for those who either fail or refuse to signify monolithically. It is a space in which identities exist in a constant state of transition.[148] Anzaldúa proposed that *neplanta* – as a site in which realities clash, idealised goals are not met and thresholds are crossed – also becomes a place for self-redefinition.[149] Indeed, the in-between can be a space for social transformation and an opportunity to put

[143] *Goodwin v United Kingdom* (n 15) para 90; *I v United Kingdom* (n 15) para 70.
[144] *L v Lithuania* (n 96) para 57.
[145] *Nunez v France* (n 100) 4.
[146] AnaLouise Keating (ed), *The Gloria Anzaldúa Reader* (Duke University Press, 2009) 322.
[147] Gloria Anzaldúa, *Borderlands / La Frontera: The New Mestiza* (Aunt Lute Books, 1999) 25–26.
[148] Cynthia Weber, *Queer International Relations: Sovereignty, Sexuality and the Will to Knowledge* (Oxford University Press, 2016) 157–59.
[149] Gloria Anzaldúa, 'Let Us Be the Healing of the Wound: The Coyolxauhqui Imperative – La sombra y el sueño' in AnaLouise Keating (ed), *The Gloria Anzaldúa Reader* (Duke University Press, 2009) 303–17, at 310.

aside epistemological certainties.[150] It can be made a site where it is even possible to reconceive the human.[151]

For some, the in-between position might not be queer enough, to the extent that it does not yet materialise the non-belonging to a gender identity (in a queer way of transcending the idea of sex). In the gender in-between, individuals are still intelligible as either men or women, even if the belonging to each category is intermittent and temporary. Nevertheless, the in-between is a site for potential changes. If this intermediate position is not just the consequence of the rejection of a request to belong to the sex binary, but is re-claimed as a desired path to challenge an imposed binary existence, it could become a powerful tool to *queer* gender identities.

I finish this section posing the following question: What would happen if a trans individual requests of the Court to be recognised as a woman in certain legal aspects, and as a man in others? The case law clearly shows that the Court has allowed states to treat trans individuals in that exact way, when they fail to fulfil certain requirements for gender recognition. Nonetheless, it would be rather queer of the Court to explicitly validate such a requested in-between existence.

IX. Conclusion

As discussed throughout the chapter, the Court has defined and re-defined the legal meaning of sex through the years. It has certainly not carried out a queer reconstruction of this notion, but it has recognised that the meaning of sex can be re-shaped. Before the reconstruction of the meaning of sex in 2002, none of the applicants saw their gender recognised by the Court. From a human rights perspective, the rulings of the Court were unsatisfactory, since they refused to acknowledge a violation of rights. On the other hand, in those early cases, the Court inadvertently opened up the possibility of existence beyond neatly fixed binary genders. The strong belief in a biological reality of sex led the Court to allow the law to treat transsexual individuals as both men and women, depending on the legal area. The main problem with this reasoning was that the gender in-between was imposed on individuals who wanted to belong to one side of the sex binary. However, the validation of the existence of a space in-between the genders can be queerly rescued from these rulings.

As to the re-creation of sex in 2002, the Court has been praised for the recognition of transsexuals' rights.[152] Indeed, the rights claimed by Christine Goodwin

[150] Judith Butler, *Undoing Gender* (Routledge, 2004) 228.

[151] ibid.

[152] Whittle, *Respect and Equality* (n 10) xix. See also Anna Śledzińska-Simon, 'Transgender Rights on the Move: Towards Recognition and Gender-Neutral Definition of Parenthood' in Carlo Casonato and Alexander Schuster (eds), *Rights on the Move: Rainbow Families in Europe* (Conference Proceedings, Trento, October 2014) 311–26, at 313.

and Ms I were granted by the Court and crossing the boundary of the sexes became an accepted legal fiction. While the Court still believed that there were biological factors that forbid a 'real' change of sex, the transition was considered to be good enough to grant it legal value. The rigidity of the gender categories proved to be more flexible than originally thought and the limit between the binary sexes could be crossed.

Nevertheless, these judgments had a clear normalising effect. The recognition of rights and sexes came at the price of reinforcing binary genders and heterosexuality. After these rulings, transsexual individuals who had fulfilled all the requirements were granted recognition as heterosexual members of the desired sex. Surgery became the path adopted by the Court to reconstruct the limit of the sex binary after allowing the transsexual to cross it. Moreover, those transsexual individuals who had not undergone genital surgery failed to have their gender recognised, but this was portrayed as merely a temporary situation, since trans people were conceived as necessarily wishing to modify their genitalia.

It took the Court almost 15 years to engage with trans identities that challenged the imposed causality between genitalia and sex. Until the judgment rendered on *AP, Garçon and Nicot v France*,[153] the possibility of gender recognition detached from genitalia seemed to be unthinkable within the Court's case law. Between 2002 and 2017, the only option left to trans identities who resisted genital surgery was to embrace the place that belonged to the pre-operative transsexual. Trans individuals who did not desire surgery could exist in-between the genders, in an intermediate position of intermittently moving across the sex boundary. To some extent, this situation has been revised by the Court in 2017. Gender recognition can no longer be made dependent on genital surgery. However, the refusal to be subjected to a medical diagnosis of a mental disorder can still lead to a life in-between genders.

[153] *AP, Garçon and Nicot v France* (n 21).

3

(Homo)Sexuality before the Court

I. Introduction

As discussed in the previous chapters, queer theory is a deconstructive technique that contests the stability of identity categories, such as gender and sexuality.[1] While in Chapter 2 I made use of queer theory to analyse how the case law of the European Court of Human Rights has constructed (and re-constructed) the category of gender, this chapter will follow a similar path concerning sexuality. An awareness of the regulatory power of the law over the construction of sexual identities marks the starting point of this analysis.[2] The law plays an important role in the demarcation of the boundaries of accepted/unaccepted sexualities,[3] which takes place both by granting privileged status to those sexualities that accommodate to the norm(al), as well as by exercising juridical power to punish those sexual practices that deviate from it.[4] While the old criminalisation of sodomy focused on the prohibition of certain sexual acts, making penile-vaginal (and hopefully reproductive) sex between a woman and a man the sexual norm,[5] the current differential recognition of rights for heterosexuals and homosexuals is concerned with relationships, conjugality, and the idealisation of the heterosexual couple. This kind of power of law over sexualities is normalising and disciplinarian in Foucauldian terms of bio-power.[6] As affirmed by Wayne Morgan, human rights law is not an exception to the regulatory power of law,[7] and neither is the jurisprudence of the European Court of Human Rights.

I argued in Chapter 2 that the Court did not engage with the notion of gender until it met the transsexual applicant, and the same is true regarding sexuality

[1] Annamarie Jagose, *Queer Theory: An Introduction* (Melbourne University Press, 1996) 3; Carl F Stychin, *Law's Desire: Sexuality and the Limits of Justice* (Routledge, 1995) 141 and 145; Jeffrey Weeks, *The Language of Sexuality* (Routledge, 2011) 146.

[2] Stychin, *Law's Desire* (n 1) 1, 7 and 156; Carlos A Ball, 'Sexual Ethics and Postmodernism in Gay Rights Philosophy' (2002) 80 *North Carolina Law Review* 371, at 404–5.

[3] William N Eskridge, 'Law and the Constitution of the Closet: American Regulation of Same-Sex Intimacy, 1880–1946' (1997) 82 *Iowa Law Review* 1007, at 1094–96.

[4] Vikki Bell, *Interrogating Incest: Feminism, Foucault and the Law* (Routledge, 1993) 159.

[5] Ngaire Naffine, 'The Body Bag' in Ngaire Naffine and Rosemary Owens (eds), *Sexing the Subject of Law* (Law Book Co, 1997) 79–93, at 91.

[6] Aleardo Zanghellini, 'Queer, Antinormativity, Counter-normativity and Abjection' (2009) 18 *Griffith Law Review* 1, at 6.

[7] Wayne Morgan, 'Queering International Human Rights Law' in Carl Stychin and Didi Herman (eds), *Sexuality in the Legal Arena* (Athlone, 2000) 208–25, at 211–12.

and the homosexual subject. The Court's concern over sexuality started when it met the homosexual and his criminalisation in Northern Ireland.[8] In *Dudgeon v United Kingdom*, the applicant complained about the violation of human rights suffered due to the existence of legislation criminalising same-sex sexuality in Northern Ireland. In this ground-breaking judgment from 1981, the Court decided that same-sex sexuality was indeed a subject that belonged to the realm of human rights law.[9] It ruled that the criminalisation of same-sex sexuality in private was a violation of the right to respect for private life, protected by the European Convention on Human Rights.[10] The Court considered that Jeff Dudgeon's homosexuality was an aspect of his *personality*, and this understanding was foundational for granting the applicant's sexual behaviour protection under the Convention.[11] Since the *Dudgeon* judgment, homosexuality has been understood by the Court as a protected manifestation of sexuality.

This case became the cornerstone of a diverse case law on the topic of homosexuality. Almost the exact same ruling to that rendered in *Dudgeon* was reiterated by the Court in the subsequent cases of *Norris* and *Modinos*, which also dealt with the criminalisation of homosexuality, on those occasions in Ireland and Cyprus. In each of these cases the Court ruled that the mere existence of legislation criminalising sexual activity between consenting adult men was a violation of the Convention.[12]

This chapter is about the Court's encounters with sexuality and how its case law on the topic constructed homosexuality as a *sexual identity* that is worthy of legal protection through human rights. The chapter is divided into nine sections. Section II will focus on the sexuality of the subject of the European Convention on Human Rights. Sections III to V will develop the claim that the protection of homosexuality within the Court's case law is grounded in its understanding as a valid sexual identity. Then, sections VI and VII will discuss how the Court has conceived this homosexual identity, focusing on different characteristics attached to this conception. Section IX will analyse some of the consequences of this construction, as well as a potential path to *queer* this understanding of sexuality. Lastly, conclusions are drawn in section IX.

II. The (Hetero)Sexual Subject of Human Rights

While the Convention does not mention the notion of sexuality, the idea of the subject of human rights as a sexual being is evident. In fact, the European

[8] *Dudgeon v United Kingdom*, Series A no 45, 22 October 1981.
[9] Leslie Moran, *The Homosexual(ity) of Law* (Routledge, 1996) 175.
[10] *Dudgeon v United Kingdom* (n 8) para 63.
[11] Paul Johnson, *Homosexuality and the European Court of Human Rights* (Routledge, 2012) 50.
[12] *Dudgeon v United Kingdom* (n 8) para 63; *Norris v Ireland*, Series A no 142, 26 October 1988, para 47; *Modinos v Cyprus*, Series A no 259, 22 April 1993, para 26.

Convention on Human Rights has been said to disclose the (hetero)sexuality of its human subject when regulating the right to marry and to found a family in Article 12. The text of the Convention reads: 'Men and women of marriageable age have the right to marry and to found a family, according to the national laws governing the exercise of this right'.[13] I agree with Robert Wintemute that the wording of the Article does not restrict the right to marry to heterosexual individuals,[14] since it only enshrines the right of men and women to marry, without demanding for men to marry women and vice versa. However, the Court has rejected this interpretation, finding in Article 12 the source of the heterosexuality of the subject of human rights. In the *Schalk and Kopf* judgment (which will be analysed in-depth in Chapter 5), the Court held that the appropriate interpretation of Article 12 of the Convention was to protect marriage as the heterosexual union of a man and a woman. It stated that 'regard must be had to the historical context in which the Convention was adopted. In the 1950s marriage was clearly understood in the traditional sense of being a union between partners of different sex'.[15]

Therefore, through the protection of heterosexual marriage as a human right, the Court constructed the subject of human rights – the one entitled to every right established in the Convention – as a heterosexual individual. As it flows from Article 12, the heterosexual subject conceived by the Convention has the human right to marry a person of the 'opposite' sex and to engage in reproductive sexuality in order to found a family. Nevertheless, even if heterosexuality is the sexuality of the true subject of the Convention, the Court has extended the protection of human rights to the homosexual as well, as will be discussed throughout this chapter.

III. The Protection of Another Sexual Identity

It is a well-accepted understanding that the rationale behind the Court's protection of homosexuality is its conception as a private matter. This is not only the view of legal academics, such as Nicholas Bamforth,[16] but it is also an understanding shared by socio-legal scholars such as Michele Grigolo and Paul Johnson.[17] However, I will propose that a different reading of the case law can offer a more

[13] Convention for the Protection of Human Rights and Fundamental Freedoms (adopted 4 November 1950, entered into force 3 September 1953) 213 UNTS 221 ('European Convention on Human Rights'), Art 12.

[14] Robert Wintemute, 'Strasbourg to the Rescue? Same-Sex Partners and Parents' in Robert Wintemute and Mads Andenæs (eds), *Legal Recognition of Same-Sex Partnerships: A Study of National, European and International Law* (Hart, 2001) 713–29, at 728.

[15] *Schalk and Kopf v Austria*, Application no 30141/04, ECHR 2010, para 56.

[16] Nicholas Bamforth 'Sexual Privacy and the European Convention on Human Rights' (1997) 56 *Cambridge Law Journal* 480, at 482.

[17] Michele Grigolo, 'Sexualities and the ECHR: Introducing the Universal Sexual Legal Subject' (2003) 14 *European Journal of International Law* 1023, at 1023, 1027 and 1029; Paul Johnson, 'An Essentially Private Manifestation of Human Personality: Constructions of Homosexuality in the European Court of Human Rights' (2010) 10 *Human Rights Law Review* 67, at 87, 93, 94 and 97.

compelling explanation of the Court's protection of homosexuality. I believe that it is the Court's understanding of homosexuality as a sexual identity which acts as the grounds for validating homosexuality as a human rights issue.

The majority of the Court's rulings dealing with same-sex sexuality have been decided from a perspective centred on the right to respect for private life. In fact, the Court explicitly tended to base these decisions on the belief that sexuality is an important part of an individual's private life.[18] Nonetheless, the scope of the right to a private life in Article 8 of the Convention is much wider than the traditional conception of privacy. As explained by Harris, O'Boyle, Bates and Buckley, the right to respect for private life is a broad concept that lacks clarity as to its precise definition and scope.[19] Some of the more clear guidance offered by the Court can be found in the *Niemietz v Germany* judgment, which reads:

> The Court does not consider it possible or necessary to attempt an exhaustive definition of the notion of 'private life'. However, it would be too restrictive to limit the notion to an 'inner circle' in which the individual may live his own personal life as he chooses and to exclude therefrom entirely the outside world not encompassed within that circle. Respect for private life must also comprise to a certain degree the right to establish and develop relationships with other human beings.[20]

This explanation underscores that the notion of private life within the Convention extends beyond the narrower Anglo-American idea of privacy.[21] This interpretation is shared by many legal scholars who have identified different areas covered by the notion of private life, such as privacy, personal information, certain aspects of personal integrity, environmental concerns, social life, migration issues, and personal autonomy.[22] The Court itself has highlighted that, within the notion of private life recognised in Article 8, it is possible to find the right to define one's own identity. According to the Court:

> Under Article 8 of the Convention in particular, where the notion of personal autonomy is an important principle underlying the interpretation of its guarantees, protection is given to the personal sphere of each individual, including the right to establish details of their identity as individual human beings.[23]

[18] *Dudgeon v United Kingdom* (n 8) para 60; *ADT v United Kingdom*, Application no 35765/97, ECHR 2000-IX, para 25; *Gas and Dubois v France*, Application no 25951/07, ECHR 2012, para 37.

[19] David J Harris and others, *Law of the European Convention on Human Rights*, 2nd edn (Oxford University Press, 2009) 364.

[20] *Niemietz v Germany*, Series A no 251-B, 16 December 1992, para 29.

[21] Harris and others, *Law of the European Convention on Human Rights* (n 19) 364.

[22] Noel Whitty, Thérèse Murphy and Stephen Livingstone, *Civil Liberties Law: The Human Rights Act Era* (Oxford University Press, 2001) 293–94; NA Moreham, 'The Right to Respect for Private Life in the European Convention on Human Rights: A Re-Examination' (2008) 1 *European Human Rights Law Review* 44; Harris and others, *Law of the European Convention on Human Rights* (n 19) 364–71; Robin CA White and Clare Ovey, *The European Convention on Human Rights*, 5th edn (Oxford University Press, 2010) 357–401.

[23] *Christine Goodwin v United Kingdom* (GC), Application no 28957/95, ECHR 2002-VI, para 90.

Even if this wide conception of private life was not fully articulated in these terms until 2002,[24] this understanding of private life has underpinned the Court's case law on homosexuality from the start.

The analysis of some of the earliest cases concerning homosexuality illustrates the claim that sexual identity, rather than sexual privacy, has been the protected value behind the protection of same-sex sexuality. This analysis begins with the already mentioned *Dudgeon* judgment, and then turns to examine *ADT v United Kingdom*. Lastly, the discussion will focus on the original twin cases regarding homosexuality in the British armed forces: *Smith and Grady v United Kingdom* and *Lustig-Prean and Beckett v United Kingdom*.

A. The Sexual Identity of Jeff Dudgeon

Paul Johnson has provided a sophisticated analysis of the Court's case law on homosexuality and has become the strongest supporter of the proposition that the main reason behind the Court's protection of homosexuality is its private character.[25] He affirmed that not only is privacy the reason behind the protection granted by the Court to homosexuality, but that the homosexual individual has been constructed as a private subject by the Court.[26] Given this situation, Johnson has gone so far as to suggest that the Court's case law has recreated the social relations of the closet, since the protection granted to homosexuality appeared to be subject to its private character, leading to the assimilation of privacy with secrecy.[27]

It is true that the seclusion in which homosexual acts were assumed to take place helped to stress the arbitrary character of the legislation criminalising homosexual sex. In the *Dudgeon* ruling, the Court explicitly held that the legislation in Northern Ireland was unacceptable under the Convention, since it did not acknowledge the distinction between private and public sex. The Court emphasised that 'the offences are committed whether the act takes place in public or in private'.[28] However, the main focus of the Court was on the person behind the acts.

As discussed in Chapter 1 following a Foucauldian conception of sexuality, it was not until the nineteenth century that homosexuality came to be conceived as an identity, when the sin of sodomy stopped being understood as merely a

[24] See *Pretty v United Kingdom*, Application no 2346/02, ECHR 2002-III, para 61; *Mikulić v Croatia*, Application no 53176/99, ECHR 2002-I, para 53; *Goodwin v United Kingdom* (n 23) para 90.

[25] Johnson, 'An Essentially Private Manifestation of Human Personality' (n 17) 76 and 83.

[26] ibid 82. I have actually supported this understanding elsewhere. See Damian A Gonzalez-Salzberg, 'The Making of the Court's Homosexual: A Queer Reading of the European Court of Human Rights' Case Law on Same-Sex Sexuality' (2014) 65 *Northern Ireland Legal Quarterly* 371.

[27] Johnson, 'An Essentially Private Manifestation of Human Personality' (n 17) 85 and 93; Johnson, *Homosexuality and the European Court of Human Rights* (n 11) 104–5.

[28] *Dudgeon v United Kingdom* (n 8) para 39.

practice, and began to be considered as the sexual expression of a specific kind of person, the homosexual. In Foucault's words:

> Homosexuality appeared as one of the forms of sexuality when it was transposed from the practice of sodomy onto a kind of interior androgyny, a hermaphrodism of the soul. The sodomite had been a temporary aberration; the homosexual was now a species.[29]

Without explicitly supporting a social constructionist perspective, the Court also adopted a distinction between identities and sinful acts in the *Dudgeon* judgment. Two dissenting judges attempted to justify Northern Ireland's criminalisation of homosexuality through the sinful character of the acts. Dissenting Judge Zekia stated that: 'Christian and Moslem religions are all united in the condemnation of homosexual relations and of sodomy'.[30] Dissenting Judge Walsh agreed with Judge Zekia, arguing that the view of sodomy as an unnatural sexual practice was held by Jewish, Christian and Muslim cultures.[31] Nevertheless, the majority of the Court viewed homosexuality as an identity, rather than a sinful act. For the Court, homosexuality was to be understood as 'an essentially private manifestation of the human personality'.[32]

Even though the Court did not use the term 'identity', but rather referred to homosexuality as a manifestation of *personality*, its subsequent case law confirmed the interpretation that the protection granted to Jeff Dudgeon in 1981 was based on an understanding of homosexuality as a *personal identity*. Indeed, the *Dudgeon* case became a precedent referenced by the Court on different occasions in which it wanted to affirm that personal identity was a notion covered by the right to respect for private life.[33]

Furthermore, the Court connected the notions of homosexual acts and homosexual identity, emphasising that the performance of the prohibited acts was motivated by the applicant's predisposition towards them.[34] The Court presented Jeff Dudgeon's dilemma in the following way:

> [E]ither he respects the law and refrains from engaging – even in private with consenting male partners – in prohibited *sexual acts to which he is disposed by reason of his homosexual tendencies*, or he commits such acts and thereby becomes liable to criminal prosecution.[35]

[29] Michel Foucault, *The History of Sexuality: An Introduction* (Penguin, 1978) 43.

[30] *Dudgeon v United Kingdom* (n 8), dissenting opinion of Judge Zekia, para 1.

[31] ibid, partially dissenting opinion of Judge Walsh, para 17.

[32] ibid para 60.

[33] See *Goodwin v United Kingdom* (n 23) para 77; *I v United Kingdom* (GC), no 25680/94, 11 July 2002, para 57; *SH and others v Austria*, Application no 57813/00, 1 April 2010, para 93; *Gross v Switzerland*, Application no 67810/10, 14 May 2013, joint dissenting opinion of Judges Raimondi, Jočienė and Karakaş, para 6.

[34] This conflation is emphasised by the distinction between 'homosexual tendency' and 'homosexual acts' drew upon by dissenting Judge Walsh in his attempt to validate the domestic criminalisation of homosexual acts. *Dudgeon v United Kingdom* (n 8), partially dissenting opinion of Judge Walsh, para 13.

[35] *Dudgeon v United Kingdom* (n 8) para 41 (emphasis added).

Therefore, the Court conceived the criminalisation of homosexual acts as the criminalisation of homosexuality, since homosexual acts were a manifestation of such an identity. These acts were a consequence of his homosexual tendencies, an expression of his human personality.[36] This is the reason why the Court dismissed the arguments offered by the state for maintaining the criminalisation in question. It held that such justifications were outweighed by the detrimental effects which the existence of such a provision had on the 'life of a person of homosexual orientation like the applicant'.[37] To summarise, it might have been easier for the Court to render its ruling since homosexual acts were prohibited in Northern Ireland even in private. However, it was the conception of homosexuality as a type of personality which deserved protection that provided the rationale for the judgment.

B. Privacy vs Identity in *ADT v United Kingdom*

A similar reading is possible of the Court's ruling in *ADT v United Kingdom*, which concerned group homosexual sex. In *ADT*, the Court held that legislation criminalising consensual sexual acts between more than two adult men was also a violation of the right to respect for private life.[38] In this case, the applicant was convicted of gross indecency. The police had found videotapes in his home that contained images of him and other adult men having group sex. Nevertheless, the Court found that the sexuality of the applicant was protected by the right to respect for private life.

Once again, Johnson made a strong argument as to the importance the Court placed on privacy.[39] Indeed, the Court highlighted that the sexuality of the applicant was truly private, since he and his sexual partners desired to remain anonymous, keeping their sexuality hidden.[40] When justifying its ruling, the

[36] In fact, Leslie Moran argued that the expressions 'homosexual tendencies' and 'personality' have been used by dissenting Judge Walsh to highlight that the majority judgment conceived homosexuality as an identity. Moran, *The Homosexual(ity) of Law* (n 9) 176.

[37] *Dudgeon v United Kingdom* (n 8) para 60.

[38] *ADT v United Kingdom* (n 18) paras 38–39.

[39] Johnson, *Homosexuality and the European Court of Human Rights* (n 11) 104–5.

[40] The strong link between privacy and secrecy reappeared in the Court's decision on admissibility in *F v United Kingdom*. On that occasion, the Court ruled that the prohibition on criminalising same-sex sexuality did not forbid extraditions to states with draconian punishments for homosexual acts, when a judicial conviction was unlikely for 'closet' homosexuals. *F v United Kingdom* (Dec), Application no 17341/03, 22 June 2004. However, while seemingly not changing its stance on extraditions, the Court has recently affirmed that 'sexual orientation constitutes a fundamental aspect of an individual's identity and conscience and that it should not demand individuals requesting international protection grounded on sexual orientation to conceal it'. Author's own translation from the French original: 'Par ailleurs, la Cour estime que l'orientation sexuelle constitue un aspect fondamental de l'identité et de la conscience d'un individu et qu'il ne saurait dès lors être exigé de personnes déposant une demande de protection internationale fondée sur leur orientation sexuelle qu'elles dissimulent cette dernière'. *IK. v Switzerland* (Dec), Application no 21417/17, 19 December 2017, para 24.

Court expressly characterised the applicant's sexual practices as private, because they were performed in private:

> It is true that the activities were recorded on videotape, but the Court notes that the applicant was prosecuted for the activities themselves, and not for the recording, or for any risk of it entering the public domain. The activities were therefore genuinely 'private'.[41]

Certainly, the fact that the homosexual practices took place on the private side of the private/public divide was a central element in deciding the case.

Nonetheless, the Court also affirmed that the main issue of the case was not the risk of the recording entering the public domain, but the fact that the legislation allowed the criminalisation of homosexual acts. The Court highlighted that 'the applicant was prosecuted for the activities themselves'.[42] Furthermore, the judgment emphasised that heterosexual group sex would have been treated differently by the domestic legislation,[43] demonstrating that the issue was not truly about the private/public distinction of the activities, but rather about the sexuality of those involved. In fact, the sexual identity of the applicant was present from the beginning of the judgment and it underpinned the Court's ruling. The description of the case actually began by stating: 'The applicant is a practising homosexual',[44] and the Court also emphasised that the applicant 'had gone to some lengths not to reveal his sexual orientation'.[45] This indicates that the case was not simply about sexual acts, but concerned the acts of a person with a clear sexual identity.

The understanding of homosexuality as an identity permeates the whole case law developed by the Court. Clear traces of this conception of homosexuality can be observed in several cases. For instance, in *Norris v Ireland*, the Court expressed the view that: 'Mr Norris is an active homosexual'.[46] The same can be seen in *Modinos v Cyprus*, where the Court declared: 'The applicant is a homosexual'.[47] Once again this is evident in *Sutherland v United Kingdom*, when the Court affirmed: 'He had his first homosexual encounter … with another person of his age who also was homosexual'.[48] This understanding was also present in *F v United Kingdom*, in which the Court stated: 'due to the fact that he is a homosexual',[49] and in *IIN v The Netherlands*, when the Court mentioned: 'on account of his homosexuality'.[50] Therefore, all the applicants in those cases *are* homosexuals. In all these occasions,

[41] *ADT v United Kingdom* (n 18) para 37.
[42] ibid.
[43] ibid para 19.
[44] ibid para 8.
[45] ibid para 25.
[46] *Norris v Ireland* (n 12) para 9.
[47] *Modinos v Cyprus* (n 12) para 7.
[48] *Sutherland v United Kingdom* (striking out) (GC), Application no 25186/94, 22 March 2001, para 11.
[49] *F v United Kingdom* (n 40) 10.
[50] *INN v The Netherlands* (Dec), Application no 2035/04, 9 December 2004, 12.

the homosexuality of the applicants was not used to refer to sexual acts, neither was it aimed at mentioning a personal characteristic, but homosexuality was used to describe a type of person.[51]

C. Incitement to Discourse

While the Court's early case law discussed the possibility of criminalising homosexual sex, this section will now explore how the Court has dealt with homosexual individuals forced to 'confess' their homosexuality by a state policy. Between 1999 and 2009, the Court decided a group of cases in which coming out of the closet was also the cause of being driven out of the military.[52] In two original cases, the Court examined the United Kingdom's policy which banned homosexuals from the armed forces, and which included intrusive investigations into those suspected of 'homosexuality' and the consequent discharge of every individual identified as homosexual.

The state policy that was analysed by the Court had the paradoxical effect of forcing members of the armed forces both inside and outside the closet. If originally the 'homosexual ban' silenced homosexual individuals, locking them inside the closet, simultaneously, it forced homosexuals to come out, through invasive investigations. The sexuality of the homosexual was, at the same time, forced into self-censorship and disclosure. This state practice can be analysed by applying a Foucauldian understanding of the political incitement to speak about sex.[53] According to Foucault, the need to regulate the sexuality of individuals requires knowledge about their sexuality, making it essential for sex to become a public issue.[54] In these particular cases, the confessions demanded from the members of the armed forces about their sexuality, and the investigation aimed at finding out whether the confessions were truthful, were the means to access knowledge about their sexuality.[55] For the state, the incitement to discourse superseded the obligation to remain in the closet, but the escape from the closet also meant discharge from the armed forces.

The Court decided that both the 'homosexual ban' policy and the investigations pursued to establish the sexuality of those discharged were violations of the

[51] Although I do not want to overstate the relevance of these statements made by the Court in the 'Facts' section of the mentioned judgments (where the Court relies heavily on the narrative provided by the applicants), I believe that they were interesting to note, as they contribute to the overall construction of a homosexual identity performed by the Court.

[52] This type of military policy in which 'coming out' was a reason for discharge from the armed forces was certainly not unique in the United Kingdom, but mirrored policies of other countries. See Stychin, *Law's Desire* (n 1) 91–100; Carl F. Stychin, 'To Take Him "At His Word": Theorizing Law, Sexuality and the US Military Exclusion Policy' (1996) 5 *Social and Legal Studies* 179.

[53] Foucault, *The History of Sexuality* (n 29) 21.

[54] ibid 25–26.

[55] ibid 63.

right to respect for private life.[56] The Court held that there were no convincing reasons for supporting the exclusion of homosexual individuals from the armed forces, and that the manner in which the investigations were conducted was an unjustifiable interference into private life.[57] Consequently, the protection granted to the homosexual members of the armed forces was not based on the concealment of their sexuality, but was founded on the disclosure of a protected sexual identity.[58]

It is on this point that Johnson made the strongest claim about the protection of homosexuality based on privacy.[59] In the *Smith and Grady* case, the applicants complained that the blanket prohibition on homosexual individuals in the armed forces not only entailed a violation of the right to respect for their private life, but it also interfered with their right to express their sexuality.[60] However, the Court refused to find a violation of the applicants' freedom of expression, arguing that this element was subsidiary to the right to respect for their private life.[61] Given this decision, Johnson argued that the Court's failure to analyse a violation of freedom of expression was a clear display of its fixation with understanding homosexuality as a private matter.[62]

While Johnson's argument regarding this case is appealing, the rationale behind the Court's rulings in these cases can be better understood as based on the conception of homosexuality as a protected identity. First, the Court accepted that the discursive practice followed by the state, in which the confession was used to produce knowledge about sexuality, actually produced this truth. According to the Court: 'The policy results in an immediate discharge from the armed forces once an *individual's homosexuality is established and irrespective of the individual's conduct*'.[63] Thus, the Court considered that the process of confession was

[56] *Lustig-Prean and Beckett v United Kingdom*, Application nos 31417/96 and 32377/96, September 1999, paras 64, 104 and 105; *Smith and Grady v United Kingdom*, Application nos 33985/96 and 33986/96, ECHR 1999-VI, paras 71, 111 and 112.

[57] However, the Court has been criticised for seemingly accepting the right of the states to investigate the sexuality of the members of the armed forces, since it only objected to the intrusive means used by the United Kingdom, but not to the investigations themselves. Johnson, *Homosexuality and the European Court of Human Rights* (n 11) 108.

[58] This opinion was reiterated in the analogous *Beck* and *Perkins* cases, and was the rationale for reaching friendly settlements in the *Brown* and *Hunt and Miller* cases, after the Ministry of Defence abandoned its contentious policy in 2000. *Beck, Copp and Bazeley v United Kingdom*, Application nos 48535/99, 48536/99 and 48537/00, 22 October 2002; *Perkins and R v United Kingdom*, Application nos 43208/98 and 44875/98, 22 October 2002; *Brown v United Kingdom* (friendly settlement), Application no 52770/99, 29 July 2003; *Hunt and Miller v United Kingdom* (friendly settlement), Application nos 10578/05 and 10605/05, 23 June 2009.

[59] Another strong case for understanding that these judgments portrayed homosexuality as a private matter was developed by Michael Kavey. Michael Kavey, 'The Public Faces of Privacy: Rewriting Lustig-Prean and Beckett v. United Kingdom' in Eva Brems (ed), *Diversity and European Human Rights: Rewriting Judgments of the ECHR* (Cambridge, 2012) 293–325.

[60] *Smith and Grady v United Kingdom* (n 56) paras 124 and 126.

[61] ibid para 127.

[62] Johnson, 'An Essentially Private Manifestation of Human Personality' (n 17) 93 and 94.

[63] *Lustig-Prean and Beckett v United Kingdom* (n 56) para 86; *Smith and Grady v United Kingdom* (n 56) para 93 (emphasis added).

not aimed at investigating individuals' sexual conduct, but at establishing their sexual identity.[64] Then, this confessed identity became the subject matter of the case and the Court decided that depriving individuals of their job based on their sexual identities was unjustifiable. In particular, the Court stressed the high level of protection deserved by those embracing a homosexual identity, as it compared homophobic bias to negative attitudes towards those of a different race, origin or colour.[65]

To summarise, this section developed the argument that the Court protects homosexuality due to its understanding of it as an identity, rather than because it is a private activity.[66] The following section will engage with the protection granted by the Court to homosexuality within the public sphere. This discussion also strengthens the claim that privacy cannot be the basis for protecting sexuality, since it cannot successfully explain why homosexuality has been granted protection beyond the private sphere.

IV. Homosexuality as a Public Identity

The majority of the Court's rulings dealing with same-sex sexuality have been decided from a perspective centred on the right to respect for private life. In fact, it was not until 2007 and 2010 that the Court had to examine cases that concerned homosexuality in the public sphere.[67] On these occasions, the Court dealt with governmental bans imposed on marches organised to draw public attention to discrimination based on sexual orientation, which took place in the capital cities of Poland and Russia. In *Bączkowski and others v Poland*, the Court explicitly recognised that sexuality was not just a private matter, but that the right to publicly express one's sexual identity was also protected by the Convention.[68] This point was made even clearer in *Alekseyev v Russia*, in which the Court reaffirmed the right of individuals to openly identify themselves as gays and lesbians.[69] In both cases, the Court found a violation of the right to assembly independently and in

[64] According to McGhee, the objective pursued by the state's investigations was to establish the sexual identity of the members of the armed forces and not to uncover the existence of actual homosexual conduct. Derek McGhee, *Homosexuality, Law and Resistance* (Routledge, 2001) 34–35. See also Nicholas Bamforth, 'Sexual Orientation Discrimination after Grant v South-West Trains' (2000) 63 *Modern Law Review* 694, at 716.

[65] *Lustig-Prean and Beckett v United Kingdom* (n 56) para 90; *Smith and Grady v United Kingdom* (n 56) para 97.

[66] In his later work, Johnson has also highlighted the importance the Court granted to homosexuality as an identity in the *Dudgeon* case. Paul Johnson, 'Sociology and the European Court of Human Rights' (2014) 62 *Sociological Review* 547, at 558–61.

[67] Before them, the *Scherer* case concerned freedom of expression, but it was rendered inadmissible by the Court due to technical reasons. *Scherer v Switzerland*, Series A no 28, 25 March 1994.

[68] *Bączkowski and others v Poland*, Application no 1543/06, 3 May 2007.

[69] *Alekseyev v Russia*, Application nos 4916/07, 25924/08 and 14599/09, 21 October 2010, para 84.

conjunction with the prohibition of discrimination based on sexual orientation.[70] The Court held that the authorities' refusal to allow the marches in question was an unjustified interference with the right to peaceful assembly. Furthermore, the fact that the refused authorisations were linked to the strong opinions against same-sex sexuality of the Mayors of the cities provided the evidential basis for the Court to find that the bans were discriminatory in character.[71]

Through these rulings, the Court demonstrated that homosexuality was a protected public characteristic. This point was clearly stated by the Court in the *Alekseyev* judgment, when it rejected the government's view that homosexuality was merely a private issue:

> [I]t was not the behaviour or the attire of the participants that the authorities found objectionable but the very fact that they wished to openly identify themselves as gay men or lesbians, individually and as a group. The Government admitted, in particular, that the authorities would reach their limit of tolerance towards homosexual behaviour when it spilt over from the strictly private domain into the sphere shared by the general public.[72]

The Court's rejection of the state's argument showed that the grounds for understanding homosexuality as a human rights issue were not limited to the protection of a private sexuality. On the contrary, the rationale behind the protection of homosexuality was its conception as a coherent identity, regardless of its private or public character.

The public protection of a homosexual identity was also strongly supported by the Court in the *Bączkowski* ruling. In that case, the Court justified the relevance of the right of peaceful assembly by referring to *pluralism* as one of the hallmarks of a democratic society and it emphasised the importance of the recognition of different identities as a requirement for pluralism.[73] The Court affirmed:

> For pluralism is also built on genuine recognition of, and respect for, diversity and the dynamics of cultural traditions, ethnic and cultural identities, religious beliefs and artistic, literary and socio-economic ideas and concepts. The harmonious interaction of persons and groups with varied identities is essential for achieving social cohesion.[74]

Therefore, the protection of the applicants' right to peaceful assembly in public was grounded in the understanding of homosexuality as an identity worthy of public protection.

[70] *Bączkowski and others v Poland* (n 68) para 101; *Alekseyev v Russia* (n 69) para 110. A very similar decision was adopted in the *Genderdoc-M v Moldova* case, in which a non-governmental organisation was refused authorisation from the Mayor of Moldova's capital city to hold a peaceful demonstration to call for the adoption of laws to protect the members of the LGBT community from discrimination. On that occasion, the Court also found violations of the right to freedom of peaceful assembly, both by itself and in conjunction with the prohibition of discrimination. *Genderdoc-M v Moldova*, Application no 9106/06, 12 June 2012.

[71] *Bączkowski and others v Poland* (n 68) paras 68, 100 and 101; *Alekseyev v Russia* (n 69) paras 86–88 and 109–110.

[72] *Alekseyev v Russia* (n 69) para 82.

[73] *Bączkowski and others v Poland* (n 68) para 63.

[74] ibid para 62.

Nonetheless, probably the Court's most emphatic support to the public character of homosexuality took place in 2017, when it decided *Bayev and others v Russia*. On that occasion, the Court examined whether Russia's legislative ban on the promotion of homosexuality and non-traditional sexual relations among minors was compatible with the Convention. The Court found Russia's legal ban to be in breach of freedom of expression by itself and also in conjunction with the prohibition of discrimination.[75] In particular, it rejected the government's attempts to justify the legislative provisions at stake as serving the protection of public morals, public health or the rights of others. The Court affirmed that such laws actually reinforced stigma and prejudice and encouraged homophobia.[76] In no uncertain terms, it asserted the existence of clear European consensus on the recognition of individuals' right to openly identify themselves as belonging to a sexual minority and to promote their own rights and freedom.[77] In other words, the Court left no room for doubt as to the public character of homosexuality.

A. The Protection of the Public Homosexual

The protection of a homosexual identity not only requires states to respect homosexual individuals, but also for them to take actions to ensure that others respect LGBT rights. The Court has dealt with the protection of homosexuality from discriminatory acts in the public sphere on different occasions, establishing a clear level of protection against homophobia. The following discussion of the cases *Vejdeland and others v Sweden*, *Mladina dd Ljubljana v Slovenia* and *Eweida and others v United Kingdom* illustrates the approach adopted by the Court. In all these cases, the Court had to decide whether the states' reactions following homophobic acts offered an appropriate protection of the human rights of the public homosexual subject. The first of these judgments was *Vejdeland*, issued by the Court in 2012.[78] In this case, the Court evaluated whether a conviction imposed by a Swedish tribunal for homophobic speech was compatible with the right to freedom of expression. The domestic conviction had been imposed for the distribution of leaflets stating that homosexuality was 'a deviant sexual proclivity' with a 'morally destructive effect on the substance of society'. The Court considered that the expressions in question constituted serious and prejudicial allegations, and decided that the conviction imposed was justified, since it could be understood as necessary in a democratic society for the protection of the reputation and rights of others.[79] Consequently, the Court confirmed that freedom of expression did not

[75] *Bayev and others v Russia*, Application nos 67667/09, 44092/12 and 56717/12, 20 June 2017, paras 84 and 92.
[76] ibid para 83.
[77] ibid para 66.
[78] *Vejdeland and others v Sweden*, Application no 1813/07, 9 February 2012.
[79] ibid paras 8, 54 and 58–60.

include the liberty to resort to homophobic hate speech,[80] thereby recognising a certain degree of protection for homosexual individuals in the public sphere.

The case of *Mladina dd Ljubljana* was also about homophobic speech. However, this time the restriction on speech imposed by the domestic authorities was not against homophobic expression, but against offensive speech used to attack homophobic remarks. During the Slovenian parliamentary debate on the legal regulation of same-sex relationships, a Member of Parliament referred to homosexuals as an undesirable section of the population.[81] Additionally, his speech was reinforced by the use of tones and gestures aimed at parodying how homosexual men were supposed to act and speak.[82] In response to this performance, a political magazine published an article in which it criticised the politician's speech claiming that it constituted

> the typical attitude of a cerebral bankrupt who is lucky to be living in a country with such a limited pool of human resources that a person of his characteristics can even end up in Parliament, when in a normal country worthy of any respect he could not even be a janitor in the average urban primary school.[83]

Following publication of the article, the parliamentary deputy brought an action before the domestic courts against the magazine, alleging to have suffered mental distress as a consequence of the publication. The domestic court not only ordered the magazine to pay damages, but it also concluded that his parliamentary speech should not be considered offensive to homosexuals.[84] After unsuccessful appeals, the publisher of the magazine claimed before the European Court of Human Rights that the domestic judgments amounted to a violation of freedom of expression.

The Court agreed with the publisher and held that the domestic courts had failed to strike a fair balance between the competing interests in the case.[85] The judgment emphasised that the controversial statement of the magazine was constructed as a counterpoint to the politician's remarks, which could be regarded as promoting negative stereotypes.[86] In particular, the Court highlighted that while describing the parliamentary deputy as a *cerebral bankrupt* 'could legitimately be considered offensive',[87] the statement 'did not amount to a *gratuitous* personal attack'.[88] Therefore, the Court affirmed that freedom of expression allows resort to offensive language when it is used to defend the public homosexual from homophobic speech.

[80] ibid. On this point see the critical analysis by Johnson, who criticises the Court for not being clear in the inclusion of the acts of the applicants within the notion of 'hate speech'. See Johnson, *Homosexuality and the European Court of Human Rights* (n 11) 176–81.
[81] *Mladina dd Ljubljana v Slovenia*, Application no 20981/10, 17 April 2014, paras 39 and 44.
[82] ibid paras 5, 44.
[83] ibid para 7.
[84] ibid paras 13 and 14.
[85] ibid paras 47–49.
[86] ibid para 44.
[87] ibid para 43.
[88] ibid para 46 (emphasis added).

The final judgment to be discussed is *Eweida and others v United Kingdom*. On this occasion, the Court decided four different applications, two of which concerned LGBT rights.[89] The applicants, Ms Ladele and Mr McFarlane, complained about sanctions taken against them at their places of work, as a result of their objection to performing professional services which they considered to condone same-sex partnerships. While the decision of the Court favoured the protection of LGBT rights in both cases, that of Ms Ladele exemplifies best the protection which the Court offered to the public homosexual individual.

Ms Ladele worked for a local authority as a registrar of births, death and marriages. Ever since the domestic legislation allowing same-sex civil partnerships had come into force, she had refused to perform her professional duties regarding this type of legal union. She claimed that, as an orthodox Christian, she believed that marriage could only be the union of one man and one woman for life and that same-sex civil partnerships were contrary to God's law. Given her refusal to conduct civil partnerships, the local authority adopted disciplinary measures that ended with Ms Ladele losing her job, and the domestic courts upheld the legality of this decision. These courts affirmed that Ms Ladele's religious beliefs did not exempt her from acting according to the prohibition of discrimination on the basis of sexual orientation. Before the Strasbourg Court, the applicant claimed that the proceedings against her, and the lack of judicial protection afforded to her, amounted to discrimination based on her religious convictions. The Court held that there was no violation of the rights of the applicant, since it considered that the domestic authorities,both the local authority which brought the disciplinary proceedings and the domestic courts which rejected her discrimination claim, acted within their margin of appreciation.[90] Consequently, the Court confirmed that states were allowed to protect the public homosexual from being discriminated against on grounds of their sexuality.

However, Judges Vučinić and De Gaetano disagreed. They affirmed that '[i]nstead of practising the tolerance and the "dignity for all" it preached, the Borough of Islington pursued the doctrinaire line, the road of obsessive political correctness'.[91] According to these judges, 'a combination of back-stabbing by her colleagues and the blinkered political correctness of the Borough of Islington (which clearly favoured "gay rights" over fundamental human rights) eventually led to her dismissal'.[92] The distinction between 'gay rights' and 'fundamental human rights' drawn by the dissenting judges is worth of further reflection. This distinction was not made between *gay rights* and *religious people's rights*. Rather, it aimed at excluding 'gay rights' from the category of fundamental human rights. The dissenting judges appeared to believe that, unlike the right of an orthodox Christian to discriminate, the right of the public homosexual individual to be free from discrimination is still not a fundamental human right.

[89] *Eweida and others v United Kingdom*, Application nos 48420/10, 59842/10, 51671/10 and 36516/10, 15 March 2013.
[90] ibid para 106.
[91] ibid, joint partly dissenting opinion of Judges Vučinić and De Gaetano, para 7.
[92] ibid joint partly dissenting opinion of Judges Vučinić and De Gaetano, para 5.

To sum up, all the cases discussed in this section dealt with homosexuality in the public sphere. The first ones concerned homosexuality as a public matter, while the remaining three referred to the protection deserved by the public homosexual individual.[93] These judgments illustrate the Court's conception of homosexuality as an identity worthy of legal protection not only in the private sphere, but also in public. The following sections will focus on how this protected homosexual identity has been constructed by the Court.

V. The Court's (Western) Understanding of Sexuality

The Court's conception of homosexuality as a sexual identity worthy of protection is not truly unexpected, as it fits with the model of sexualities adopted by Western societies. On the one hand, this sexual model places different sexual practices in a clear hierarchy,[94] and on the other hand, it favours the recognition of certain sexual identities over others, as lucidly express by Eve Kosofsky Sedgwick:

> It is a rather amazing fact that, of the very many dimensions along which the genital activity of one person can be differentiated from that of another (dimensions that include preference for certain acts, certain zones or sensations, certain physical types, a certain frequency, certain symbolic investments, certain relations of age or power, a certain species, a certain number of participants, etc. etc. etc.), precisely one, the gender of object choice, emerged from the turn of the century, and has remained, as the dimension denoted by the now ubiquitous category of 'sexual orientation'.[95]

These views on sexuality seem to be reproduced by the Court's case law when dealing with sexualities that extend beyond the heterosexual/homosexual binary, such as sadomasochism and incest.

A. Sadomasochism before the Court

In 1997, the Court decided the case of *Laskey, Jaggard and Brown v United Kingdom*, in which it examined whether the criminalisation of consensual sadomasochism

[93] The protection of homosexual individuals within the public sphere is an area of fast development within the Court's jurisprudence. For instance, within the last few years, the Court has ruled that the procedural limb of Art 3 of the Convention, in conjunction with Art 14, establishes the obligation to investigate the existence of homophobic motives behind attacks against LGBT individuals. Conversely, the Court has also found that public remarks on a TV show that suggested that a gay male public figure could be considered to be a woman did not amount to defamation, if they were intended as a 'joke' and lacked discriminatory intent. *Identoba and others v Georgia*, Application no 73235/12, 12 May 2015, paras 77 and 81; *MC and AC v Romania*, Application no 12060/12, 12 April 2016, paras 124–25; *Sousa Goucha v Portugal*, Application no 70434/12, 22 March 2016, paras 49, 55 and 66–67.

[94] Gayle Rubin, 'Thinking Sex: Notes for a Radical Theory of the Politics of Sexuality' in Richard Parker and Peter Aggleton (eds), *Culture, Society and Sexuality: A Reader* (Routledge, 2007) 150–87.

[95] Eve Kosofsky Sedgwick, *Epistemology of the Closet* (California University Press, 1990) 8.

should be allowed in a democratic society.[96] The Court answer in the affirmative, ruling that individuals could be criminalised for enjoying sadomasochism in the privacy of their own homes. The legal basis of the ruling was that the criminalisation of sadomasochism was aimed at the protection of health.[97] The Court accepted that sadomasochistic practices could be considered an intimate aspect of individuals' private life:

> In the present case, the applicants were involved in consensual sado-masochistic activities for purposes of sexual gratification. There can be no doubt that sexual orientation and activity concern an intimate aspect of private life.[98]

Nevertheless, that was not considered sufficient grounds for granting protection to sadomasochism. In fact, the Court reasoned that: 'not every sexual activity carried out behind closed doors necessarily falls within the scope of Article 8'.[99]

Eight years later, in 2005, the Court revisited the topic of sadomasochism. In *KA and AD v Belgium*, it examined whether a criminal conviction imposed on two individuals for assault occasioning bodily harm during sadomasochistic practices was compatible with respect for their human rights.[100] Once again, the Court decided that the imposition of a conviction for sadomasochistic practices was permissible in a democratic society. Nonetheless, the rationale for the judgment was different from the previous case. While the decision in *Laskey, Jaggard and Brown* was based on the general protection of health, in *KA and AD*, the Court found that the value in need of protection were the rights and freedoms of those actually hurt during sadomasochism.[101] In particular, the main factor in deciding the case was the lack of respect for the decision of the person being harmed to stop the practices.[102] The Court affirmed:

> If a person can demand the right to perform sexual practices as freely as possible, the limit which must be found is the respect for the will of the 'victim' of these practices, whose own right to free choice for the modalities of expressing their sexuality must also be guaranteed. This means that the practices should take place in conditions which allow such respect, and this was not case.
>
> In fact, in light of the elements kept by the court of appeal, it appears that the commitment of the applicants towards intervening and stopping the practices immediately when the 'victim' did not agree to them anymore were not respected.[103]

[96] *Laskey, Jaggard and Brown v United Kingdom*, Reports of Judgments and Decisions 1997-I, 19 February 1997.

[97] ibid.

[98] ibid para 36.

[99] ibid.

[100] *KA and AD v Belgium*, Application nos 42758/98 and 45558/99, 17 February 2005.

[101] ibid para 87.

[102] ibid para 85.

[103] ibid. Author's own translation from the original paragraph in French: 'Si une personne peut revendiquer le droit d'exercer des pratiques sexuelles le plus librement possible, une limite qui doit trouver application est celle du respect de la volonté de la "victime" de ces pratiques, dont le propre droit au libre choix quant aux modalités d'exercice de sa sexualité doit aussi être garanti. Ceci implique

That is to say, the Court clearly upheld the ability of the state to criminalise non-consensual sadomasochistic practices.

Unfortunately, this was the only clear assertion made by the Court. Whether the possibility of enjoying sadomasochistic practices is protected by human rights remains uncertain. On the one hand, it can be argued that the blanket prohibition on sadomasochism has been overturned by the Court. If this were not the case, the Court could have just confirmed the *Laskey, Jaggard and Brown* precedent, reiterating the wide power of the state to criminalise sadomasochism. On the contrary, the Court resorted to the lack of consent underpinning the practices in order to prove that the specific case of sadomasochism was rightfully decided. Therefore, the Court only confirmed that nobody can be subjected to sadomasochistic acts against their own will. On the other hand, it is also evident that the Court abstained from explicitly affirming that consensual sadomasochism could not be criminalised by the state. Indeed, the Court continued to show its disapproval of sadomasochism by referring to those at the receiving end of the stick (almost literally) as the 'victim'.[104]

In conclusion, the legal status of sadomasochism is now unclear, since it is not beyond dispute whether states can actually criminalise these sexual practices at their own discretion. Nevertheless, what became apparent was that, in the eyes of the Court, sadomasochism has failed to reach the status of a protected sexual identity,[105] even if performed in private between consensual adults. It can be inferred that the fluidity of desire that queer theory proposes is still at odds with a law that continues to conceive protected sexualities through the heterosexual/homosexual binary.[106]

B. The Court's View on Incestuous Siblings

Another sexual topic that came under the gaze of the Court was incest. In the *Stübing v Germany* judgment, the Court confirmed the validity of German legislation criminalising incestuous practices. The Court held that the criminalisation of consensual sexual acts between adult siblings was not a violation of the right

que les pratiques se déroulent dans des conditions qui permettent un tel respect, ce qui ne fut pas le cas. En effet, à la lumière notamment des éléments retenus par la cour d'appel, il apparaît que les engagements des requérants visant à intervenir et arrêter immédiatement les pratiques en cause lorsque la « victime » n'y consentait plus n'ont pas été respectés'.

[104] ibid paras 55, 57, 81 and 85.

[105] As to the BDSM (Bondage, Domination, Sado-Masochism) community assertions of sadomasochism as an identity see Michel Foucault, 'Sex, Power, and the Politics of Identity' in Paul Rabinow (ed), *Ethics: Essential Works of Michel Foucault 1954–1984* (Penguin, 2000) 163–73, 167–70; Chris Ashford, 'Barebacking and the "Cult of Violence": Queering the Criminal Law' (2010) 74 *Journal of Criminal Law* 339, at 357.

[106] Carol Johnson, 'Heteronormative Citizenship and the Politics of Passing' (2002) 5 *Sexualities* 317, at 329.

to respect for private life.[107] It considered that incest 'concerns a question about the requirement of morals' and individual states were better positioned than the Court itself to decide how to confront the issue of incestuous relationships between consenting adults.[108] In order to reach a decision, the Court surveyed the domestic legislation of the states belonging to the Council of Europe and found that, while 24 states criminalised consensual incestuous sexual acts, 20 of them did not. Nonetheless, the Court noted that none of the states allowed siblings to get married. Then, linking sex and marriage, the Court reasoned that 'a broad consensus transpires that sexual relationships between siblings are neither accepted by the legal order nor by society as a whole'.[109]

This was certainly an odd path for the Court to reach a decision regarding consensus, since it subordinated the legality of consensual sexuality to the current rules of the institution of marriage. If this same reasoning was to be applied to homosexuality or group sex, it could also lead to validating their criminalisation. In fact, when the Court came to examine same-sex sexuality and group homosexual sex, it decided in favour of their protection under the Convention (as discussed above in this chapter) despite these practices not being in conformity with the rules of marriage. This gives grounds to thinking that, perhaps, it was the Court's own revulsion towards the violation of the incest taboo which allowed it to reach the decision to validate the domestic criminalisation.[110]

Following this decision, incest became another sexual practice that the Court allowed to be criminalised, even if practised in private. As was the case with sadomasochism, the Court accepted that incestuous sexual acts could be private. In the Court's own words:

> It follows from the above principles that the domestic authorities enjoy a wide margin of appreciation in determining how to confront incestuous relationships between consenting adults, notwithstanding the fact that this decision concerns an intimate aspect of an individual's private life.[111]

However, the private and consensual character of these activities was not sufficient grounds to secure their protection under the Convention.

C. The 'Triumph' of a Homosexual Identity

Gayle Rubin has argued that Western societies place sexual practices in a hierarchy. On the top of this hierarchy the only practice to be found is monogamous

[107] *Stübing v Germany*, Application no 43547/08, 12 April 2012.
[108] ibid para 61.
[109] ibid.
[110] John R Spencer, 'Incest and Article 8 of the European Convention on Human Rights' (2013) 72 *Cambridge Law Journal* 5, at 7.
[111] *Stübing v Germany* (n 107) para 61.

heterosexual reproductive sex performed in the privacy of the conjugal home.[112] Therefore, it is not surprising that, as discussed in section II above, reproductive sexuality is the only sexuality that appears clearly protected by the European Convention on Human Rights. Similarly, sadomasochism is definitely at the bottom of the sexual hierarchy,[113] and the Court's decision to allow the general criminalisation of sadomasochism in *Laskey, Jaggard and Brown* lends credibility to Rubin's analysis. The Court's approach to incest also supports Rubin's argument concerning the prohibition of incestuous practices. She argued that Biblical sexual taboos are the roots of the Western system of hierarchies regarding sexual practices and the prohibition of incest is one that has survived the years.[114] Thus, the Court's case law came to confirm and reinforce the existence of the hierarchy of sexual practices discussed by Rubin. On the one hand, married heterosexual sex appears as the only sexuality that the Court considered to have been contemplated in the original text of the Convention. On the other hand, States Parties have been granted the approval of the Court to criminalise sexual acts that appear at the bottom of the scale, such as incest or sadomasochism.

As to homosexuality, it escaped the Court's condemnation. According to Rubin's analysis, which was originally published in 1984,[115] homosexuality was only verging on respectability. Therefore, it is almost surprising that in 1981 the Court expressly granted homosexuality protection through human rights, including it as an identity within the legal system of the Convention.[116] A persuasive explanation for the Court's protection of homosexuality is that in the Western model of sexuality, the heterosexual/homosexual binary overshadows other possible sexual identities. As discussed above, within Western thought, sexual identities have been conceived in terms of the gender of the desired sexual partner, ignoring other dimensions along which sexuality extends.[117] Consequently, the Court can be seen as adopting the model for the classification of sexualities made available to it by Western culture: the heterosexual/homosexual binary.

Within the Western model heterosexuality appears as the norm(al). However, for heterosexuality to be the norm, the existence of homosexuality is indispensable. As discussed in previous chapters, intelligible subjects are created through a

[112] Rubin, 'Thinking Sex' (n 94) 161.

[113] ibid.

[114] ibid 159.

[115] Gayle Rubin, 'Thinking Sex: Notes for a Radical Theory of the Politics of Sexuality' in Carole S Vance (ed), *Pleasure and Danger: Exploring Female Sexuality* (Routledge & Kegan, 1984) 267–319.

[116] *Dudgeon v United Kingdom* (n 8).

[117] Sedgwick, *Epistemology of the Closet* (n 95) 8–9; Patrick Califia, 'Gay Men, Lesbians, and Sex: Do It Together' in Iain Morland and Anabelle Willox (eds), *Queer Theory* (Palgrave Macmillan, 2005) 22–27, at 25; Nikki Sullivan, *A Critical Introduction to Queer Theory* (New York University Press, 2003) 38. As to the distinction between sexual acts and sexual identities, see Kenji Yoshino, 'The Epistemic Contract of Bisexual Erasure' (2000) 52 *Stanford Law Review* 353, at 371; Steven Seidman, *The Social Construction of Sexuality* (Norton & Company, 2003) 43.

process that has, as a logical need, the simultaneous creation of the non-subject, the other.[118] Both identities subsist in an asymmetrical dyad as norm/other. For heterosexuality to be kept as the paradigmatic example of sexuality, both identity categories need to subsist. Even more, both identities should be fixed with a clear strict limit between them. Otherwise, the coherence and stability of the sexual system would be at risk. Consequently, these binary sexualities have been conceived as sexual orientations; rigid categories that allow maintaining their coherence as identities,[119] as well as that of the adopted sexual model.

The sexual subject of human rights law has been constructed following this model. The Court started shaping the subject of human rights as a sexual individual with the *Dudgeon* case, since the sexuality of individuals was never truly discussed by the Court until it was faced with homosexuality. In that moment, the Court began the construction of both the homosexual and the heterosexual subjects. This process shaped homosexual individuals as the other, consolidating the heterosexual as the norm(al).[120] Within the Court's case law, the most evident construction of the homosexual other took place in the dissenting opinions in the *Dudgeon* case. Dissenting Judges Matscher and Walsh in their respective judgments expressed their conviction that the homosexual subject could not even be compared to the heterosexual individual. Judge Matscher affirmed: 'The difference of character between homosexual conduct and heterosexual conduct seems obvious, and the moral and social problems to which they give rise are not at all the same'.[121] And Judge Walsh agreed, making reference to 'those who seek to blur the essential difference between homosexual and heterosexual activities'.[122] One technique for preserving the Western model of sexuality within the Court's case law is to ensure that the homosexual individual does not become entitled to the full enjoyment of human rights. If that were to happen, the stability of the heterosexual identity, as the true subject of human rights, would be jeopardised by the blurring of the dividing line between the self and the other.[123]

The remainder of this chapter will explore in-depth how the Court has shaped, in particular, the notion of homosexuality. The focus will be on the characteristics granted to homosexuality through the Court's case law and how this construction also has consequences for the conception of heterosexuality.

[118] Judith Butler, *Bodies that Matter: On the Discursive Limits of Sex* (Routledge, 1993) xi.

[119] See Nico J Beger, *Tensions in the Struggle for Sexual Minority Rights in Europe: Que(e)rying Political Practices* (Manchester University Press, 2009) 104–5.

[120] See Diana Fuss (ed), *Inside/Out: Lesbian Theories, Gay Theories* (Routledge, 1991) 2; Ki Namaste, 'The Politics of Inside/Out: Queer Theory, Poststructuralism, and a Sociological Approach to Sexuality' (1994) 12 *Sociological Theory* 220, at 226; Larry Catá Backer, 'Queering Theory: An Essay on the Conceit of Revolution in Law' in Leslie Moran, Daniel Monk and Sarah Beresford (eds), *Legal Queeries: Lesbian, Gay and Transgender Legal Studies* (Cassell, 1998) 185–203, at 188.

[121] *Dudgeon v United Kingdom* (n 8), dissenting opinion of Judge Matscher p. 32.

[122] ibid, partially dissenting opinion of Judge Walsh, para 20.

[123] Gonzalez-Salzberg, 'The Making of the Court's Homosexual' (n 26) 385–86.

VI. The Construction of a Sexual Predisposition

Edward Stein has offered an interesting framework for analysing key aspects of individuals' sexuality.[124] He highlighted three specific ongoing discussions, each focusing on a different aspect of human sexuality. These disputes are the ones regarding essentialism/constructionism, nature/nurture, and determinism/voluntarism. The first concerns the source of the categories of sexual identity; the second refers to the source of individuals' sexuality; and the third discusses whether this sexuality is a matter of choice. This framework can be applied to examine how the Court has understood the sexuality of the applicants that went to Strasbourg.

The study of sexual behaviour as a field of scientific enquiry has developed in the Western world since the end of the nineteenth century. A small number of researchers made use of medical and psychological insights in an attempt to better comprehend and explain human sexuality.[125] With a strong focus on 'deviant' sexual behaviour, sexuality became understood as an essential aspect of human personality.[126] The framework developed at the time to provide an explanation about the source of sexualities is known as 'essentialism'. An essentialist perspective would understand sexual identities as universally valid, existing in different times and places.[127] While essentialism might remain the dominant framework for understanding the nature of sexual life in both scientific realms and popular culture, since the mid-twentieth century social scientists have developed an alternative view: social constructionism.[128] In opposition to an essentialist view, social constructionism believes sexual identities to be culturally-dependent, having emerged within specific historical contexts.[129] A paradigmatic constructionist approach is that adopted by Michel Foucault when proposing homosexual and heterosexual identities as a product of nineteenth-century Western thought.[130]

As to whether the Court has adopted a side in the essentialist/constructionist debate, Grigolo and Morgan suggested that the Court has resorted to essentialist

[124] Edward Stein, 'The Essentials of Constructionism and the Construction of Essentialism' in Edward Stein (ed), *Forms of Desire: Sexual Orientation and the Social Constructionist Controversy* (Routledge, 1990) 325–53.

[125] Sonia Corrêa, Rosalind Petchesky and Richard Parker, *Sexuality, Health and Human Rights* (Routledge, 2008) 84.

[126] Momin Rahman, 'Querying the Equation of Sexual Diversity with Modernity: Towards a Homocolonialist Test' in María Amelia Viteri and Manuela Lavinas Picq (eds), *Queering Paradigms V: Queering Narratives of Modernity* (Peter Lang AG, 2015) 91–111, at 96.

[127] Stein, 'The Essentials of Constructionism and the Construction of Essentialism' (n 124) 325.

[128] Steven Epstein, 'Gay Politics, Ethnic Identity: The Limits of Social Constructionism' in Edward Stein (ed), *Forms of Desire: Sexual Orientation and the Social Constructionist Controversy* (Routledge, 1990) 239–93, at 250; Corrêa, Petchesky and Parker, *Sexuality, Health and Human Rights* (n 125) 109; Rahman, 'Querying the Equation of Sexual Diversity with Modernity' (n 126) 101; Matthew Waites, 'The Fixity of Sexual Identities in the Public Sphere: Biomedical Knowledge, Liberalism and the Heterosexual/Homosexual Binary in Late Modernity' (2005) 8 *Sexualities* 539–69, at 540.

[129] Stein, 'The Essentials of Constructionism and the Construction of Essentialism' (n 124) 325.

[130] Foucault, *The History of Sexuality* (n 29) 43.

understandings of homosexuality.[131] By contrast, Johnson argued that the Court's discourse in this area has been 'both multifarious and unstable', which he interpreted as a reflection of the competing discourses that coexist in Europe concerning the source of sexual categories.[132] I am inclined to agree with Johnson. I believe the Court has not clearly endorsed a side of the essentialist/constructionist debate, since it has not dealt expressly with how and when sexual identities have emerged. Nonetheless, the Court has engaged with issues closely related to the sources of sexual identities. It has dealt with the question regarding the source of the sexuality of individuals, the 'nature versus nurture' debate.

The question of whether the sexuality of individuals is an innate characteristic or whether it is learned or acquired through life has been addressed by the Court on different occasions. The Court's first clear answer came in 1999, when it issued the judgments in the cases of *Smith and Grady* and *Lustig-Prean and Becket*.[133] As discussed above, these were the two original cases concerning the United Kingdom's policy prohibiting homosexuals from serving in the armed forces. In these rulings, the Court explicitly adopted the 'nature' side of the debate. The Court affirmed that: 'the applicants were discharged on grounds of their innate personal characteristics'.[134] In other words, the Court's viewpoint was that the homosexuality of the applicants had its origin in nature.

However, Moran, Morgan and Johnson have affirmed that the Court's belief in homosexuality as an inherent quality of individuals could already be found in the *Dudgeon* case.[135] According to Morgan, the Court's conception of homosexuality as innate was pointed out by Judge Walsh in his dissenting opinion in *Dudgeon*.[136] On that occasion, the dissenting judge affirmed that the majority of the Court understood the applicant to be 'a male person who is by nature homosexually predisposed or oriented'.[137] Similarly, Johnson found the inherent character of homosexuality within *Dudgeon* when the Court referred to homosexuality as 'an essentially private manifestation of human personality'.[138]

This understanding of sexuality based in nature could also suggest an essentialist perspective on sexual identities. According to Stein, it would not be possible to support an understanding of individuals' sexuality as innate and, at the same time, hold the belief in the social construction of sexual identities.[139]

[131] Grigolo, 'Sexualities and the ECHR' (n 17) 1027; Morgan, 'Queering International Human Rights Law' (n 7) 218–19.

[132] Johnson, 'An Essentially Private Manifestation of Human Personality' (n 17) 73.

[133] *Smith and Grady v United Kingdom* (n 56); *Lustig-Prean and Beckett v United Kingdom* (n 56).

[134] *Lustig-Prean and Beckett v United Kingdom* (n 56) para 86; *Smith and Grady v United Kingdom* (n 56) para 93.

[135] Moran, *The Homosexual(ity) of Law* (n 9) 178–79; Morgan, 'Queering International Human Rights Law' (n 7) 218; Johnson, *Homosexuality and the European Court of Human Rights* (n 11) 50.

[136] Morgan, 'Queering International Human Rights Law' (n 7) 218.

[137] *Dudgeon v United Kingdom* (n 8), partially dissenting opinion of Judge Walsh, para 13.

[138] Johnson, *Homosexuality and the European Court of Human Rights* (n 11) 50; *Dudgeon v United Kingdom* (n 8) para 60.

[139] Stein, 'The Essentials of Constructionism and the Construction of Essentialism' (n 124) 330.

Therefore, following Stein's reasoning, if the Court believes in nature as the source of individuals' homosexuality, by definition, it would be adopting an essentialist perspective. Nonetheless, I am not convinced of this conclusion.

The Court's belief in the innate character of sexuality seems to have been abandoned a few years later in the first two of a group of cases against Austria concerning the differential age of consent for male homosexual sex, on the one hand, and for heterosexual and lesbian sex, on the other.[140] In the *L and V v Austria* and the *SL v Austria* judgments, the Court stated that very weighty reasons needed to be offered in order to justify a differential age of sexual consent and that such justification had not been provided in the cases. Consequently, the Court ruled that the existence of a differential age of consent was discriminatory on grounds of sexual orientation.[141]

In these cases, the Court appeared to have left behind its belief in the innate character of sexuality. When examining the cases, the Court referred to a decision by the European Commission of Human Rights, which had dealt with the issue of unequal age of consent in the United Kingdom. The Court affirmed:

> In the *Sutherland* case, the Commission, having regard to recent research according to which sexual orientation is usually established before puberty in both boys and girls and to the fact that the majority of member States of the Council of Europe have recognised equal ages of consent, explicitly stated that it was 'opportune to reconsider its earlier case-law in the light of these modern developments'.[142]

In this passage, the Court adopted the conclusions of the Commission, which had relied on an understanding of sexuality as somehow acquired at some stage through life before puberty. That is to say, the Court did not refer to homosexuality as a quality that exists from birth, as it had previously done, but as a characteristic that is established before puberty. Thus, the Court seemed to abandon its firm conviction in nature as the source of sexuality.

Nevertheless, the Court's clear support for the understanding of nature as the source of sexuality appeared once again in its judgment in *Alekseyev*, which was discussed in section IV. In its ruling, the Court rejected the government's arguments that 'homosexuality was a result of a conscious, and antisocial, choice'.[143] While defending the importance of public debate concerning sexualities, the Court affirmed that this type of discussion: 'would also clarify some common points of confusion, such as whether a person may be *educated* or enticed *into or*

[140] *L and V v Austria*, Application nos 39392/98 and 39829/98, ECHR 2003-I; *SL v Austria*, Application no 45330/99, ECHR 2003-I; *BB v United Kingdom*, Application no 53760/00, 10 February 2004; *Woditschka and Wilfling v Austria*, Application nos 69756/01 and 6306/02, 21 October 2004; *Ladner v Austria*, Application no 18297/03, 3 February 2005; *Wolfmeyer v Austria*, Application no 5263/03, 26 May 2005; *HG and GB v Austria*, Application nos 11084/02 and 15306/02, 2 June 2005; *RH v Austria*, Application no 7336/03, 19 January 2006.

[141] *L and V v Austria* (n 140) para 54; *SL v Austria* (n 140) para 46.

[142] *SL v Austria* (n 140) para 39. Similar wording in *L and V v Austria* (n 140) para 47.

[143] *Alekseyev v Russia* (n 69) para 86.

out of homosexuality, or opt into or out of it voluntarily'.[144] From this sentence, it is possible to infer that the Court was, once again, embracing the understanding of sexuality as inherent, given its rejection of the idea that homosexuality could be learned.[145] The Court's stance appeared even more clearly in the *Bayev and others* ruling,[146] when addressing Russia's attempt at justifying its legislation banning the 'promotion of homosexuality'. As a response to the government's claim that the legislation was enacted as a precaution against the conversion of minors to a homosexual 'life style',[147] the Court asserted:

> The Government were unable to provide any explanation of the mechanism by which a minor could be enticed into '[a] homosexual lifestyle', let alone science-based evidence that one's sexual orientation or identity is susceptible to change under external influence. The Court therefore dismisses these allegations as lacking any evidentiary basis.[148]

In conclusion, the Court seemed to have settled on the nature side of the nature/nurture divide.

The statements from the *Alekseyev* and *Bayev and others* judgments also addressed the question of whether sexuality has been considered by the Court as a matter of choice or as something beyond individuals' will, suggesting the latter understanding. While the Court might not always have been clear as to its stance on the nature/nurture debate, its position in the discussion about whether sexuality is predisposed or voluntary has been firm. In its first encounter with the homosexual subject in the *Dudgeon* case, one of the reasons the Court found for ruling in favour of the applicant was the conviction that his sexuality was beyond his choice. When analysing the applicants' situation under the criminalisation of homosexual acts in Northern Ireland, the Court held:

> [E]ither he respects the law and refrains from engaging – even in private with consenting male partners – in prohibited *sexual acts to which he is disposed by reason of his homosexual tendencies*, or he commits such acts and thereby becomes liable to criminal prosecution.[149]

The Court constructed the applicant's sexuality as beyond his will. He was considered to be 'disposed' to the sexual acts he performed; hence, he was not to be criminalised for them.

[144] ibid (emphasis added).

[145] Also in 2010, but in a case not dealing with LGBT rights, the Court confirmed its understanding of sexual orientation as an innate or inherent characteristic stating that: 'it is unsurprising that the Court has considered to constitute "other status" characteristics which, like some of the specific examples listed in the Article, can be said to be personal in the sense that they are *innate or inherent*. Thus in *Salgueiro da Silva Mouta* … § 28, it found that sexual orientation was "undoubtedly covered" by Article 14'. *Clift v United Kingdom*, Application no 7205/07, 13 July 2010, para 57 (emphasis added).

[146] Nevertheless, in this case, dissenting Judge Dedov clearly supported the understanding of individuals' sexuality as partly determined by social life and social relations. *Bayev and others v Russia* (n 75), dissenting opinion of Judge Dedov, 42.

[147] ibid para 74.

[148] ibid para 78.

[149] *Dudgeon v United Kingdom* (n 8) para 41 (emphasis added).

Conversely, the conception of homosexuality as a voluntary characteristic appeared only once within the Court's judgments, expressed by a dissenting judge in the *Dudgeon* case. Within this judgment, dissenting Judge Walsh developed his own theory of homosexuality. He reasoned that there were different types of homosexuality, some of which are allegedly innate and others culturally acquired. According to this theory, within the cases in which homosexuality is not innate, there is a clear element of choice in individuals' sexual orientation. In his own words:

> The fact that a person consents to take part in the commission of homosexual acts is not proof that such person is sexually orientated by nature in that direction … It is known that many male persons who are heterosexual or pansexual indulge in these activities not because of any incurable tendency but for sexual excitement.[150]

In the opinion of Judge Walsh, there could be an element of choice in sexuality. It seems that some people just decide to indulge in homosexuality. At the same time, the fact that sexuality as a matter of choice has only appeared in a peculiar dissenting opinion comes to reinforce the idea that the Court itself has understood the sexuality of individuals as a characteristic to which they are predisposed.

In sum, the Court's construction of homosexuality has certainly been multifarious.[151] The Court does not seem to have engaged with the essentialist/constructionist question, and seems to have supported different understandings regarding the nature/nurture debate. Nevertheless, its position regarding whether homosexuality is a matter of choice seems to be more clear. The Court has understood homosexuality as a predisposition. The next section will discuss another element of the sexuality of individuals, as conceived by the Court: whether sexuality is a characteristic that can be changed.

VII. A (Mutable) Immutable Sexuality

The idea that sexuality is an immutable characteristic is far from being universally accepted.[152] Therefore, the Court's anxiety about the rigidity of sexuality should not come as a surprise. As discussed in section V, the Court operates within a legal framework in which heterosexuality continues to be sanctified. The heterosexual subject remains the only true subject of human rights and this understanding

[150] ibid, partially dissenting opinion of Judge Walsh, para 13.

[151] Johnson, 'An Essentially Private Manifestation of Human Personality' (n 17) 73.

[152] Janet Halley, 'The Politics of the Closet: Towards Equal Protection for Gay, Lesbian, and Bisexual Identity' (1989) 36 *UCLA Law Review* 915, at 934. See also Shane Phelan, 'Queer Liberalism?' (2000) 94 *American Political Science Review* 431, at 434; Didi Herman, 'Are We Family Yet? Lesbian Rights and Women's Liberation' (1990) 28 *Osgoode Hall Law Journal* 789, at 813; Judith Butler, 'Imitation and Gender Insubordination' in Diana Fuss (ed), *Inside/Out: Lesbian Theories, Gay Theories* (Routledge, 1991) 13–31, at 23.

has been validated by the Court. Consequently, any threats to the construction of heterosexuality can be seen as a reason for concern. A paradigmatic example of a threat is the latent fluidity of the categories of heterosexuality and homosexuality. The 'potential for mutability that undermines heterosexual identity', in Janet Halley's words,[153] is the issue that will be explored in this section.

Both Morgan and Johnson have argued that in the *Dudgeon* case, the Court supported the notion that individuals' sexuality is rigidly fixed.[154] While the Court did not make this understanding explicit, it seems plausible, since the idea of sexuality as fluid was only raised by two dissenting judges. For Judge Zekia and Judge Walsh, homosexuality could be either mutable or immutable, depending on whether it could be cured or not. Both judges drew heavily on the idea of homosexuality as pathology.[155] In particular, Judge Walsh affirmed:

> A distinction must be drawn between homosexuals who are such because of some kind of innate instinct or pathological constitution judged to be incurable and those whose tendency comes from a lack of normal sexual development or from habit or from experience or from other similar causes but whose tendency is not incurable.[156]

That is to say, Judge Walsh diagnosed certain homosexuals as incurable, while others might still have hope of being treated. The diagnosis in these curable cases seemed to be much more complex. However, the Judge took the opportunity to explain that sexuality can be changed (or cured) when the source of the 'tendency' proceeds from abnormal sexual development, from habit, from experience, or 'from other similar causes' (maybe boredom or fashion).

Nonetheless, I will argue that the dissenting opinion of Judge Walsh presents a truly *queer* conception of sexuality, in an otherwise very conservative judgment. In one of the most interesting paragraphs, Judge Walsh stated: 'It is known that many male persons who are heterosexual or pansexual indulge in these activities not because of any incurable tendency but for sexual excitement'.[157] And he used this well-known 'fact' to justify his support for maintaining the criminalisation of homosexual sex, in order to preserve the 'moral ethos of the community', under threat from activities such as homosexuality.[158]

Various appealing elements can be rescued from this opinion. First, the reference to 'pansexual' individuals has been the only clear mention of a sexual identity beyond the heterosexual/homosexual binary that can be found in the

[153] Janet Halley, 'Misreading Sodomy: A Critique of the Classification of "Homosexual" in Federal Equal Protection Law' in Julia Epstein and Kristina Straub (eds), *Body Guards: The Cultural Politics of Gender Ambiguity* (Routledge, 1991) 351–78, at 367.

[154] Morgan, 'Queering International Human Rights Law' (n 7) 218; Johnson, *Homosexuality and the European Court of Human Rights* (n 11) 50.

[155] *Dudgeon v United Kingdom* (n 8), dissenting opinion of Judge Zekia, para 4 and partially dissenting opinion of Judge Walsh, para 13.

[156] ibid, partially dissenting opinion of Judge Walsh, para 13.

[157] ibid.

[158] ibid, partially dissenting opinion of Judge Walsh, para 14.

jurisprudence of the Court. Secondly, a desire for homosexuality was manifest throughout the Judge's opinion. On five different occasions he referred to engaging in male homosexual sex by making use of the verb *to indulge*.[159] Lastly, Judge Walsh offered a fluid conception of heterosexuality, which did not exclude a heterosexual desire for same-sex sexuality. He predicated that it was common knowledge that many heterosexual men just could not resist engaging in homosexual sex. Even though their heterosexual identity should impose some sort of obstacle, this difficulty is overcome by their excitement, which makes them surrender to desire. In fact, it seemed to be the irresistible character of homosexual sex that justified his appeal to preserve its criminalisation. Perhaps, the fear of a criminal punishment was seen as the only path for stopping heterosexuals from succumbing to homosexuality. Thus, while the Court might have supported a conception of sexuality as rigidly fixed, the latent mutability of heterosexuality was a clear concern in the mind of Judge Walsh.

A. The Court's (Mutable) Understanding of Sexuality

Another clear appearance of a mutable sexuality within the Court's case law can be found in the *Salgueiro da Silva Mouta* case. On that occasion, the Court had to decide whether making the sexuality of the parents of a child a determining factor at the time of awarding parental responsibility was compatible with the Convention.[160] For the first time in its jurisprudence, the Court affirmed that sexual orientation was a prohibited category of discrimination and, consequently, ruled that the decision of the domestic courts to deny parental responsibility of a child due to the sexuality of the father was discriminatory.[161]

It is interesting that the flexibility of sexual desire underpinned this case, but the Court decided to ignore it. According to the facts, the applicant had been married to a woman and had had a child with her. After seven years of marriage, the applicant separated from his wife and started living in an intimate relationship with a man.[162] Nonetheless, when the Court examined the case, the sexuality of the applicant appeared as undoubtedly homosexual, ignoring his rather heterosexual past. The judgment reads:

> The Court reiterates its earlier finding that the Lisbon Court of Appeal, in examining the appeal lodged by M.'s mother, introduced a new factor when making its decision as to the award of parental responsibility, namely the applicant's homosexuality.[163]

[159] ibid, partially dissenting opinion of Judge Walsh, paras 3, 4, 7 and 13. Also dissenting Judge Zekia refers to *indulging* in homosexuality. *Dudgeon v United Kingdom* (n 8), dissenting opinion of Judge Zekia, para 4.

[160] *Salgueiro da Silva Mouta v Portugal*, Application no 33290/96, ECHR 1999-IX.

[161] ibid para 36.

[162] ibid para 9.

[163] ibid para 33.

The homosexuality of the applicant appeared as a fact, and the possibility of a change in his sexuality was completely absent from the analysis of the case. Thus, heterosexuality remained immutable, since the applicant had always been homosexual.[164]

The immutable character of sexuality might have been challenged when the Court accepted that individuals can modify their sex through a gender transition process in the *Goodwin* and *I* cases of 2002. An obvious question would be whether individuals who had changed their legal sex had consequently modified their sexual orientation, since sexuality is conceived as a relational concept dependent on gender. The answer that can be inferred from the case law is certainly contradictory and depends on the period of jurisprudence under consideration. As discussed in Chapter 2, during the 1980s and 1990s, the Court refused to recognise that individuals could modify their sex. During this period, transsexual applicants were understood as homosexuals when having a relationship with individuals of the sex 'opposite' to that which (the Court refused to recognise) had been acquired by the transsexual. This can be observed in the Court's denial of the right of trans women to marry men and trans men to marry women.[165]

As argued by the Court, the refusal to allow marriage between two people of the same sex is, actually not founded on their sexes, but on their sexualities. With express reference to *Corbett v Corbett* and quoting Justice Ormrod, the denial of the right to marry a person of the same sex is due to the incapability of 'consummating the marriage in the context of ordinary and complete sexual intercourse'.[166] Thus, the denial of transsexuals' right to marry was based on the assumption that they could not perform 'ordinary' sexual intercourse. Since it is safe to assume that 'ordinary' sex is heterosexual sex, and sexuality has been considered by the Court to be binary heterosexual/homosexual, transsexual individuals were denied the right to marry because they were considered to be homosexuals.

Because transsexual people were understood as homosexuals while their sex was considered to be immutable, it is only logical to infer that if their sex was considered to have changed, their sexual orientation would follow. In other words, keeping the sexual attraction to one sex, while changing the sex of belonging, means the amendment of sexual orientation along the heterosexual/homosexual binary. Following this understanding, after the Court amended its case law so

[164] The mutability of sexuality was also a topic present in the Grand Chamber's decision of *ME v Sweden*, but was not discussed, since the case was struck from the list as the state conferred on the applicant, who was at risk of expulsion, permanent residence in Sweden. *ME v Sweden* (GC) (striking out), Application no 71398/12, 8 April 2015, paras 15, 16 and 19. See also the judgment of the Chamber, where the mutability of the applicant's sexuality presents a different dimension, as his spouse is described as a transsexual woman who was at the time of the application undergoing transition. *ME v Sweden*, Application no 71398/12, 26 June 2014, paras 15, 16 and 57.

[165] *Rees v United Kingdom*, Series A no 106, 17 October 1986; *Cossey v United Kingdom*, Series A no 184, 27 September 1990; *Sheffield and Horsham v United Kingdom*, Reports of Judgments and Decisions 1998-V, 30 July 1998.

[166] *Sheffield and Horsham v United Kingdom* (n 165) para 27.

as to recognise that transsexual individuals could actually transition sex, sexual orientation should have become mutable. That is to say, if a transsexual woman performed sexual intercourse with a man, the Court would have considered such practice as homosexual when gender transition was not recognised, and heterosexual afterwards.

Nevertheless, when in 2002 the Court decided to acknowledge that transsexual persons could transition sex, it did so basing its understanding on transsexual individuals as essentially heterosexual. As discussed in Chapter 2, since 2002 transsexual people have been understood by the Court as heterosexual. This was the actual reason for allowing surgery to change sex. According to the new case law of the Court, transsexual individuals always would have been heterosexual, since this was a requirement for establishing transsexuality. Therefore, even though gender has then become mutable, sexuality would not be. Consequently, sexual orientation was originally conceived as immutable, and it should have become mutable when gender transitioning was recognised by the Court (since sexuality based on gender is a relational concept). However, the rejection of homosexuality (the homophobia of the law) kept sexuality seemingly immutable.

On the other hand, this topic remains open to debate, since the subsequent case law of the Court dealing with pre-operative transsexual applicants might not be consistent with the re-discovered heterosexuality of transsexual individuals. In *L v Lithuania*, the Court did not impose on the state the obligation to allow the applicant to enter into a marriage with an individual of the 'opposite' sex to that which would be acquired through transition.[167] This put into question how heterosexual the applicant was conceived to be. Furthermore, if Mr L, a pre-operative transsexual man, could not enter into heterosexual marriage until his sex was duly attained, his sexuality also became dependent on his transition and was, therefore, mutable. In other words, (straight) transsexuals might not be as heterosexual as understood by the Court in 2002, but their heterosexuality was made dependent on their transition. In conclusion, for as long as surgery determined sex, sexuality was less immutable that the Court assumed it to be.

Lastly, the Court was faced with a seemingly clear case of mutable sexuality when it declared inadmissible the case of *Wena and Anita Parry v United Kingdom* in 2006.[168] This ruling will be discussed in-depth in Chapter 5, but at this stage I will focus on the issue of the fluidity of sexuality present in the case. The applicants, Wena and Anita Parry, were a married couple who had three children. More than 30 years into their marriage, the first applicant underwent a gender affirming process. However, Wena was unable to obtain full legal recognition of her gender unless she put an end to her marriage with Anita, as the British legislation at the time did not allow for same-sex marriage. The case reached the Court because the applicants considered that the domestic legislation was imposing an unjustified interference on their right to respect for private and family life. That is, they

[167] *L v Lithuania*, Application no 27527/03, ECHR 2007-IV, para 64.

[168] *Parry v United Kingdom* (Dec), Application no 42971/05, ECHR 2006-XV.

had to choose between Wena obtaining full recognition of her gender transition and continuing their marriage. Even the Court recognised this situation, when it expressed: 'The legislation clearly puts the applicants in a quandary – the first applicant must, invidiously, sacrifice her gender or their marriage'.[169]

At this point, I am interested in analysing how the Court interpreted not Wena's, but Anita's sexuality. The Court found the application to be inadmissible, since it considered that it was within the discretion of the state to restrict the institution of marriage to different-sex couples. In reaching this decision the Court affirmed that the state 'cannot be required to make allowances for the small number of marriages where both partners wish to continue notwithstanding the change in gender of one of them'.[170] The Court thereby realised that there are situations in which a heterosexual relationship might become a homosexual one, due to the change in the gender of one of the parties in the relationship. As I have argued, it is not clear whether the Court understood the sexuality of the transsexual person as having changed or not. Nonetheless, it is evident that the Court considered that Anita, the *cissexual* partner, had changed her sexuality in this specific context.[171] Therefore, a heterosexual cissexual applicant made the Court face the mutability of sexuality. However, the Court did not dare to mention this apparent change in its decision.

The mutability of sexuality is likely to remain unmentioned in the Court's case law. A plausible reason for this is that acknowledging the mutability of sexuality will not only mean that homosexuality is not a stable identity, but that the heterosexual subject of human rights has a much more fluid sexual identity than once assumed, and this lack of fixity of heterosexuality is inconsistent with the Western sexual model.[172]

VIII. Narratives of Homosexual Identity

As discussed through the chapter, *Dudgeon* marked the beginning of the Court's engagement with the sexual subjects of human rights and their binary existence as self/other (heterosexual/homosexual). The homosexual individual was conceived through the Court's case law as the opposite counterpart of the true subject of human rights law, the heterosexual. The Court's construction of a homosexual identity through its case law is a clear display of the power of the law to regulate, contain and constrain the legal sexuality of the subject that claims human rights.[173]

[169] ibid 10.

[170] ibid 12–13.

[171] The term 'cissexual' has made its appearance in the Court's jurisprudence in the *Hämäläinen v Finland* case. *Hämäläinen v Finland* (GC), Application no 37359/09, 16 July 2014, paras 111–12.

[172] For a discussion regarding how the immutability of heterosexuality actually depends on the stability of homosexuality, see Halley, 'Misreading Sodomy' (n 153) 361 and 367.

[173] See Carl F Stychin, 'Essential Rights and Contested Identities: Sexual Orientation and Equality Rights Jurisprudence in Canada' (1995) 8 *Canadian Journal of Law and Jurisprudence* 49, at 56; Lisa Gotell, 'Queering Law: Not by Vriend' (2002) 17 *Canadian Journal of Law and Society* 89, at 108.

It led to the construction of rigid binary sexual identities, understood as (mostly) innate, predisposed and immutable, as was examined in sections VI and VII. As discussed above, other sexual acts have not been understood as identities, and no further sexual identities have yet been claimed before the Court. If the notion of bisexuality has sporadically appeared in the rulings of the Court, it was only when referring to fragments of domestic decisions or international soft law instruments;[174] and an undefined reference to 'pansexuality' has only appeared in the partially dissenting opinion of a single judge.[175] It was not until 2010 that the Court showed a degree of willingness to open the sexual binary, when it made reference to gays, lesbians and 'any other sexual minority',[176] but this simple mention has not had any legal consequences in the Court's case law thus far.[177]

Nevertheless, the Court cannot be held solely responsible for the restrictive conception of human sexuality delineated by the case law. The construction of homosexuality as an identity worthy of protection through human rights led to maintaining the ongoing dynamic of self/other. Because of the protection granted to the homosexual other through the case law, this identity has been continuously reclaimed (and therefore reinforced) by applicants who brought cases to the Court. Applicants who self-identify as homosexuals to request the protection of their rights act as an essential part of the process that allows the continuous construction of the homosexual identity as the other. Ironically, homosexual applicants willingly construct their sexuality as a fixed characteristic beyond the individual's control in order to obtain protection from the Court.[178]

In fact, the truth about sexuality produced by the case law is heavily based on the value of the first-person narrative presented by the applicants. The ritual of confession, one of the most important techniques for the production of truth,[179] is clearly present within the procedures before the Court. The production of the truth about (homo)sexuality, discussed in sections VI and VII, depends on

[174] *Scherer v Switzerland* (n 67); *Laskey, Jaggard and Brown v United Kingdom* (n 96) paras 11 and 47; *TN v Denmark*, Application no 20594/08, 20 January 2011, para 65; *EG v United Kingdom*, Application no 41178/08, 31 May 2011, para 45; *Rubio Dosamantes v Spain*, Application no 20996/10, 21 February 2017, para 46.

[175] *Dudgeon v United Kingdom* (n 8), partially dissenting opinion of Judge Walsh.

[176] *Alekseyev v Russia* (n 69) para 84.

[177] A similar reference, this time to 'various sexual minorities', has been made by the Court in the more recent case *Identoba and others v Georgia*, but again it seemed to lack any clear meaning. In this case, a group of demonstrators on the International Day Against Homophobia were attacked by counter-demonstrators. The Court found that the lack of positive measures adopted by the state entailed its international responsibility under the Convention. In particular, the Court declared violations of the right to freedom of peaceful assembly, in conjunction with the prohibition of discrimination, and of the right to personal integrity, also in conjunction with the prohibition of discrimination. *Identoba and others v Georgia* (n 93) para 97.

[178] Concerning the strategic use of claims relying on essentialist understandings of sexual identities to secure successful litigations see Waites, 'The Fixity of Sexual Identities in the Public Sphere' (n 128) 556; Rahman, 'Querying the Equation of Sexual Diversity with Modernity' (n 126) 101–2.

[179] Foucault, *The History of Sexuality* (n 29) 61–62.

the applicants' confession. Applicants confess their sexuality to the Court, by explaining the restrictions the state imposed upon them based on this sexuality. Within this ritualised procedure, the Court acts as the authority that requires the confession, evaluates the truth behind it, and judges it through its rulings. The truth of the confessed sexuality is validated by the Court's judgment and, in turn, it shapes the conception of the homosexual subject.

Furthermore, the homosexual applicants that appeared to confess their sexuality to the Court became defined by their sexual identity. As discussed in section III, within the Court's jurisprudence a homosexual act is understood as the manifestation of a type of personality: the homosexual. The sexuality of the homosexual is not only relevant for their sexual acts, but it permeates every aspect of their personality. This process almost perfectly proves the accuracy of Foucault's reflections:

> Nothing that went into his total composition was unaffected by his sexuality. It was everywhere present in him: at the root of all his actions because it was their insidious and indefinitely active principle.[180]

The sexual identity of individuals has become extremely important for the enjoyment of human rights. Consensual sex turned out to be so much more than just sex. As it is a display of a type of person, sexual acts grew into the grounds for denying the enjoyment of human rights. Within the Court's case law, sexuality has become relevant for topics as diverse as parenting, marriage, pensions and inheritance tax. This will be the topic of Chapters 4 and 5.

Nonetheless, the power of confession may also offer a future path for deconstructing the Court's categorical approach to sexuality. Applicants that bring different sexual narratives to the Court can offer alternative conceptions of sexualities that expose the limitations of the heterosexual/homosexual binary to comprehend human sexuality.[181] New sexual confessions can play an important role in bringing visibility to the existence of queer sexualities that decentre gender as the focus of sexual desire and behaviour.[182] In turn, this can lead to an understanding of sexualities far beyond the traditional Western binary.

[180] ibid 43.

[181] Elizabeth Sara Lewis, 'Pegging, Masculinities and Heterosexualities: How Narratives of Men Who Enjoy Being Penetrated by Women Can Contribute to Social Transformation and to Queering the Hidden Homosexual Norm in Queer Studies' in María Amelia Viteri and Manuela Lavinas Picq (eds), *Queering Paradigms V: Queering Narratives of Modernity* (Peter Lang AG, 2015) 241–63, at 243; Terry Threadgold, 'Performing Theories of Narrative: Theorizing Narrative Performance' in Joanna Thornborrow and Jennifer Coates (eds), *The Sociolinguistics of Narrative* (John Benjamins, 2005) 261–78, at 264.

[182] Lewis, 'Pegging, Masculinities and Heterosexualities' (n 181) 243; Matthew Waites, 'Critique of "Sexual Orientation" and "Gender Identity" in Human Rights Discourse: Global Queer Politics Beyond the Yogyakarta Principles' (2009) 15 *Contemporary Politics* 137, at 152.

IX. Conclusion

Queer theory highlights that the binary model of sexuality in terms of the gender of the desired sexual partner is a historical construction that restricts and regulates sexuality, ignoring dimensions along which sexuality actually extends.[183] It overshadows possible sexualities that are less concerned with constructing an identity grounded in people's genitalia. However, this is the sexual model widely accepted by Western culture and, as discussed throughout the chapter, this is the conception of sexuality adopted by the Court.

The Court has affirmed that the actual subject of the Convention is the heterosexual individual, and it has understood homosexuality as a sexual identity also worthy of the protection of human rights. This protected homosexual identity (and, in turn, its heterosexual counterpart) was shaped by the Court through its case law. It was constructed as predisposed and (most likely) innate. As well, both homosexuality and heterosexuality have been conceived (and re-conceived) as rigidly fixed. As discussed in Chapter 2, the Court has recognised that gender cannot be conceived as an immutable category. While this lack of fixity of gender should have had clear consequence for the understanding of sexuality, I have argued in section VII above that when the Court was faced with sexualities that did not fit the rigidly fixed binary model it opted to ignore their apparent mutability. It might have been the Court's concern over the potential mutability of heterosexuality that acted as the foundation for confirming the immutability of homosexuality.

The fact that protection for sexual acts needs to be requested in terms of fixed sexual identities means that other sexualities remain excluded. Butler has explained that the construction of identities through the binary understanding of self/other also means producing a domain of what is left aside, that which is not conceivable within the self/other universe.[184] Therefore, while the heterosexual subject is the true subject of human rights and the homosexual individual can claim protection as the needed other, those who fail to fit within these binary identities are, in principle, precluded from being successful before the Court. Indeed, those who have claimed protection of other private sexual practices, such as sadomasochism or incest, found their claims rejected by the Court.

Nevertheless, as I argued in the previous section, one of the main reasons for the Court's adoption of the heterosexual/homosexual categorical approach to sexuality is the fact that the homosexual identity continues to be reclaimed. This means that the sexual binary is reinforced by the appearance of applicants before the Court requesting protection based on their homosexuality. Consequently, the logic of the protection of human rights might leave an alternative path to challenge this binary conception. Given the value of confession in the Court's

[183] Sedgwick, *Epistemology of the Closet* (n 95) 8–9; Califia, 'Gay Men, Lesbians, and Sex: Do It Together' (n 117) 25; Sullivan, *A Critical Introduction to Queer Theory* (n 117) 38.
[184] Butler, *Bodies that Matter* (n 118) xi.

construction of sexuality, a possible strategy to overcome the categorical model could consist of future applicants appearing before the Court and demonstrating the incapacity of the fixed binary sexual identities to comprehend their sexualities. The challenge to make the Court overcome its restrictive approach might be huge, as the recognition of the fluidity of sexuality would jeopardise the assumed stability of heterosexuality. Nonetheless, the place of confession as a ritual of discourse within the Court's procedure provides the means for introducing narratives of sexualities that exist beyond the heterosexual/homosexual binary. In fact, in the *Alekseyev* case, the Court has already (maybe inadvertently) made reference to the existence of other sexual identities, when it mentioned 'the right of individuals to openly identify themselves as gay, lesbian or *any other sexual minority*'.[185] It would be for future applicants, through the confession of their experienced sexualities, to provide content to the recognition of these other sexual minorities.

[185] *Alekseyev v Russia* (n 69) para 84 (emphasis added). This expression seems to have become part of the Court's constant case law when dealing with LGBT rights. As I mentioned above (text to n 179), it has been reiterated in *Identoba and others v Georgia* and, more recently, in *Bayev and others v Russia*. *Identoba and others v Georgia* (n 93) para 97; *Bayev and others v Russia* (n 75) para 66.

4

LGBT Families and Non-discrimination

I. Introduction

While Chapters 2 and 3 discussed how the European Court of Human Rights has constructed the notions of gender and sexuality through its case law, Chapters 4 and 5 will focus on how these legal constructions have had consequences for the enjoyment of human rights, as the Court continues to validate the denial of certain rights based on the gender and sexual identities of individuals. The focus of these two chapters will be on 'family rights', since this has become the most recurrent topic in the Court's jurisprudence dealing with LGBT[1] rights. Within the Court's case law, family rights are still conceived as specifically gendered and (hetero) sexualised and, in turn, so is the human entitled to them. Chapter 4 will focus on the conception of the family under the Convention and on how the prohibition of discrimination under Article 14 has been deployed through the case law to provide some degree of protection for LGBT family rights. In fact, claims to equality and non-discrimination have been the preferred legal strategy for LGBT people to pursue inclusion within the institution of the family. Chapter 5 will complement this examination through an in-depth exploration of two of the most current demands brought to Strasbourg by LGBT families: that of marriage and parenting rights.

The right to be recognised as family is now the central claim in LGBT politics within the Council of Europe.[2] Under the European Convention on Human Rights, the family as a protected institution appears twice, in different articles. Article 8(1) establishes: 'Everyone has the right to respect for his private and family life, his home and his correspondence'. And Article 12 states: 'Men and women of marriageable age have the right to marry and to found a family, according to the national laws governing the exercise of this right'. However, it is not possible to find a definition of family within the Convention. On the contrary, other international instruments, such as the Universal Declaration of Human Rights or the International Covenant on Civil and Political Rights, have described the family as 'the natural and fundamental group unit

[1] As discussed in Chapter 1, I use the acronym LGBT to refer to lesbians, gays, bisexuals and trans people.

[2] Nico J Beger, *Tensions in the Struggle for Sexual Minority Rights in Europe: Que(e)rying Political Practices* (Manchester University Press, 2009) 173.

of society';[3] hence, presenting it as a pre-social institution, grounded in nature, which requires recognition and protection from the law, given its fundamental character. Because the Convention does not make such a declaration, the meaning and membership of the family within the Council of Europe remains open to discussion and negotiation. This is nothing but coherent, as the notion of the family is a historical construct that has varied in meaning and organisation in different times and places.[4] Family ties can be understood to comprise the links that Butler defined as kinship; that is, socially alterable sets of arrangements that institute and organise relationships of various kinds to address fundamental forms of human dependency aimed at the reproduction of material life. This includes the ritualisation of practices concerning births, child-rearing, generational ties, deaths, and relations of emotional dependency and support alliances, encompassing the regulation of sexuality through sanctions and taboos.[5]

Naomi Cahn has explained how the law plays a crucial role in the social construction of families

> by defining who can marry whom (from same-sex couples to sixteen-year-olds), assigning parenthood and identifying the father and mother, determining who can make decisions on behalf of a child, establishing when parental rights can and should be terminated, as well as by providing legal protections for the privacy of relationships defined as families, protections for family members based on their status, and a structure to allocate decision making with respect to the parent, child, and state.[6]

In our times, marriage and parenthood are the two social and legal bonds considered to be the pillars of the family,[7] and as such have been recognised under the protection of family life granted by the Convention.[8] While it is clear that the Court's jurisprudence has supported the existence of a hierarchy of relationships within the protection of family rights, with the heterosexual nuclear family, established through marriage and parenthood, clearly at the top,[9] other relationships should not be assumed to be excluded from recognition as families under the Convention.

[3] Both Art 16(3) of the UDHR and Art 23(1) of the ICCPR establish: 'The family is the natural and fundamental group unit of society and is entitled to protection by society and the State'. In fact, it was the clear intention of some of the drafters of the Declaration to present the family as a natural institution. See Johannes Morsink, 'Women's Rights in the Universal Declaration' (1991) 13 *Human Rights Quarterly* 229, at 236–39.

[4] Shulamith Firestone, *The Dialectic of Sex: The Case for Feminist Revolution* (Bantam Books, 1972) 74–76; Gerda Lerner, *The Creation of Patriarchy* (Oxford University Press, 1986) 216–17.

[5] Judith Butler, *Antigone's Claim: Kinship Between Life and Death* (Columbia University Press, 2000) 72; Judith Butler, 'Is Kinship Already Heterosexual' (2002) 13 *Differences: A Journal of Feminist Cultural Studies* 14, at 14–15.

[6] Naomi Cahn, 'The New Kinship' (2012) 100 *Georgetown Law Journal* 367, at 381.

[7] Martha Albertson Fineman, *The Neutered Mother, the Sexual Family and other Twentieth Century Tragedies* (Routledge, 1995) 150–51.

[8] David J Harris, Michael O'Boyle, Ed Bates and Carla Buckley, *Law of the European Convention on Human Rights*, 2nd edn (Oxford University Press, 2009) 374.

[9] Bernadette Rainey, Elizabeth Wicks and Clare Ovey, *The European Convention on Human Rights*, 7th edn (Oxford University Press, 2017) 373.

This chapter will make use of insights from queer theory to analyse both the notion of the family within the Court's case law, as well as the prohibition of discrimination as the main strategy deployed by LGBT individuals to claim inclusion within the family. An understanding of family ties as social arrangements has allowed LGBT families to somehow fit within the human rights notion of the family. However, the inclusion achieved has had its shortcomings. On the one hand, the Court continues to idealise the heterosexual married couple and their children, allowing states to privilege its members. On the other hand, the strategies leading to inclusion have required LGBT families to mimic traditional family structures. It is, therefore, possible to argue that, under the Convention, family rights are still conceived as belonging to the realm of the *heterosexual matrix*.

The idea of the heterosexual matrix, developed by Butler, refers to a net of cultural intelligibility through which bodies are naturalised. This cultural network subjects the comprehensibility of bodies to their performance of stable genders defined through the compulsory practice of heterosexuality.[10] According to Butler, the *heterosexualisation* of desire both requires and institutes the production of a discrete and asymmetrical gender opposition: men and women. As a result, intelligible individuals are those that maintain relations of coherence and continuity between performed genders and culturally imposed sexual desire.[11] This heterosexual matrix can be found embedded into norms, institutions and practices that naturalise and enforce the requirement of asymmetric opposed genders and compulsory heterosexuality. This heterosexual matrix is connected to the notion of *heteronormativity*, discussed in Chapter 1. I argued then that heteronormativity should be understood as a broad concept that refers to the institutions, discourses and practices that naturalised heterosexuality, making it appear as a natural, coherent and privileged sexuality.[12] This includes other normative ideals, such as the conception of sexuality itself as a human imperative; couplehood as the paradigmatic type of intimate relationship; reproduction as an irresistible natural drive; and cissexuality as the assumed gender norm.[13] All these *normativities* can actually be understood as manifestations of the heterosexual matrix.

[10] Judith Butler, *Gender Trouble: Feminism and the Subversion of Identity*, 2nd edn (Routledge, 1999) 194. Butler acknowledged that the idea of the heterosexual matrix is based on the notions of 'compulsory heterosexuality', developed by Adrianne Rich, and 'heterosexual contract', used by Monique Wittig. See Adrianne Rich, 'Compulsory Heterosexuality and Lesbian Existence' (1980) 5 *Signs* 631; Monique Wittig, *The Straight Mind and Other Essays* (Beacon Press, 1992).

[11] Butler, *Gender Trouble* (n 10) 23.

[12] Lauren Berlant and Michael Warner, 'Sex in Public' (1998) 24 *Critical Inquiry* 547, at 548.

[13] Eve Kosofsky Sedgwick, *Tendencies* (Routledge, 1994) 7; Ela Przybylo, 'Masculine Doubt and Sexual Wonder' in Karli June Cerankowski and Megan Milks (eds), *Asexualities: Feminist and Queer Perspectives* (Routledge, 2014) 442–81, 448; Robin Bauer, 'Non-Monogamy in Queer BDSM Communities: Putting the Sex Back into Alternative Relationship Practices and Discourse' in Meg Barker and Darren Langdridge (eds), *Understanding Non-Monogamies* (Routledge, 2010) 142–53, at 145; Katherine M Franke, 'Theorizing Yes: An Essay on Feminism, Law, and Desire' in Martha Albertson Fineman, Jack E Jackson and Adam P Romero (eds), *Feminist and Queer Legal Theory: Intimate Encounters, Uncomfortable Conversations* (Ashgate, 2009) 29–44, at 30–31; Michael Warner (ed), *Fear of a Queer Planet: Queer Politics and Social Theory* (University of Minnesota Press, 1993) ix; Greta R Bauer, Rebecca Hammond,

I will argue that this heterosexual matrix permeates the Court's conception of the family, parenthood and marriage and, consequently, the enjoyment of family rights. This has become evident in discrimination cases, in which the Court has compared the heterosexual married couple with same-sex couples, in order to decide whether denying to the latter those privileges that are granted to the former, constituted discriminatory treatment. Similarly, the heterosexual matrix is present when the Court allows states to 'protect' the traditional nuclear family by depriving other family formations from benefiting from equal rights. Section II will provide a discussion of the prohibition of discrimination under the Convention and its use by LGBT families in their quest for family rights. Following this, section III will focus on the privileges granted to the heterosexual married couple that are denied to same-sex couples and section IV will discuss the Court's validation of the protection of the traditional family as a legitimate goal of state policy. After discussing the Court's engagement with the privileged traditional family, sections V and VI will put forward a number of difficulties that arise when making use of human rights strategies for advancing LGBT claims concerning family rights, with a specific focus on the use of the prohibition of discrimination. Lastly, the Conclusion will provide a summary of the arguments discussed throughout the chapter.

II. The Prohibition of Discrimination under the Convention

The prohibition of discrimination is enshrined in Article 14 of the Convention, which states:

> The enjoyment of the rights and freedoms set forth in this Convention shall be secured without discrimination on any ground such as sex, race, colour, language, religion, political or other opinion, national or social origin, association with a national minority, property, birth or other status.

Since its early case law the Court has clarified that the aim of the prohibition of discrimination is to protect equality of treatment in the enjoyment of the rights recognised by the Convention.[14] It affirmed that the principle of equality is not breached by every differential treatment that is carried out, but only by distinctions lacking of an objective and reasonable justification.[15] To determine whether such a justification exists, the Court examines whether the performed distinction pursues a 'legitimate aim' and if there is a reasonable relationship of proportionality

Robb Travers, Matthias Kaay, Karin M Hohenadel and Michelle Boyce, '"I Don't Think This is Theoretical; This is Our Lives": How Erasure Impacts Health Care for Transgender People' (2009) 20 *Journal of the Association of Nurses in AIDS Care* 348, at 356; Cristina Richie, 'Lessons from Queer Bioethics: A Response to Timothy F Murphy' (2016) 30 *Bioethics* 365, at 366.

[14] *Case relating to Certain Aspects of the Laws on the Use of Languages in Education in Belgium'* (Merits), Series A no 6, 23 July 1968, para 10.

[15] ibid; *National Union of Belgian Police v Belgium*, Series A no 19, 27 October 1975, para 46.

between the means employed and the aim sought to be realised.[16] While it has not explicitly acknowledged it, the Court has interpreted that the prohibition of discrimination established by the Convention reflects the Aristotelian notion of distributive justice, which imposes the need to treat like cases alike and dissimilar cases differently.[17]

However, it is not always evident which are the steps followed by the Court when it examines, in particular cases, whether a state has breached the prohibition of discrimination. In fact, scholars disagree as to which steps and how many of them are followed by the Court in order to decide whether there has been discriminatory treatment in violation of Article 14 of the Convention.[18] I will argue that in the majority of cases, the methodology of the Court seems to be a four-tier system. The first step taken by the Court consists of the analysis of whether the case falls within the ambit of a human right protected by the Convention (the 'within the ambit' test). This is because Article 14 is not a generic anti-discrimination guarantee, but only protects the enjoyment of Convention rights without discrimination.[19] There is no need for the measure under analysis to have breached a substantive Convention right, but only for the matter to be covered within the general scope of a Convention article.[20] It is worth mentioning that the Court has not provided clear criteria to establish how an issue falls within the Convention when a right has not been breached,[21] but it has repeatedly stressed that the ambit encompasses those activities in which the state has opted to engage in an effort to enhance the protection of Convention rights and freedoms, even if the state was under no obligation to do so under the Convention.[22] Since this leaves the Court a wide margin of discretion to evaluate the extension of the 'ambit' in each case, the applicability of Article 14 will be dependent upon the ability of the applicant to persuade the Court that their particular case passes the 'within the ambit' test. Examples of matters falling within the general scope of

[16] *Case relating to Certain Aspects of the Laws on the Use of Languages in Education in Belgium*' (n 14) para 10; *Marckx v Belgium*, Series A no 31, 13 June 1979, para 33.

[17] Aristotle, *Nicomachean Ethics* (Roger Crisp ed and tr, Cambridge University Press, 2004) xxii and 86. Some judges, in their separate opinions, have actually made reference to this being the Court's interpretation under Art 14. See *Fábián v Hungary*, Application no 78117/3, 5 September 2017, joint concurring opinion of Judges O'Leary and Koskelo, para 10; *Khamtokhu and Aksenchik v Russia* (GC), Application nos 60367/08 and 961/11, ECHR 2017, dissenting opinion of Judge Pinto de Albuquerque, para 19.

[18] Harris and others, *Law of the European Convention on Human Rights* (n 8) 579–600; Clare Ovey and Robin CA White, *The European Convention on Human Rights*, 4th edn (Oxford University Press, 2006) 419–29; Robin CA White and Clare Ovey, *The European Convention on Human Rights*, 5th edn (Oxford University Press, 2010) 551–64; Paul Johnson, *Homosexuality and the European Court of Human Rights* (Routledge, 2012) 123–26.

[19] Nicholas Bamforth, Maleiha Malik and Colm O'Cinneide, *Discrimination Law: Theory and Context* (Sweet & Maxwell, 2008) 673.

[20] Harris and others, *Law of the European Convention on Human Rights* (n 8) 580–81.

[21] Rainey et al, *The European Convention on Human Rights* (n 9) 642.

[22] Aaron Baker, 'The Enjoyment of Rights and Freedoms: A New Conception of the "Ambit" under Article 14 ECHR' (2006) 69 *Modern Law Review* 714, at 716 and 734.

the Convention for the applicability of Article 14 have been the right to adopt, the right to succeed to a tenancy agreement, or the right to obtain a residence permit, as will be discussed in different cases analysed through Chapters 4 and 5.

The second stage of the Court's analysis under Article 14 consists of establishing whether the applicant has suffered a differential treatment compared to that given to other individuals in analogous circumstances (the 'analogous situation' test). As mentioned above, a specific treatment of individuals will only be in breach of the equality principle when similar cases are not treated alike, or when dissimilar cases are given the same type of treatment.[23] Nonetheless, the analysis of this step seems to be missing from the Court's decision in numerous cases.[24] The step tends to be made explicit by the Court mostly when it finds that the differential treatment under consideration was justified, due to the applicant not being in a relevantly similar situation to those treated more favourably.[25] That is to say, the Court expressly analyses whether the applicant was in analogous circumstances to other individuals when it believes that they were not similar enough to be compared to each other, in order to justify that there has been no discrimination. There is no exhaustive list of circumstances that allows proving the existence of an 'analogous situation', but the Court has stated that Article 14 only prohibits differences in treatment that are based on an identifiable, objective or personal characteristic, by which persons or groups of persons are distinguishable from one another.[26] While Article 14 sets out specific grounds which constitute such a status, that enumeration is illustrative and not exhaustive.[27] In fact, the Court has established that the categories of sexual orientation and gender identity are protected characteristics concerning the prohibition of discrimination, even though they do not appear listed in Article 14.[28]

Once the Court is convinced that there has been a difference in treatment in analogous circumstances ('analogous situation' test), which falls within the ambit of a protected right ('within the ambit' test), it proceeds to the evaluation of whether this distinction was justified. This is analysed in the third and fourth steps. Moreover, there is a shift as to the burden of proof in these last steps. Once an applicant has shown the existence of a difference in treatment, it is for the

[23] *Thlimmenos v Greece* (GC), Application no 34369/97, ECHR 2000-IV, para 44; *DH and others v Czech Republic* (GC), Application no 57325/00, ECHR 2007-IV, para 175; *Carson and others v United Kingdom*, Application no 42184/05, 4 November 2008, para 77.

[24] Harris and others, *Law of the European Convention on Human Rights* (n 8) 583; Johnson, *Homosexuality and the European Court of Human Rights* (n 18) 125.

[25] For example, see *Gas and Dubois v France*, Application no 25951/07, ECHR 2012, para 68; *X and others v Austria* (GC), Application no 19010/07, 19 February 2013, para 109.

[26] *Clift v United Kingdom*, Application no 7205/07, 13 July 2010, para 55; *Fábián v Hungary* (n 17) para 113.

[27] *Salgueiro da Silva Mouta v Portugal*, Application no 33290/96, ECHR 1999-IX, para 28; *Clift v United Kingdom* (n 26) para 55.

[28] *Salgueiro da Silva Mouta v Portugal* (n 27) paras 28 and 36; *PV v Spain*, Application no 35159/09, 30 November 2010, para 30; *Identoba and others v Georgia*, Application no 73235/12, 12 May 2015, para 96.

state to convince the Court that such a distinction was justified.[29] As mentioned above, the case law of the Court has established that a difference in treatment is discriminatory if it has no objective and reasonable justification. That happens when differential treatment does not pursue a legitimate aim, or when there is no reasonable relationship of proportionality between the means employed and the aim sought to be realised.[30] Therefore, the third stage of the examination consists of analysing whether the differential treatment pursues a legitimate aim (the 'legitimate aim' test). However, in most cases the Court seems to simply accept the aims pursued by the state, and proceeds to decide the case based on the analysis of the fourth stage.[31]

The fourth and last step is the examination of whether the measure under analysis can be considered to be proportionate (the 'proportionality' test). The Court has established that states enjoy a margin of appreciation in assessing whether and to what extent differences in otherwise similar situations justify differential treatment. The margin of appreciation doctrine refers to a certain degree of discretion left by the Court to States Parties when adopting measures that fall within the area of a Convention right.[32] This means that the Court will refuse to find a violation of a human right when it considers a state measure to fall within this 'margin of appreciation'. The scope of this margin will vary depending on the circumstances of the case. For instance, where there is no consensus between the Member States of the Council of Europe as to how a specific situation should be regulated, the margin of appreciation is considered to be wider. On the contrary, the Court has asserted that distinctions based on sexual orientation require very weighty reasons by way of justification, narrowing the scope of the discretion of states in this area.[33] In fact, the Court has affirmed that in cases in which the margin of appreciation afforded to the state is narrow, such as where there is a difference in treatment based on sexual orientation, the principle of proportionality does not merely require the measure chosen to be suitable for realising the aim sought, but the state must also show that in order to achieve its legitimate aim it was necessary to exclude people based on their sexuality from the scope of application of the measure.[34]

[29] *DH and others v Czech Republic* (n 23) para 177; *Timishev v Russia*, Application nos 55762/00 and 55974/00, ECHR 2005-XII, para 57; *Chassagnou and others v France* (GC), Application nos 25088/94, 28331/95 and 28443/95, ECHR 1999 III, para 92.

[30] *Karner v Austria*, Application no 40016/98, ECHR 2003-IX, para 37; *Fretté v France*, Application no 36515/97, ECHR 2002-I, para 34; *EB v France* (GC), Application no 43546/02, 22 January 2008, para 91.

[31] *Salgueiro da Silva Mouta v Portugal* (n 27) para 30; *Karner v Austria* (n 30) para 40; *Fretté v France* (n 30) para 38.

[32] Harris and others, *Law of the European Convention on Human Rights* (n 8) 11. For a discussion on the complexities concerning the doctrine of the 'margin of appreciation', see George Letsas, 'Two Concepts of the Margin of Appreciation' (2006) 26 *Oxford Journal of Legal Studies* 705. As to a critical discussion on the use of this doctrine in cases concerning LGBT rights, see Frances Hamilton, 'Why the Margin of Appreciation Is Not the Answer to the Gay Marriage Debate' (2013) 1 *European Human Rights Law Review* 47.

[33] *Karner v Austria* (n 30) para 37.

[34] ibid para 41.

Nevertheless, as many issues regarding LGBT rights are also situated in areas lacking European consensus, the Court has reserved for itself a wide discretion for deciding in each case whether it will grant states a wide or a narrow margin of appreciation. Indeed, the Court has supported contradictory statements in cases concerning discrimination based on sexual orientation. In a number of cases, the Court has held that a distinction based on sexual orientation is discriminatory in itself. In its own words, the Court has stated that 'if the reasons advanced for a difference in treatment were based solely on the applicant's sexual orientation, this would amount to discrimination under the Convention'.[35] However, at other times the Court seemed to pull back from this statement, resorting to the lack of European consensus to accept differential treatment based on sexual orientation. The Court has highlighted that

> there remain issues where no European consensus has been reached, such as granting permission to same-sex couples to adopt a child … and the right to marry, and the Court has confirmed the domestic authorities' wide margin of appreciation in respect of those issues.[36]

Therefore, the Court appears to have adopted a swinging criterion regarding the prohibition of discrimination based on sexual orientation. In judgments that have affirmed that the differential treatment performed was unacceptable, the Court stated that a distinction based on this characteristic was completely forbidden. On the contrary, in rulings that have validated a difference in treatment, the Court affirmed that there are issues in which the lack of consensus between states allowed them a wide margin of appreciation to decide for themselves on the compatibility between the measure and the Convention.

The majority of the cases concerning discrimination against LGBT families have been decided by the Court at either the second stage ('analogous situation' test) or the fourth one ('proportionality' test) of the analysis under Article 14. The cases decided at the second stage were based on the consideration that same-sex couples were not similar enough to married heterosexual couples. On the other hand, the cases decided on the fourth step were decided after evaluating whether states were justified to privilege a particular type of kinship through a diverse range of measures. The following sections will engage with examples of both of these situations. Section III will focus on the failure of same-sex couples to be considered similar enough to different-sex couples and section IV will deal with cases in which the Court had to assess whether the protection of the 'family in the traditional sense' entitled states to treat LGBT families in a less favourable manner.

[35] *Kozak v Poland*, Application no 13102/02, 2 March 2010, para 92. This idea had been already sketched by the Court in its ruling *EB v France*, and has been reaffirmed by the Court in its judgments on *Genderdoc-M v Moldova* and *X and others v Austria*, *EB v France* (n 30) para 93; *Genderdoc-M v Moldova*, Application no 9106/06, 12 June 2012, para 51; *X and others v Austria* (n 25) para 99.

[36] *Alekseyev v Russia*, Application nos 4916/07, 25924/08 and 14599/09, 21 October 2010, para 83.

III. The Privileged Heterosexual Married Couple

In a series of cases, the Court has been called to examine benefits that states were reserving for the privileged married (heterosexual) couple to decide whether their denial to same-sex couples amounted to discrimination. The Court has been adamant on its view of marriage as a special institution that confers a particular status on those who enter into it and which gives rise to specific social, personal and legal consequences.[37] This special character attributed to marriage has been used by the Court to justify differential entitlement of rights. However, as will be discussed in Chapter 5, the Court remains of the idea that states are free to deny access to the institution of marriage based on sexuality. Therefore, when marriage can be nothing but heterosexual, it is possible to argue that a differential entitlement of rights based on marriage is actually based on sexuality.

A group of three judgments appears as the clear example of restrictions in the enjoyment of human rights allowed by the Court on the basis of (heterosexual) marriage. The cases were *Courten v United Kingdom*, *MW v United Kingdom* and *Manenc v France*, all of which concerned the denial of certain benefits to surviving same-sex partners. In its rulings, the Court followed the four-tier system for claims under Article 14, but it ended the analysis at the second stage ('analogous situation' test),[38] or by way of a summary decision which concluded that the distinction was within the discretion of the state.[39] The cases *Courten* and *MW*, both against the United Kingdom, were similar and had the same outcome. The first was about the unsuccessful claim for an exemption from inheritance tax following the death of a same-sex cohabiting partner,[40] while the second concerned the refusal of bereavement benefits after the death of a same-sex partner.[41] The applicants submitted that the refusal to extend a benefit available to (heterosexual) married couples to same-sex couples who were legally unable to marry was contrary to the prohibition of discrimination in conjunction with the right to the peaceful enjoyment of possessions. However, the Court recalled that not every difference in treatment amounts to discrimination. It must be established that other persons in an analogous or relevantly similar situation enjoy preferential treatment, and that there is no reasonable or objective justification for this distinction. In the *Courten* and *MW* cases, the Court concluded that the applicants were not in an analogous situation to married couples. It affirmed that 'notwithstanding social changes, marriage remains an institution that is widely accepted as conferring a particular status on those who enter it and, indeed, it is singled out for special treatment under Article 12 of the Convention'.[42] It then held that the promotion of (heterosexual) marriage,

[37] *Burden v United Kingdom* (GC), Application no 13378/05, ECHR 2008, para 63.

[38] *Courten v United Kingdom* (Dec), Application no 4479/06, 4 November 2008, 6; *MW v United Kingdom* (Dec), Application no 11313/02, 23 June 2009, 6.

[39] *Manenc v France* (Dec), Application no 66686/09, 21 September 2010, 9–10.

[40] *Courten v United Kingdom* (n 38).

[41] *MW v United Kingdom* (n 38).

[42] *Courten v United Kingdom* (n 38) 5. See also *MW v. United Kingdom* (n 38) 5.

by way of limited benefits for surviving spouses, could not be said to exceed the margin of appreciation afforded to states. The Court also examined the claim of the applicants that they were legally unable to enter into marriage or a civil partnership, since the facts of the case predated the coming into force of the legislation allowing for the recognition of same-sex partnerships. Nevertheless, it ruled that the state could not be criticised for its failure to introduce earlier the legislation enabling the applicants to obtain the benefits conferred on the survivor of a civil partnership.[43]

The *Manenc* case was very similar to *Courten* and *MW*, but on this occasion the refusal of a survivor's pension had an added element in that the applicant was bound to his partner by a French civil partnership (PACS).[44] The Court held that couples bound by civil partnership were not in an analogous situation to those who had married, and the fact that the applicant was not legally allowed to marry was considered to be insufficient to place him in such a situation. Consequently, the Court ruled that the distinction between married couples and those bound by civil partnership had a legitimate aim – the protection of the family based on marriage – and was within the margin of appreciation of the state.[45]

There are two main problems with these rulings of the Court: first, the validation of benefits based on marriage; and, second, the use of the institution of marriage to privilege heterosexuality. As to the first problem, queer theorists have lucidly argued that granting economic benefits based on marriage means considering other relationships to be less worthy.[46] In particular, Michael Warner has emphasised that attaching privileges to the institution of marriage means that other intimate relationships, including cohabiting partnerships, are not recognised by the law as having the same rights and validity as married couples.[47] However, as affirmed by Warner, it is certainly possible to imagine the extension of these privileges to other kinds of households and intimate relations, uncoupling them from the institution of marriage,[48] or even to uncouple them from couplehood altogether.[49]

Concerning the second problem, the Court continued to privilege the heterosexual institution of marriage and, by doing so, kept considering sexuality as a

[43] As will be discussed in Chapter 5, only since its judgment in *Oliari and others v Italy* from July 2015 has the Court found states to be under the positive obligation to provide for alternative means of legal recognition to same-sex couples. *Oliari and others v Italy*, Application nos 18766/11 and 36030/11, 21 July 2015.

[44] *Manenc v France* (n 39).

[45] ibid 9.

[46] Michael Warner, *The Trouble with Normal: Sex, Politics, and the Ethics of Queer Life* (Harvard University Press, 2000) 82; Aeyal Gross 'The *Burden* of Conjugality' in Eva Brems (ed), *Diversity and European Human Rights: Rewriting Judgments of the ECHR* (Cambridge University Press, 2013) 265–92, at 281.

[47] Warner, *The Trouble with Normal* (n 46) 96.

[48] ibid 108 and 117–18.

[49] Aeyal M Gross, 'Sex, Love, and Marriage: Questioning Gender and Sexuality Rights in International Law' (2008) 21 *Leiden Journal of International Law* 235, at 246–47 and 252; Gross, 'The *Burden* of Conjugality' (n 46) 281.

valid reason for states to differentiate between individuals. The differential treatment based on sexuality appeared disguised by the difference between married and unmarried couples. Nonetheless, when same-sex marriage is legally forbidden by states, the benefits deriving from the institution are also denied based on sexual orientation, not just marital status. Stating that the distinction is based on marriage seems to be merely a masquerade. In fact, in each of these cases the Court failed to analyse whether the attribution of privileges based on marital status acted as a clear case of indirect discrimination based on sexual orientation. The prohibition of indirect discrimination has been established in the Court's case law,[50] and refers to seemingly neutral practices or policies that in themselves do not involve impermissible discrimination, but that affect detrimentally and disproportionately the members of a specific group.[51] While the Court presented the economic privileges as based on a neutral and objective element (the existence or not of a marriage), the fact that individuals could be banned from accessing marriage based on their sexuality means that same-sex couples could be precluded from obtaining such privileges because their sexuality made them unable to marry. Given that sexual orientation has been widely accepted by the Court as a prohibited category of discrimination, a benefit denied on the grounds of marriage must be understood (at least) as a case of indirect discrimination based on sexual orientation when marriage is not open to same-sex couples.

By contrast, the Court resorted to an argument of vicious circularity in which the applicants were considered to be different from married couples because they were not married, while rendering unproblematic the fact that they were banned from marrying because the states considered them to be different to heterosexual couples.[52] In a nutshell, they were different because they were not married and they could not marry because they were different. According to the Court, this distinction (allegedly based on marital status, but actually based on sexuality) allowed for the differential enjoyment of human rights. Therefore, hiding behind the privileged institution of marriage, the Court considered that individuals could be made entitled to different rights depending on their sexuality.

A. A (Seeming) Change of Criteria

In 2016, the Court (implicitly) acknowledged that its reasoning in judgments concerning privileges for heterosexual married couples had been problematic, when it decided *Taddeucci and McCall v Italy*. On that occasion, the Court examined

[50] *DH and others v Czech Republic* (n 23) para 184; *Horváth and Kiss v Hungary*, Application no 11146/11, 29 January 2013, para 105.

[51] Harris and others, *Law of the European Convention on Human Rights* (n 8) 607; William A Schabas, *The European Convention on Human Rights: A Commentary* (Oxford University Press, 2017) 566.

[52] A similar criticism has been raised by Johnson regarding the *Manenc* case and by Gross regarding the *Burden* case. Johnson, *Homosexuality and the European Court of Human Rights* (n 18) 137; Gross, 'The *Burden* of Conjugality' (n 46) 277–78.

the domestic legislation that only allowed married couples to benefit from a residence permit on family grounds, even though marriage remained restricted to different-sex couples. The applicants, a bi-national Italian/New-Zealand same-sex couple, complained of discrimination based on sexual orientation as the legislation did not allow the non-Italian partner to benefit from a residence permit, which led them to abandon Italy and settle in the Netherlands. The Court evaluated the fact that the legislation banned the members of any unmarried couple, regardless of sexuality, to qualify as family members for the purpose of a residence permit. Nevertheless, this time it reasoned that while different-sex couples could circumvent such a restriction by getting married, this possibility was forbidden to same-sex couples. It stated that the situation of same-sex couples could not be compared to that of a heterosexual couple who, for personal reasons, do not wish to contract a marriage.[53] That is to say, with regard to eligibility for a residence permit for family reasons, the applicants were treated in the same way as persons in a significantly different situation from theirs, namely, a different-sex couple who out of choice decides not to get married.[54] Consequently, the Court found the legislation to be discriminatory, as it failed to treat same-sex couples differently from unmarried different-sex couples, without an objective and reasonable justification.[55]

As pointed out by dissenting Judge Sicilianos, this decision did not follow the Court's previous case law, which allowed states to negate benefits to same-sex couples, as long as those were awarded only to married different-sex couples.[56] However, Judge Sicilianos needed not to worry. This ruling did not necessarily mean that the Court was to forbid distinctions based on the sexuality of individuals (if duly disguised as marital-based). On the contrary, it is possible to infer that the Court's decision was based on the understanding that, at the time of the facts, the state was not providing any form of legal recognition for same-sex couples, which had become an obligation under the Convention, as will be discussed in Chapter 5. In fact, the Court affirmed that it was

> precisely the lack of any possibility for same-sex couples to enter into a form of legal recognition of their relationship which placed the applicants in a different situation from that of unmarried heterosexual couples.[57]

Conversely, when states allow same-sex couples access to the legal recognition of their relationship, the Court does not require the institution to offer the same rights as those made available through marriage.[58] Therefore, while the ruling

[53] *Taddeucci and McCall v Italy*, Application no 51362/09, 30 June 2016, para 84.
[54] ibid para 85.
[55] ibid paras 96 and 99.
[56] ibid, partly dissenting opinion of Judge Sicilianos, para 10.
[57] ibid para 95.
[58] *Schalk and Kopf v Austria*, Application no 30141/04, ECHR 2010, para 109; *Chapin and Charpentier v France*, Application no 40183/07, 9 June 2016, para 51; *Orlandi and others v Italy*, Application nos 26431/12, 26742/12, 44057/12 and 60088/12, 14 December 2017, para 195.

in *Taddeucci and McCall v Italy* stands as a good starting point to put an end to allowing differential rights based on the sexuality of individuals, it does not necessarily mean that the jurisprudence of the Court has radically changed (yet).

It is possible to affirm that, despite the rhetoric, the Court continues to consider heterosexuality to be a privileged characteristic of family rights. While the ability to subject residence permits to the sexuality of family members seems now beyond the discretion of States Parties, the situation might not be the same for economic benefits or even for parenting rights, as will be discussed in Chapter 5.

IV. The Protection of the 'Family in the Traditional Sense'

To repeat, the Court has played its part in the process of idealisation of the reproductive married couple as the paradigmatic family unit. This has not only been present in rulings in which the Court has failed to see same-sex couples as similar enough to married heterosexual couples, but also in a series of cases in which the reason given by the state as the basis for differential treatment was actually the protection of a specific type of family: the traditional family. The first ruling in this line of jurisprudence was *Mata Estevez v Spain*,[59] which was a very similar case to those discussed in the previous section. The Court dealt with the refusal of a claim to a pension for surviving spouses made by the surviving partner of a same-sex couple. The reason for the refusal by the domestic authorities was the fact that, according to the legislation, survivors' pensions were conditional on the existence of a lawful marriage, and same-sex couples were legally unable to marry. However, the applicant complained that the difference in treatment between married couples and same-sex couples, who were legally forbidden from marrying, was unjustified discrimination, which violated his right to respect for private and family life. The Court conducted the four-tier analysis for discrimination. First, it affirmed that long-term same-sex relationships did not fall within the scope of family life, a stance that the Court would finally revise in 2010.[60] Nonetheless, the Court accepted that the case could be considered under the right to respect for private life. It did not pay much attention to the 'analogous situation' test on this occasion, but continued with the examination regarding the aim pursued by the legislation. The Court noted that the legislation relating to eligibility for survivors' allowances had a legitimate aim: 'the protection of the family based on marriage bonds'.[61] It then decided that the difference in treatment performed could be considered to fall within the state's margin of appreciation; therefore, it did not constitute a discriminatory interference with the applicant's private life.[62]

[59] *Mata Estevez v Spain* (Dec), Application no 56501/00, ECHR 2001-VI.

[60] *Schalk and Kopf v. Austria* (n 58) para 94; *PB and JS v Austria*, Application no 18984/02, 22 July 2010, para 30.

[61] *Mata Estevez v Spain* (n 59) 5.

[62] ibid.

The protection of a specific type of family as a legitimate aim of state policy was also considered in the *Karner* and *Kozak* cases. On those occasions, the Court examined whether individuals were entitled to succeed to the tenancy contract of a deceased same-sex partner, or if such a right could be limited by the state to different-sex partners. In particular, the Court had to decide whether the differential treatment of same-sex and different-sex partners, regarding the right to succeed to a tenancy agreement, was discriminatory. In both the *Karner* and the *Kozak* cases, the Court followed the four-tier analysis. As to whether the facts of the case fell 'within the ambit' of a right protected by the Convention, the Court decided that the relationship between the applicants and their partners fell within the right to respect for their home and, in the latter case, with the right to respect for their private life.[63] The Court then focused its analysis on whether the differential treatment pursued a legitimate aim and if there was a reasonable relationship of proportionality between the means employed and the aim sought to be realised. As to the aim pursued by the state, in *Karner* the Court accepted that the 'protection of the family in the traditional sense' was legitimate.[64] Similarly, in *Kozak* the Court accepted that the protection of the family founded on a 'union of a man and a woman was a weighty and legitimate reason which might justify a difference in treatment'.[65] Nonetheless, the Court affirmed that since the distinction was based on the sexual orientation of the applicants, the margin of appreciation afforded to the state in order to justify the distinction was narrow. Consequently, particularly serious reasons by way of justification needed to be given by the state to prove that the measure adopted was necessary to achieve the legitimate aim.[66] In these cases, the Court held that no convincing or compelling reason had been advanced by the state to justify the distinction in treatment between same-sex and different-sex partners and, therefore, there had been a violation of the prohibition of discrimination regarding the applicants' rights.[67]

While the applicants were successful in their claims in two of the three cases discussed, in all three of them the Court accepted that the protection of the traditional family was a weighty and legitimate reason which might justify detrimental treatment of same-sex couples. Moreover, the Court avoided recognising that same-sex couples could constitute families.[68] In the *Mata Estevez* case, the Court affirmed: 'long-term homosexual relationships between two men do not

[63] *Karner v Austria* (n 30) para 33; *Kozak v Poland* (n 35) paras 83–84.

[64] *Karner v Austria* (n 30) para 40.

[65] *Kozak v Poland* (n 35) para 98.

[66] *Karner v Austria* (n 30) paras 37 and 40; *Kozak v Poland* (n 35) paras 92 and 99.

[67] *Karner v Austria* (n 30) paras 42–43; *Kozak v Poland* (n 35) para 99.

[68] Although, in the *Kozak* case, the Court could be seen to be on the verge of acknowledging same-sex couples as families, as it asserted: 'the State, in its choice of means designed to protect the family and secure, as required by Article 8, respect for family life must necessarily take into account developments in society and changes in the perception of social, civil-status and relational issues, including the fact that there is not just one way or one choice in the sphere of leading and living one's family or private life'. *Kozak v Poland* (n 35) para 98.

fall within the scope of the right to respect for family life protected by Article 8 of the Convention'.[69] Consequently, while same-sex couples were granted protection through the right to respect for their home and private life, the Court felt that, at the time, it could deny that these couples were bound by ties of kinship.

However, as I mentioned above, the European Convention on Human Rights differs from other international human rights instruments regarding its conception of the family. While the Universal Declaration of Human Rights and the International Covenant on Civil and Political Rights present the family as a pre-social and fundamental institution that deserves recognition, the Convention is silent on the matter. In fact, in the three cases just discussed, the Court did not refer to the 'protection of the family' as a legitimate aim, which would have implied that the family of human rights was a unique monolithic institution. Rather, the traditional family was referred to as the 'family in the traditional sense', the 'family based on marriage bonds', and the family based on the 'union of a man and a woman'. It was presented as one type of family among others. The fact that the traditional family has been understood as merely one type of family is compatible with the idea of the family as a social construction.[70] That is, the family is the result of social arrangements that change through time, instead of a pre-social institution that can only adopt one 'natural' form.[71]

The Court has acknowledged the social and evolving construction of the family, when it affirmed that certain forms of kinship that differ from the heterosexual couple should be considered to be families. An early (and timid) example of the Court broadening the scope of kinship took place in 1997, with the recognition that a couple composed of a transsexual man and a cissexual woman, and their child conceived through artificial insemination, were linked by 'de facto family ties'.[72] Another example was the decision of the Court to modify its jurisprudence in 2010, whereby it began to acknowledge that 'there is not just one way or one choice in the sphere of leading and living one's family … life',[73] which led to recognising that cohabiting same-sex couples should also be considered to be families.[74]

Notwithstanding the conception of the family as a social construction, and the evolution experienced by the institution within the Court's case law, the Court has continued to validate the protection of the traditional family as a legitimate aim of state policy. However, it is certainly problematic that the Court accepts as

[69] *Mata Estevez v Spain* (n 59) 4.

[70] See Katherine O'Donovan, *Family Law Matters* (Pluto Press, 1993) 30; Richard Collier, *Masculinity, Law and the Family* (Routledge, 1995) 77 and 80.

[71] See Loveday Hodson, 'Family Values: The Recognition of Same-Sex Relationships in International Law' (2004) 22 *Netherlands Quarterly of Human Rights* 33, at 34.

[72] *X, Y and Z v United Kingdom*, Reports of Judgments and Decisions 1997-II, 22 April 1997, para 37.

[73] *Kozak v Poland* (n 35) para 98.

[74] *Schalk and Kopf v Austria* (n 58) para 94. Later on, the requirement of 'cohabitation' would be dropped, but only in so far as it did not jeopardise the idea of 'stability' of the couple. See *Vallianatos and others v Greece* (GC), Application nos 29381/09 and 32684/09, ECHR 2013, para 73; *Oliari and others v Italy* (n 43) para 169; *Pajić v Croatia*, Application no 68453/13, 23 February 2016, para 67.

legitimate aims the protection of 'the family in the traditional sense' (as in *Karner*), 'the family based on marriage bonds' (as in *Mata Estevez*), or the family founded on a 'union of a man and a woman' (as in *Kozak*). There are two main objections to this: the exclusionary character of the traditional family, and the fact that its alleged protection is actually an attempted justification for treating other forms of kinship detrimentally. As to the first objection, Michel Foucault has explained that the traditional family has been constructed as the model of legitimate sexuality,[75] providing means to favour reproductive sexuality, while policing non-procreative sexualities.[76] Since the traditional family is an exclusionary ideal that privileges only the reproductive heterosexual couple,[77] it is unjustifiable in law for the Court to consider its protection a legitimate state objective. The protection of a particular type of kinship that is based on the exclusion of LGBT individuals is an aim of state policy that the Court should have expressly and critically analysed, instead of just accepting it as a self-evident legitimate aim.

The second objection refers to a further exclusion validated by the Court when it accepts that the 'protection of the family in the traditional sense' is a legitimate aim within the analysis of discrimination. When the Court consents to the protection of the traditional family as a legitimate aim for justifying unequal treatment, it confirms that the traditional family should be entitled to privileged treatment, and this is to be achieved by treating other types of families in a different and detrimental manner. However, it is not particularly clear how forbidding other families from acquiring equal rights protects the traditional family.[78] How is the traditional family threatened by other families' enjoyment of human rights? Paraphrasing, the 'protection of the family in the traditional sense' is nothing but a smokescreen to justify depriving other types of families from enjoying equal rights. Therefore, the protection of the traditional family should never be considered a legitimate aim by the Court, as it is not aimed at protecting anybody, but rather provides an excuse for treating certain families detrimentally.

In its more recent jurisprudence the Court seemed to have realised that the protection of a specific type of family, which requires depriving others of certain rights, is difficult to square with the Convention's goal of protecting equality. While, on different occasions, it continued to affirm that the 'protection of the family in the traditional sense is, in principle, a weighty and legitimate reason which might justify a difference in treatment',[79] by 2016 it started casting doubts as to how legitimate this aim might be. In fact, it changed the way it phrases its usual validation of

[75] Michel Foucault, *The History of Sexuality: An Introduction* (Penguin, 1978) 3.

[76] ibid 3–4 and 110–11.

[77] Didi Herman, *Rights of Passage: Struggles for Lesbian and Gay Legal Equality* (University of Toronto Press, 1994) 146.

[78] See Drucilla Cornell, *At the Heart of Freedom: Feminism, Sex and Equality* (Princeton University Press, 1998) 177. See also Baroness Hale in *M v Secretary of State for Work and Pensions* [2006] UKHL 11, para 113.

[79] See *X and others v Austria* (n 25) para 138; *Vallianatos and others v Greece* (n 74) para 83.

this goal, which now reads: 'the protection of the traditional family *may, in some circumstances*, amount to a legitimate aim'.[80]

The most evident challenge to the validation of privileges for the traditional family has appeared in the Court's judgment on the *Bayev and others v Russia* case. As discussed in Chapter 3, in *Bayev and others* the Court ruled that Russia's legislative ban on the promotion of non-traditional sexual relations among minors was incompatible with the Convention. To reach this decision, one of the arguments examined by the Court was Russia's claim that the imposed restriction on freedom of expression was aimed at the protection of 'traditional family values'.[81] The Court rejected this claim, reiterating that there is more than just one way when it comes to leading one's family life.[82] However, it decided to provide stronger support to its decision, by adding that:

> [F]ar from being opposed to family values – many persons belonging to sexual minorities manifest allegiance to the institutions of marriage, parenthood and adoption, as evidenced by the steady flow of applications to the Court from members of the LGBT community who wish to have access to them.[83]

In other words, even though the Court mentioned that there should be multiple acceptable ways in which to live one's family life and none of those should benefit from additional privileges, its justification for the protection of non-traditional sexualities seemed to heavily rely on the idea that the way many LGBT individuals chose to live their family life was actually akin to the traditional family. This assimilation of LGBT politics with the traditional values of a heterosexual culture is what queer theory has labelled *homonormativity*.

V. Homonormativity as an LGBT Strategy

My argument is that the diminishing protection the Court granted to the traditional nuclear family came hand in hand with the realisation that LGBT families could fit that same family model in all but the sexuality of the couple. As discussed above, *heteronormativity* is used to refer to 'the institutions, structures of understanding, and practical orientations that make heterosexuality seem not only coherent – that is, organized as a sexuality – but also privileged'.[84] Based on this notion, Lisa Duggan made use of the term *homonormativity* to designate LGBT politics that far from contesting heteronormative assumptions and institutions

[80] *Taddeucci and McCall v Italy* (n 53) para 93 (emphasis added).
[81] *Bayev and others v Russia*, Application nos 67667/09, 44092/12 and 56717/12, 20 June 2017, paras 46, 48 and 65.
[82] ibid para 67.
[83] ibid para 67.
[84] Berlant and Warner, 'Sex in Public' (n 12) 548.

uphold and sustain them.[85] Homonormative strategies have achieved a certain degree of success before the Court. Examples of this type of LGBT politics include the demand to be accepted in the military; the recognition of partnership rights, including the struggle for same-sex marriage; and participation in carefully scheduled and pre-approved pride marches.[86] They are characterised by a rejection of queer's take on the celebration of proliferating forms of sexual dissidence, in favour of state-endorsed institutions and practices.[87] Human rights victories become the desired goals, leaving aside the possibility of more progressive and radical changes.[88] In sum, homonormativity seeks to redefine inclusion and equality in (restrictive) liberal terms that equate these ideals with formal access to the institutions of domestic privacy.[89]

Homonormativity promotes a demobilised LGBT constituency and a privatised and depoliticised culture anchored in consumption and domesticity.[90] The desired domesticity is modelled after the traditional nuclear family, simply expanded to recognise that some LGBT people can also fit the 'ideal'. Homonormative families are also monogamous stable couples who desire to raise children together and only differ from the original model in that they happen to be of the same sex.[91] This homonormative type of LGBT family is the one that the Court seemed to have in mind when it took its stronger stance against the 'protection of the traditional family' in *Bayev and others*. Far from being a threat to the traditional family, homonormative LGBT families reinforce it as the ideal to be achieved.

A similar (homonormative) interpretation is possible of the Court's ruling in *Taddeucci and McCall*, which was discussed in section III.A. The Court found it discriminatory that, for the purpose of residence permits on family grounds, same-sex couples and unmarried heterosexual couples were treated equally, even though same-sex couples were not allowed to marry. This decision can actually be read as a sanction against the state for not allowing the (domesticated) homosexual couple to duly register their relationship. The judgment revealed the Court's

[85] Lisa Duggan, *The Twilight of Equality: Neoliberalism, Cultural Politics, and the Attack on Democracy* (Beacon Press, 2003) 50. The term was already used in queer theory previous to Duggan's formulation, but with a different meaning. Susan Stryker, 'Transgender History, Homonormativity, and Disciplinarity' (2008) 100 *Radical History Review* 145, at 145.

[86] Duggan, *The Twilight of Equality* (n 85) 62; Nikita Dhawan, 'Homonationalism and State-phobia: The Postcolonial Predicament of Queering Modernities' in María Amelia Viteri, and Manuela Lavinas Picq (eds), *Queering Paradigms V: Queering Narratives of Modernity* (Peter Lang, 2015) 51–68, at 52–53.

[87] Duggan, *The Twilight of Equality* (n 85) 65–66; Diane Richardson, 'Claiming Citizenship? Sexuality, Citizenship and Lesbian/Feminist Theory' (2000) 3 *Sexualities* 255, at 268.

[88] Carl F Stychin, 'Same-Sex Sexualities and the Globalization of Human Rights Discourse' (2004) 49 *McGill Law Journal* 951, at 967; Dianne Otto, 'Resisting the Heteronormative Imaginary of the Nation-State: Rethinking Kinship and Border Protection' in Dianne Otto (ed), *Queering International Law: Possibilities, Alliances, Complicities, Risks* (Routledge, 2017) 236–57, at 256.

[89] Duggan, *The Twilight of Equality* (n 85) 50–51 and 65–66.

[90] ibid 50.

[91] Richardson, 'Claiming Citizenship?' (n 87) 268; Cynthia Weber, *Queer International Relations: Sovereignty, Sexuality and the Will to Knowledge* (Oxford University Press, 2016) 110.

firm belief that rights can be rightfully attached to couples who 'regularise their situation', ideally through marriage but also through civil partnerships.

While *Manenc v France* exposed that married couples need not be treated equally to registered same-sex couples, *Taddeucci and McCall* established that the same has become true for homosexual couples, who have embraced homonormativity and desire to register their union through the means made available by the state, and 'rogue' couples who opt out of registration. In fact, in *Taddeucci and McCall*, the Court repeatedly referred to unmarried different-sex couples as couples who have decided not to 'regularise their situation', an expression used on seven different occasions throughout the judgment. As highlighted by dissenting Judge Sicilianos, the only way for heterosexual couples to achieve such a 'regularisation' was through marriage.[92] Even though married heterosexual couples remain the preferred family structure and are the only ones truly entitled to enjoy all human rights recognised in the Convention, same-sex couples who embrace domesticity by dutifully registering their partnership should be entitled to certain rights, such as access to residence permits on the grounds of family, that can be denied to different-sex couples who refuse 'regularisation'. If registered same-sex couples are not similar enough to married heterosexual ones, they are at least dissimilar to those who are unmarried out of choice. The hierarchy of family structures remains present in the Court's case law and the right sexual choices continue to be rewarded. Nonetheless, regularised (homonormative) domesticity now appears to trump heterosexuality as the most desired sexual feature, although only when coupled with heterosexuality allows for the full enjoyment of rights.

Homonormative tactics have enabled LGBT families to improve the protection of their family rights under the Convention, but these are inseparable from specific trade-offs. One of the main risks of homonormative politics is that the outcome of such strategies is an LGBT person subjected to traditional (hetero) sexual normativity.[93] Protection comes as a consequence of having adopted couplehood, monogamy, stability and domesticity as the values to be cherished by LGBT families. Moreover, while LGBT people who follow this path can achieve the satisfaction of their human rights claims (or at least of some of them), this rights discourse produces narratives that allow identifying those who are not worthy of inclusion and recognition.[94] The (homonormative) articulation of the goals of the LGBT movement de-legitimises other subjectivities, as those identities who do not conform to the prescribed narratives will find themselves further marginalised

[92] *Taddeucci and McCall v Italy* (n 53) paras 85, 91, 94, 98, partly dissenting opinion of Judge Sicilianos, paras 6 and 13.

[93] Ratna Kapur, 'The (Im)possibility of Queering International Human Rights Law' in Dianne Otto (ed), *Queering International Law: Possibilities, Alliances, Complicities, Risks* (Routledge, 2017) 131–47, at 142. See also Martha Albertson Fineman, 'The Sexual Family' in Martha Albertson Fineman, Jack E Jackson and Adam P Romero (eds), *Feminist and Queer Legal Theory: Intimate Encounters, Uncomfortable Conversations* (Ashgate, 2009) 45–63, at 45.

[94] Steven Seidman, 'From Polluted Homosexual to the Normal Gay' in Chrys Ingraham (ed), *Thinking Straight: The Power, the Promise, and the Paradox of Heterosexuality* (Routledge, 2005) 39–61, at 45; Weber, *Queer International Relations* (n 91) 110–12.

because their demands are rendered unintelligible within the terms of the available liberal framework.[95]

Arguably, the most evident strategy of homonormative politics consists of the use of the prohibition of discrimination as a tool to achieve an equal treatment to that enjoyed by heterosexual individuals and their families. This strategy claims inclusion into the status quo which, far from challenging it, leads to reinforcing and naturalising the values and dynamics of the traditional nuclear family. The queer critique of the current use of such (homonormative) rights strategies will be discussed in the following section.

VI. Problems with (Non-)Discrimination

To repeat, claiming discrimination under Article 14 of the Convention has been the most frequently used strategy of LGBT families to demand access to rights and benefits granted to the traditional nuclear family. The goal of the provision prohibiting discrimination is to redress inequality, as has been acknowledged by the Court.[96] However, the category-based approach to discrimination adopted by international human rights treaties in general, such as the European Convention on Human Rights, suffers from a series of problems that act as obstacles to achieving this goal. Nitya Iyer has highlighted that categorical approaches to discrimination are problematic as they obscure the complexity of social identities in ways that are harmful to both the specific victims of discrimination, as well as to the larger goal of redressing inequality.[97]

I have discussed in section II that, in order to claim discrimination under the Convention, applicants need to persuade the Court that they have been treated worse than others based on an identifiable characteristic by which persons are distinguishable from one another. This process of identifying with a specific characteristic requires the embracing of an identity category, such as a particular sex, race, religion or sexuality. As discussed in Chapter 1, the construction of an identity necessarily means establishing similarities and differences; those who share an identity are similar to each other, while at the same time they are different from those who do not so identify. Paradoxically, the protection from discrimination requires a persuasive claim of belonging to a specific identity category (and therefore the non-belonging to another category) in order to argue that a distinction based on such a difference should not be allowed. As stated by Joan Scott: '[e]quality might well be defined as deliberate indifference to specified differences'.[98]

[95] Kapur, 'The (Im)possibility of Queering International Human Rights Law' (n 93) 140 and 142–43.

[96] *Case relating to Certain Aspects of the Laws on the Use of Languages in Education in Belgium* (n 14).

[97] Nitya Iyer, 'Categorical Denials: Equality Rights and the Shaping of Social Identity' (1994) 19 *Queen's Law Journal* 179, at 181.

[98] Joan W Scott, 'Deconstructing Equality-Versus-Difference: Or, the Uses of Post-structuralist Theory for Feminism' (1988) 14(1) *Feminist Studies* 33, at 44.

An evident problem is that the available categories that allow protection from discrimination reflect 'the dominant perspective about what social characteristics are relevant when differentiating among people',[99] and the dominant perspective that has established the categories also determined their meaning.[100] This offers a rather restrictive view of identities, since their conception appears as pre-established and fixed.[101] However, given that claims of belonging to a specific protected identity category are more likely to be successful when they match the dominant expectation of what it means to be part of such a group, those claiming protection willingly present a (caricaturised) narrative of the identity that fits the envisioned characteristic of the group.[102] In turn, claiming protection through these categories contributes to the naturalisation of such characteristics as relevant. It reinforces identity formation in binary terms with a dominant norm and its *other*.[103]

Let's think about the concrete example of sexuality as a protected characteristic under the Convention within the ambit of family rights. As discussed in Chapter 3, the first time the Court affirmed that sexual orientation was a protected ground against discrimination was in its judgment in *Salgueiro da Silva Mouta*. The applicant in that case resorted to the prohibition of discrimination to protect his family ties with his daughter. This was a case in which a man and his former wife were engaged in a judicial battle over the parental responsibility for their child. The Portuguese courts had granted parental responsibility to the child's mother, after taking into consideration (as a negative factor) that the father was living with another man.[104] Therefore, the Court had to consider whether the decision adopted by the domestic courts amounted to discrimination based on the sexuality of the applicant. The Court understood that the applicant was homosexual (ignoring other sexual possibilities), constructing the category of 'sexual orientation' through the heterosexual/homosexual binary provided by Western culture.[105] This dominant conception of sexuality acted as the foundations of the Court's ruling that held the decision of the domestic authorities to be discriminatory. From that moment onwards, successful claims of discrimination based on sexual orientation have all carefully fitted the narrative of belonging to a fixed identity group (homosexuals), because reproducing this categorical understanding of sexuality maximises the chances of success in obtaining the protection of rights, including family rights. In turn, this strategy has reinforced the stability of both the homosexual and the heterosexual identity.[106] In brief, discrimination strategies can help

[99] Iyer, 'Categorical Denials' (n 97) 186.
[100] ibid 193.
[101] ibid 205
[102] ibid 193.
[103] Carl F Stychin, 'Essential Rights and Contested Identities: Sexual Orientation and Equality Rights Jurisprudence in Canada' (1995) 3 *Canadian Journal of Law and Jurisprudence* 49, at 63.
[104] *Salgueiro da Silva Mouta v Portugal* (n 27).
[105] As argued by Beger, sexual orientation is equated with identity, becoming a clear and fixed marker of personality. Beger, *Tensions in the Struggle for Sexual Minority Rights in Europe* (n 2) 104–5.
[106] This was discussed in detail in Chapter 3.

LGBT individuals to protect their family rights, but their use also supports the current conception of sexual and gender identities, as illustrated by the previous example. Concerning sexuality, this means, on the one hand, that heterosexuality and homosexuality subsist in their asymmetric dynamic as norm/other (while the same can be said about the cissexuality/transsexuality binary) and, on the other hand, that possible identities beyond the binary remain ignored.

As argued at the beginning of this section, a further fundamental problem with the current approach to discrimination is that it reveals the poverty of our vision of social equality.[107] This becomes evident on three different levels. First, within liberal human rights regimes it is possible for marginalised groups to obtain access to certain rights and formal equality without undermining structural inequalities.[108] Hierarchical distinctions between the traditional nuclear family and LGBT families can continue to exist, alongside successful claims for equality. This can be seen in the cases discussed in section III, where same-sex couples gained equal access to residence permits for family reasons (*Taddeucci and McCall v Italy*), but not to certain economic benefits enjoyed by the privileged nuclear family (*Manenc v France*). Secondly, success is usually the outcome of homonormative strategies. LGBT families are granted access to equal rights when they manage to persuade the Court of how similar they are to the privileged nuclear family. Indeed, this is a requirement imposed by the discrimination analysis under the Convention through the 'analogous situation' test. Lastly, strategies built upon the prohibition of discrimination have a limited potential, as their ultimate goal is to achieve an outcome that already exists: equal treatment to that enjoyed by the privileged group, in this case the heterosexual nuclear family. Consequently, they can only act as poor substitutes for radical changes capable of freeing minority groups from subjugation.[109]

Does that mean that strategies based on the prohibition of discrimination should be abandoned? I do not think so. We certainly need to be aware that these strategies help to reproduce versions of identities that support values and norms associated with what Duggan has labelled homonormativity.[110] But, at the same time, it is important to acknowledge that strategies that broaden inclusion into traditional heteronormative institutions also challenge aspects of the heterosexual matrix embedded in them. For example, the recognition that family ties are not necessarily heterosexual contributes to the intelligibility of LGBT familial bonds. Therefore, abandoning legal tactics that might lead to (even limited) victories might not be the solution either.

[107] Iyer, 'Categorical Denials' (n 97) 207.

[108] Matthew Waites, 'The Fixity of Sexual Identities in the Public Sphere: Biomedical Knowledge, Liberalism and the Heterosexual/Homosexual Binary in Late Modernity' (2005) 8 *Sexualities* 539, at 557–59; See also Momin Rahman, 'Querying the Equation of Sexual Diversity with Modernity: Towards a Homocolonialist Test' in María Amelia Viteri and Manuela Lavinas Picq (eds), *Queering Paradigms V: Queering Narratives of Modernity* (Peter Lang, 2015) 91–111, at 109.

[109] Beger, *Tensions in the Struggle for Sexual Minority Rights in Europe* (n 2) 117.

[110] Richardson, 'Claiming Citizenship?' (n 87) 268.

A. The Potential Queering of Non-discrimination Strategies

It is possible to envision queer strategies with a potential to destabilise the categorical approach to discrimination. Two, in particular, I propose here: one that makes use of queer's ability to challenge strict definitions and a second one that takes advantage of queer's celebration of differentiating from the norm. As to the first one, it builds on the possibility of making use of available legal tools while contesting the categorical approach to discrimination.[111] As claimed by Carl Stychin, it is possible to make use of identity-categories, without committing to a fixed and closed definition of them.[112] When it comes to the discrimination analysis under Article 14, the second step that needs to be fulfilled by applicants is that of persuading the Court that they can be considered to be in an 'analogous situation' to those treated more favourably. According to the case law, this requires identifying a personal characteristic by which persons (or groups of persons) are distinguishable from one another, such as sexuality or gender identity. Currently, identities such as the homosexual or the transsexual person can satisfy these requirements, since the Court has adopted an understanding of genders and sexualities made available to it by Western culture. As discussed in Chapter 3, this means that applicants coming to Strasbourg tend to provide narratives that fit the established expectations in order to obtain the Court's protection.

However, queer theory can help us highlight that there is a fundamental flaw in a system that depends on pre-conceived notions of identities, because identities are always under performative construction and cannot, therefore, be pre-established.[113] This objection can lay the foundations for claiming discrimination based on more fluid sexual and gender identities to further trouble the category-based approach to discrimination. As discussed in Chapter 3, the role that confession plays within the Court's procedure opens up a path to introduce narratives that challenge dominant perspectives on identities.[114] Queer identities that represent a subversion of categorical thinking and highlight the contingency of all boundaries can demonstrate the impossibility of encompassing subjugated

[111] Carl F Stychin, *Law's Desire: Sexuality and the Limits of Justice* (Routledge, 1995) 155–56; Matthew Waites, 'Critique of "Sexual Orientation" and "Gender Identity" in Human Rights Discourse: Global Queer Politics Beyond the Yogyakarta Principles' (2009) 15 *Contemporary Politics* 137, at 139.

[112] Stychin, *Law's Desire* (n 111) 155–56. See also Judith Butler, *Bodies that Matter: On the Discursive Limits of Sex* (Routledge, 1993) 222.

[113] Butler, *Gender Trouble* (n 10) 33 and 180; Stychin, *Law's Desire* (n 111) 146; Stephen Valocchi, 'Not Yet Queer Enough: The Lessons of Queer Theory for the Sociology of Gender and Sexuality' (2005) 19 *Gender and Society* 750, at 756.

[114] The argument can be stretched even further to claim that identities continue to be *performatively* constructed through the production and re-production of these narratives. See Judith Butler, *Undoing Gender* (Routledge, 2004) 163 and 218; Elizabeth Sara Lewis, 'Pegging, Masculinities and Heterosexualities: How Narratives of Men Who Enjoy Being Penetrated by Women Can Contribute to Social Transformation and to Queering the Hidden Homosexual Norm in Queer Studies' in María Amelia Viteri and Manuela Lavinas Picq (eds), *Queering Paradigms V: Queering Narratives of Modernity* (Peter Lang AG, 2015) 241–63, 250 and 261.

gender and sexual identities in fixed and pre-determined binary terms.[115] It would be very interesting to see how a legal instrument conceived for providing protection to subordinated groups rises to the challenge posed by identities that do not fit the originally thought categorical binaries. This strategy might not challenge structural inequality, as it demands equal treatment to that already given to privileged sexual and gender groups, but it can expand the understanding of sexual and gender identities beyond binary conceptions.

Concerning the second mentioned strategy, this one is based on challenging the criteria used to determine whether a specific group, such as LGBT families, should be considered to be in an 'analogous position' (second step of the discrimination analysis) to that of the group that benefits from a privileged treatment (the traditional nuclear family). As discussed throughout the chapter, a claim of discrimination is usually based on the lack of an equal treatment in similar circumstances. While this type of assertion of discrimination can pursue homonormative goals of assimilation into heterosexual standards, contesting the grounds on which the different treatment is based may have a more transformative effect. I have argued above that legal strategies that build upon the prohibition of discrimination necessarily failed in proposing a radical outcome, as their goal is to achieve a treatment already enjoyed by a privileged group. However, if such treatment is not demanded as a consequence of being in equal circumstances, but through questioning the criteria used to assess such circumstances, the outcome could be more significant. Even if the desired result is still to obtain an existing treatment (eg a right, a benefit), these strategies assert a more radical demand as they entail a claim for equal treatment to be adopted, despite dissimilar circumstances, in order to satisfy the principle of equality. In other words, a claim of this kind can lead to challenging the grounds upon which rights and benefits are structured, such as the heteronormative rules of kinship.

As affirmed by Michael Warner, queer theory rests upon resistance to making the norms of straight culture into the standards by which queer life should be measured.[116] While the current rules of kinship have been naturalised and are scarcely challenged, that does not make them either immutable or neutral. The use of heteronormative standards to determine family ties and to allocate rights and benefits in society certainly places LGBT individuals in a more precarious situation to those who pledge alliance to the heterosexual nuclear family. Consequently, it is possible to question whether it is justifiable to hold couplehood, monogamy, stability and domesticity, among others, as the values to be cherished to gain access to economic benefits, the right to live in a particular country, or even the possibility of being recognised as a parent. It should be up to the state to justify the legitimate aim pursued through these exclusions and I have argued already in section IV about the problematic use of the protection of the traditional family as a goal of

[115] Stychin, 'Essential Rights and Contested Identities' (n 103) 61.
[116] Warner, *The Trouble with Normal* (n 46) 88.

state policy. As to proportionality, it has been discussed as well that differences that rely on the sexuality and gender identity of individuals place upon the state the burden to prove that such exclusions were actually needed to achieve a legitimate aim. If the denial of benefits is recognised as problematic due to the use of unfair (heteronormative) standards, then LGBT individuals should be considered entitled to such benefits, regardless of their 'failure' to fulfil the imposed requirements.

VII. Conclusion

Within the European Convention on Human Rights, the family is a protected institution as it emanates from Articles 8 and 12. In contrast to the pre-social family imagined by other international instruments, the family of the Convention is a social construct that has changed and broadened in scope through time. However, even if the traditional nuclear family is not the only type of family, it remains the privileged one within the Court's case law. The heterosexual matrix continues to permeate the Court's understanding of family ties.

At the same time, the strategies deployed for challenging the heterosexual matrix tend to fall into a 'homonormative trap'. Claims for recognition of LGBT families are more often than not grounded on the similarity of these families to the privileged one. Assertions of discrimination are supported by the fact that sexual and gender identities should not be considered valid grounds for differential treatment. In fact, the Court tends to accept that distinctions based on the sexual orientation or the gender identity of individuals are unacceptable under the Convention, unless very strong reasons for justification can be provided by the state. As discussed in section VI, this encourages the applicants in Strasbourg to embrace the gender and sexual identities made available to them through binary categories, since these will offer protection to those on the problematic side of the binary (the homosexual or the trans person), so long as they can prove how similar their lifestyle is to that of the members of the heterosexual nuclear family. These strategies have managed to provide a certain degree of inclusion into heteronormative family structures, while reinforcing them as the norm. Any opportunities for radically changing the values underpinning the idealisation of the traditional family are discarded in exchange for the possibility of inclusion into the protected family of human rights.

While I support the idea that liberal rights strategies need not to be abandoned, there is certainly room for *queering* these tactics. The rejection of fixed identity categories in favour of more fluid and unstable queer identification is a possible way forward. This can lead to emphasising the insufficiency of the current categorical approach to discrimination, as it comprehends sexual and gender identities in limited binary terms that reinforce the normality of cissexuality and heterosexuality. In addition to this, putting forward claims that challenge the criteria used to determine which families are deserving of rights and benefits should also be considered. A rejection to being measured by the heteronormative values of the traditional nuclear family as a requirement for gaining access to legal recognition, protection and benefits should be further explored. Instead of arguing that LGBT families are deserving of equal treatment because they should be considered to be in a relevantly similar situation to that of heterosexual nuclear families, there is a need to emphasise that the situation of LGBT people in terms of family rights is different. However, this difference is due to the fact that the standards currently used to value the reality and validity of kinship are already heterosexual. New standards that lead to equal rights for those identities that do not fit the heterosexual matrix are required. It is true that the possibility of success when the demand is for a more fundamental change in the criteria for determining kinship is much smaller than when it comes to the inclusion of LGBT families into existing familial standards, but the outcome could be substantially more queer. Moreover, when the goals pursued are utopian, the mere fact of re-visioning institutions can contribute – if not necessarily to radical change – at least to new understandings as to what is held to be natural, normal and deviant.[117] The value of queer lies precisely in helping us think what has not yet been thought.[118]

[117] Fineman, *The Neutered Mother, the Sexual Family and other Twentieth Century Tragedies* (n 7) 232.
[118] David M Halperin, 'The Normalization of Queer Theory' (2003) 45 *Journal of Homosexuality* 339, at 343.

5

Of Marriage, Partnerships and Parenthood (and Marriage Once Again)

I. Introduction

This chapter will continue the discussion of family rights started in Chapter 4, focusing on two types of claims LGBT families have brought to the European Court of Human Rights: access to marriage (and marriage-like institutions) and parenting rights. The first part of the chapter will focus on the institution of marriage and on how the Court has constructed (and re-constructed) the meaning of marriage through its case law. It will also explore how the Court has developed a specific jurisprudence on alternative means of formal recognition for same-sex couples. The chapter will then turn its attention to the struggle experienced by LGBT individuals and couples to gain access to parenting rights. However, the focus returns to marriage as the Court has validated the existence of a special link between marriage and parenthood. The chapter will make use of queer theory to examine different assumptions that underpin both marriage and parenthood. While Chapter 4 has raised concerns about the homonormative 'danger' of embracing traditional familial practices, this chapter will query whether the inclusion of LGBT individuals into traditional family institutions can also lead to a more queer future.

The discussion needs to begin with a reminder that within human rights law, marriage is presented as an institution of extreme importance. In fact, the desirability of marriage reached its zenith with its recognition as a human right. Marriage belongs to the same group of essential rights as the right to life, due process of law, and freedom of expression. The Court has also reaffirmed the importance of marriage. It has stated that 'marriage confers a special status on those who enter into it. The exercise of the right to marry is protected by Article 12 of the European Convention on Human Rights and gives rise to social, personal and legal consequences'.[1] As discussed in Chapter 4, the Court has allowed states

[1] *Burden v United Kingdom* (GC), Application no 13378/05, ECHR 2008, para 63.

to reward those individuals who enter the institution, through granting privileges, such as tax benefits or survivors' pensions.[2]

Nonetheless, this protected institution has been subjected to strong criticism from queer theory. For instance, Michael Warner and Aeyal Gross have argued that marriage, as an institution, discriminates,[3] and this seems to be a necessary implication of the institution. According to Warner, marriage sanctifies some couples at the expense of others, since it is used by law and society to confer legitimacy upon relationships, and relationships that do not mimic the institution of marriage are considered to be less worthy.[4] That is to say, marriage appears as the ideal type of relationship and those who cannot achieve this bond are seemingly settling for a less ideal relationship, if any relationship at all.[5] The discriminatory character of marriage is also exposed by the privileges attached to the institution. As Warner highlighted, other intimate relationships, including cohabiting partnerships, are not recognised by the law as having the same rights and validity as marriage.[6] While I do not necessarily share the absolute opposition to marriage (including same-sex marriage) professed by many queer theorists,[7] I certainly agree with the queer criticism of marriage expressed by Warner. In particular, the discriminatory character currently held by the institution of marriage is evident in its exclusionary nature and in its privileged character. In other words, it is an institution that cannot be accessed by everyone, and it is used by states to grant benefits to certain couples, which are denied to unmarried individuals.

The following section will explore how the Court has played an important role in keeping the institution of marriage as privileged and heterosexually exclusive. The section will begin with a discussion of the Court's rejection of same-sex marriage, and then will focus on registered partnerships, as an institution akin to

[2] *Mata Estevez v Spain* (Dec), Application no 56501/00, ECHR 2001-VI; *Courten v United Kingdom* (Dec), Application no 4479/06, 4 November 2008.

[3] Michael Warner, *The Trouble with Normal: Sex, Politics, and the Ethics of Queer Life* (Harvard University Press, 2000); Aeyal Gross 'The *Burden* of Conjugality' in Eva Brems (ed), *Diversity and European Human Rights: Rewriting Judgments of the ECHR* (Cambridge University Press, 2013) 265–92.

[4] Warner, *The Trouble with Normal* (n 3) 82; Gross 'The *Burden* of Conjugality' (n 3) 281.

[5] Gross has taken the discrimination argument even further, seeing the discriminatory character of marriage in the message of exclusion it sends not only to those legally inhibited to participate in the institution, but also to those that are unable to take part in it due to the lack of a willing partner. Gross 'The *Burden* of Conjugality' (n 3) 281. Nonetheless, this argument seems to be extreme, since many institutions or practices sanctioned by law also require the existence of willing partners, and that does not turn them automatically into cases of discrimination. Indeed, freedom of assembly and association is a human right, but it does not entail the right to force others into associating, neither does it give raise to a valid claim of discrimination if association is refused. Even more, sexuality is a legally protected activity that tends to require the participation of willing partners and it would seem almost absurd to resort to queer theory to challenge it, based on the fact that some people might be unable to find eager partners.

[6] Warner, *The Trouble with Normal* (n 3) 96.

[7] Warner, *The Trouble with Normal* (n 3) 82; Gross 'The *Burden* of Conjugality' (n 3) 281; Reese Kelly, 'Gay Marriage. Why Now? Why at All?' in Steven Seidman, Nancy Fischer and Chet Meeks (eds), *Introducing the New Sexuality Studies*, 2nd edn (Routledge, 2011) 457–62, at 462; Dean Spade, *Normal Life: Administrative Violence, Critical Trans Politics, and the Limits of Law*, 2nd edn (Duke University Press, 2015) 31–35.

marriage that is made available to same-sex couples. Section III will make use of the deconstructive method of queer theory to examine the meaning of the heterosexuality of marriage within the Court's case law. After that, section IV will focus on the rather problematic engagement of the Court with parenthood and LGBT individuals. Lastly, the Conclusion will present some final reflections on marriage, LGBT families, domesticity, and the heterosexual matrix.

II. The Heterosexual Right to Marry

In the *Schalk and Kopf* case, the Court had to decide whether the lack of same-sex marriage in Austria was compatible with the Convention; on the one hand, with the right to marry and, on the other hand, with the right to respect for private and family life in conjunction with the prohibition of discrimination. The applicants argued that the wording of Article 12, which grants the right to marry to 'men and women', did not necessarily imply that a man could only marry a woman and vice versa. They claimed that Article 12 should be read in present-day conditions, granting same-sex couples access to marriage or, in other words, as obliging States Parties to provide for such access in their national laws.[8]

The Court was not persuaded by the applicants' argument.[9] It observed that, looked at in isolation, the wording of Article 12 might be interpreted so as not to exclude marriage between two men or two women. However, in contrast, all other substantive articles of the Convention grant rights and freedoms to 'everyone', or state that 'no one' is to be subjected to certain types of prohibited treatment. According to the Court, the choice of words in this article had to be regarded as deliberate. The Court highlighted the historical context in which the Convention was adopted, stating that in the 1950s marriage was clearly understood in the traditional sense of being a union between two partners of different sexes.[10] The Court then affirmed that it would no longer consider that the right to marry must in all circumstances be limited to different-sex spouses.[11] Nonetheless, the question whether or not to allow same-sex marriage was left to regulation by the states through their national law.[12] The Court held that Article 12 of the Convention did not impose an obligation on states to grant same-sex couples access to marriage.[13]

[8] *Schalk and Kopf v Austria*, Application no 30141/04, ECHR 2010, para 57.

[9] ibid para 58.

[10] ibid para 55.

[11] ibid para 61. It is worth mentioning that the Court's statement that it 'would no longer consider that the right to marry … must in all circumstances be limited to marriage between two persons of the opposite sex' was actually concerning. In particular, it left an appealing question unanswered, namely: Was there a time in which the Court affirmed that the right to marry needed to be restricted to different-sex couples? It would actually have been extremely problematic for a human rights court to tell the states within its jurisdiction that they had to limit the enjoyment of a human right based on the sexuality of individuals.

[12] ibid.

[13] ibid para 63.

Following the analysis of the case under Article 12, the Court proceeded to examine the issue as a possible violation of the right to respect for family life, in conjunction with the prohibition of discrimination. The Court evaluated whether the different rights conferred by marriage, compared to registered partnerships, amounted to discrimination. It affirmed that, according to its established case law, the notion of family under the Convention was not confined to marriage-based relationships and could encompass other family ties where the parties were living together out of wedlock.[14] For the first time, the Court considered that it was artificial to maintain the view that, in contrast to a different-sex couple, a same-sex couple could not enjoy 'family life' for the purposes of Article 8. Consequently the relationship of the applicants, a cohabiting same-sex couple living in a stable de facto partnership, fell within the notion of 'family life', as would the relationship of a different-sex couple in the same situation.[15]

The Court then started to perform the four-tier analysis concerning Article 14, which was discussed in Chapter 4. It accepted the premise that same-sex couples were just as capable as different-sex couples of entering into stable committed relationships. Therefore, they were to be considered in a similar situation to a different-sex couple as regards their need for legal recognition and protection of their relationship.[16] However, the Court did not continue the four-tier analysis. It did not evaluate whether the different concessions of rights pursued a legitimate aim or whether there was a relationship of proportionality between the means employed and the aim pursued. The Court limited itself to finding that there was not yet a majority of states providing for legal recognition of same-sex couples. Hence, states enjoyed a margin of appreciation in the timing of the introduction of legislation granting rights to same-sex couples.[17] Furthermore, the Court held that when states chose to provide same-sex couples with an alternative means of recognition, they were not obliged to confer a status on them which corresponds to marriage in each and every respect. Accordingly, the Court granted states a certain margin of discretion as to the rights conferred by alternative means of recognition.[18] In conclusion, the Court found no violation of the prohibition of discrimination taken in conjunction with the right to respect for family life.[19]

Only three judges, Judges Rozakis, Spielmann and Jebens, partially dissented from the majority ruling and held that there had been a violation of the Convention, given the unjustified difference in treatment of the applicants regarding the respect of their right to family life. They emphasised that the majority judgment considered that the applicants were in a similar situation to that of different-sex couples, and recognised that differences based on sexual orientation required

[14] ibid para 91.
[15] ibid para 94.
[16] ibid para 99.
[17] ibid para 105.
[18] ibid paras 108–9.
[19] ibid para 110.

serious reasons by way of justification. Therefore, they affirmed that the Court should have requested the state to provide cogent reasons for the difference in treatment.[20] They stated that, since the state did not offer any argument to justify the absence of similar rights for same-sex couples, the Court should have found a violation of Article 8 in conjunction with Article 14.[21]

There were two main problems with the approach adopted by the Court in the *Schalk and Kopf* case. On the one hand, the majority judgment was a clear example of the Court exercising its own discretion to decide the scope of the margin of appreciation left to states to protect the right to respect for family life. As pointed out by the dissenting judges, the Court rhetorically highlighted that differences based on sexual orientation required heavy reasons by way of justification, but then it demanded no reasons at all from the state for justifying its detrimental treatment. On the other hand, the exclusion of same-sex couples from the right conferred by Article 12 is certainly controversial. The denial of a human right based on the sexuality of individuals means that the particular right is conceived as a heterosexual right and, consequently, non-heterosexual individuals are rhetorically constructed as not 'human enough' to enjoy it. In fact, through the decision in *Schalk and Kopf*, the Court confirmed the heterosexuality of the subject protected by the European Convention on Human Rights.[22] Following this ruling, only heterosexual individuals can be seen as true subjects of human rights, since only they are allowed to enjoy all human rights.[23]

A. A (Homosexual-Friendly) Alternative to Marriage

To repeat, in the *Schalk and Kopf* judgment, the Court affirmed that, according to its established case law, the notion of family under the Convention was not confined to marriage-based relationships and could encompass other family ties where the parties are living together out of wedlock.[24] For the first time, the Court considered that it was artificial to maintain the view that same-sex couples could not enjoy 'family life'.[25] Thus, outsiders from the traditional family order, such

[20] ibid, joint dissenting opinion of Judges Rozakis, Spielmann and Jebens, para 8.

[21] ibid, joint dissenting opinion of Judges Rozakis, Spielmann and Jebens, paras 9–10.

[22] Damian A Gonzalez-Salzberg, 'The Making of the Court's Homosexual: A Queer Reading of the European Court of Human Rights' Case Law on Same-Sex Sexuality' (2014) 65 *Northern Ireland Legal Quarterly* 371, at 386.

[23] There is the argument that LGBT individuals have not been truly deprived of the right to marry, since everyone can still marry heterosexually. However, that argument (besides homophobic) is certainly flawed. The absurdity of the argument can be seen by an analogy with the enjoyment of another right. For instance, it would be similar to suggesting that a domestic law that prohibits criticising the government would be compatible with freedom of expression, since it still allows everyone to praise the government.

[24] *Schalk and Kopf v Austria* (n 8) para 91.

[25] ibid para 94. This was reiterated by the Court in *PB and JS v Austria*, Application no 18984/02, 22 July 2010, para 30.

as LGBT families, managed to be accepted within the Court's idea of family.[26] Notwithstanding the widening scope of the notion of the family, the Court continued to sustain a restricted and privileged view of marriage.

The Court's refusal to find States Parties under the obligation to allow for same-sex marriage led to a developing jurisprudence on alternative means of legal recognition for same-sex couples, which culminated with the Court finding States Parties under an actual obligation to provide the option of registered partnerships, when same-sex marriage was not made available by domestic laws. The first timid step of the Court on this matter took place in 2013, when it decided *Vallianatos and others v Greece*. On that occasion, the Court examined Greek domestic legislation that introduced a new form of registered partnerships that offered legal recognition to couples that did not desire to enter into marriage. However, this new type of partnerships was only available to different-sex couples, which meant that, in Greece, same-sex couples could have access to neither marriage nor civil partnerships. The Court found this specific legislation to be discriminatory against same-sex couples.[27] Nonetheless, it emphasised that there was no consensus among States Parties as to the need to introduce forms of legal recognition of same-sex relationships. That is to say, states were not considered to be under the obligation to provide for the domestic regulation of same-sex partnerships, but if (and only if) they decided to introduce legislation concerning civil partnerships, these institutions could not be limited to different-sex couples.[28]

A qualitative leap in this area took place two years later with the Court's ruling on *Oliari and others v Italy*. In this case the Court had to examine whether the European Convention on Human Rights actually imposed upon the state a positive obligation to provide for some form of legal recognition for same-sex couples, as claimed by the applicants: three Italian same-sex couples. The Court asserted that, in the absence of same-sex marriage, same-sex couples had a particular interest in the existence of some form of registered partnership within the domestic law, as this would allow them access to the legal recognition and protection of their relationships.[29] It considered that the state failed to show the existence of any public interest that could justify depriving same-sex couples of the mentioned protection and recognition and, consequently, it found Italy under the positive obligation to implement a legal framework that would allow for the registration of same-sex couples.[30]

[26] As mentioned in Chapter 4, the Court had already taken a first incipient step in that direction when deciding *X, Y and Z v United Kingdom*, which will be discussed in section IV.A.

[27] *Vallianatos and others v Greece* (GC), Application nos 29381/09 and 32684/09, 7 November 2013, para 92.

[28] ibid para 91.

[29] *Oliari and others v Italy*, Application nos 18766/11 and 36030/11, 21 July 2015, para 174.

[30] ibid para 185–87. Three concurring judges expressed their view that the findings in the case were to be seen as only applicable to the particular circumstances existing in Italy at the time, and not as establishing a general positive obligation upon states to provide for means of legal recognition for same-sex couples. However, the further development of the Court's case law, as discussed below,

At the same time, the Court affirmed that states were under no obligation to allow for same-sex marriage and that they enjoyed a certain margin of appreciation in regards to the rights conferred by the alternative means of recognition that should be provided to same-sex couples.[31] The same conclusion was reiterated by the Court almost a year later, when it ruled in *Chapin and Charpentier v France*. In that case, a same-sex couple had actually been married by a local mayor, but their marriage was subsequently declared void by the domestic courts.[32] They claimed that the lack of access to marriage and the more restricted set of rights provided by French civil partnerships (PACS), when compared to marriage, amounted to different breaches of the Convention. Notwithstanding the rejection of the claim, the Court seemed to hint at a possible jurisprudential change in the future, as it ruled that it saw no reasons to modify its understanding of the scope of states' obligations under Article 12 of the Convention (right to marry) 'given the brief period of time elapsed' since it decided this matter in other cases.[33]

This topic was revisited by the Court at the end of 2017 in *Orlandi and others v Italy*. This time the applicants were six same-sex couples who had married abroad and claimed that Italy's refusal to register their contracted marriages, as either marriage or registered partnerships, amounted to a violation of the right to marry and of the right to respect for their family life under the Convention. By the time the Court issued its judgment, the state had already amended its legislation, introducing into domestic law the institution of civil unions, which allowed for the registration of same-sex partnerships (including the registration of marriages contracted abroad as such). The Court took that legislative change into consideration and decided that a violation of the applicants' rights could be found, but only up until the moment in which the new legislation entered into force.[34] Hence, the Court confirmed that the state was under the positive obligation to provide legal recognition and protection of same-sex couples.[35] Furthermore, the Court seemed to hint strongly at a potential change of its current stance on same-sex marriage under the Convention. The judgment reads:

> The Court reiterates that States are *still* free, under Article 12 of the Convention as well as under Article 14 taken in conjunction with Article 8, to restrict access to marriage to different-sex couples.[36]

Therefore, at the end of 2017, the Court's position (still) remains that states are free to both ban and permit same-sex marriage under the Convention. Nevertheless,

together with the growing European consensus on the matter allows casting aside any uncertainties raised by such an opinion. See *Oliari and others v Italy* (n 29), concurring opinion of Judge Mahoney joined by Judges Tsotsoria and Vehabović.

[31] ibid paras 177 and 194.

[32] *Chapin and Charpentier v France*, Application no 40183/07, 9 June 2016, paras 13–20.

[33] ibid para 39. Own translation from the French original.

[34] *Orlandi and others v Italy*, Application nos 26431/12; 26742/12; 44057/12 and 60088/12, 14 December 2017, para 196.

[35] ibid paras 209–11.

[36] ibid para 192 (emphasis added).

the Court seemed adamant in finding a violation of the Convention if states that do not allow for same-sex marriage do not provide an alternative form of registration for same-sex couples.

The Court has also affirmed that states are free to restrict access to this alternative type of recognition to same-sex couples. In *Ratzenböck and Seydl v Austria*, the Court examined a claim brought by a different-sex couple alleging discrimination in the enjoyment of their right to respect for family life, as they were refused access to the institution of registered partnerships, the alternative form of legal recognition for same-sex couples established in Austria. The Court rejected the applicants' claim, ruling that this differential treatment did not amount to discrimination under the Convention. It reached such a decision reasoning that different-sex couples had access to marriage, as a means for obtaining legal recognition of their relationship, and considering that the applicants could not claim to have been affected by any difference in law that might exist between those institutions.[37]

However, two judges disagreed with the majority and issued a dissenting opinion. Judges Tsotsoria and Grozev affirmed that different-sex couples and same-sex couples should be considered to be in relevantly similar situations, which placed on the state the burden of justifying the differential treatment implemented.[38] According to the dissenting judges, 'any justification not rooted in hundreds of years of history and tradition … inevitably runs the risk of sliding into stereotypes about the "different" nature of a heterosexual and a homosexual relationship'.[39] This rather cryptic statement that concluded the dissent seemed to suggest that only longstanding traditions, such as restricting access to marriage to different-sex couples, could justify a differential treatment between different-sex and same-sex couples. In other words, while marriage could be maintained exclusively heterosexual, registered partnerships should be open to both same-sex and different-sex couples.[40]

To summarise, based on the conviction that states are free to decide whether to allow for same-sex marriage or not, the Court has developed an obligation upon states to, at least, provide for alternative means of recognition for same-sex couples. However, the Court has avoided establishing the scope of the rights that should come along with such alternative recognition. In fact, reiterating a formula adopted in *Schalk and Kopf*, the Court has usually refused to examine the difference in terms of the rights provided by marriage and by the types of

[37] *Ratzenböck and Seydl v Austria*, Application no. 28475/12, 26 October 2017, paras 41–42.

[38] ibid, joint dissenting opinion of Judges Tsotsoria and Grozev.

[39] ibid, joint dissenting opinion of Judges Tsotsoria and Grozev, 18.

[40] Furthermore, the dissenting judges affirmed that 'different-sex couples and same-sex couples are not groups of individuals which have been created by regulatory choices', but that their existence was independent of such regulation. This understanding of the sexuality of individuals as free from 'regulatory choices', coupled with their reference to the 'nature' of heterosexual and homosexual relationships, came to reinforce the ideas discussed in Chapter 3 concerning the Court's approach to sexuality. In particular, the conception of individuals' sexuality as innate, predisposed and immutable, which ignores the role played by the law (including the Court's case law) in the construction and re-construction of individuals' notions of their own sexuality.

registered partnerships adopted for same-sex couples by each state.[41] Therefore, the institution of marriage can still be used to privilege heterosexuality. However, the following section makes use of queer's deconstructive approach to interrogate how the heterosexuality of marriage has been constructed (and re-constructed) through the case law. My claim is that the privileged and heterosexual institution of marriage might not have always been as *straight* as it is assumed to be.

III. Heterosexual(ising) Marriage's History

The *Schalk and Kopf* judgment is considered to be the first occasion in which the Court affirmed the heterosexuality of marriage.[42] Nevertheless, the Court had already analysed the right to marry of LGBT individuals in the early jurisprudence on transsexuality: *Rees*, *Cossey*, *B v France*,[43] and *Sheffield and Horsham*, which were discussed in Chapter 2. In this early case law, the Court refused to find that prohibiting transsexual individuals from marrying persons of the opposite sex to that attained through gender transition was a violation of the right to marry. In the *Rees* case, it held that the right to marry referred to traditional marriage between persons of 'opposite biological sex'.[44] For the Court, this appeared to be confirmed by the wording of the article which seems mainly concerned with protecting marriage as the basis of the family.[45] The Court asserted that Article 12 establishes that the exercise of the right to marry should be subject to the national laws of the states, but that the limitations thereby introduced must not restrict or reduce the right in such a way or to such an extent that the very essence of the right is impaired.[46] Nonetheless, the Court determined that the legal impediment on the marriage of persons who were not of the opposite biological sex could not be said to have an effect of this kind.[47] The Court revisited the issue of marriage and transsexuality in the *Cossey* and *Sheffield and Horsham* cases, reaching the same conclusion.[48] The Court was not open to taking a different approach to the one adopted in *Rees*; hence, it confirmed its 'attachment to the traditional concept of marriage'.[49]

[41] *Schalk and Kopf v Austria* (n 8) para 109; *Chapin and Charpentier v France* (n 32) para 51; *Orlandi and others v Italy* (n 34) para 195.

[42] *Schalk and Kopf v Austria* (n 8) para 50.

[43] In this specific case the Court did not rule on Art 12, but many judges addressed the topic of transsexual individuals and their right to marry in their own separate opinions. *B v France*, Series A no 232-C, 25 March 1992, dissenting opinion of Judge Pinheiro Farinha, dissenting opinion of Judge Pettiti, and concurring opinion of Judge Walsh.

[44] *Rees v United Kingdom*, Series A no 106, 17 October 1986, para 49.

[45] ibid.

[46] ibid para 50.

[47] ibid.

[48] *Cossey v United Kingdom*, Series A no 184, 27 September 1990; *Sheffield and Horsham v United Kingdom*, Reports of Judgments and Decisions 1998-V, 30 July 1998.

[49] *Cossey v United Kingdom* (n 48) para 46; *Sheffield and Horsham v United Kingdom* (n 48) para 67.

In fact, in *B v France*, the judgments of three dissenting judges showed that their opposition to recognising the applicant's gender was based on their conviction in the heterosexuality of marriage.[50] According to Judge Pettiti, a consequence of the rectification of the birth certificate of the applicant would be the lack of legal obstacles for Miss B to marry and even adopt children. The consequences would be monumental: '[t]he whole civil law and inheritance law could be thrown into confusion'.[51] That is to say, the heterosexuality of marriage was the basis of Judge Pettiti's refusal to recognise Miss B's acquired gender, since her potential marriage could derange the whole legal system. What is also worth highlighting is the fragility of the civil law, implicitly assumed in the judgment, if the marriage of a transsexual woman was capable of causing such chaos.

For Judge Valticos, joined by Judge Loizou, the strict heterosexuality of marriage was also a fundamental reason for opposing the recognition of Miss B's gender: 'half-feminised men claiming the right to marry normally constituted men, and then where would the line have to be drawn?'[52] Their opinion was a clear expression of marriage as a heterosexually exclusive institution. As discussed in Chapter 4, the heterosexual matrix imposes two opposed genders as a requirement for marriage and this was not fulfilled by the applicant, who was a 'half-feminised' man and, apparently, wanted to marry a 'normally constituted' man. However, given the anxiety to avoid a violation of the matrix, the dissenting opinion failed to explain what a 'half-feminised man' and a 'normally constituted' man were, and how to recognise them to avoid this potential problem in future cases. In fact, it remains a mystery how Judge Valticos knew that Miss B wanted to marry one of these 'normally constituted men', since there is no description in the judgment of the person she wanted to marry but for the fact that his gender was registered as male. Moreover, a further question remained unanswered by Judge Valticos' ruling. He did not explain who belonged to the opposite gender to that of Miss B, which would have allowed her to marry without infringing the heterosexuality of marriage. Certainly, it was not a 'normally constituted' man. Would it have been another 'half-feminised' man, or should it have been a 'half-masculinised' woman, or was she plainly unable to marry? Whichever the case, it is evident that the early case law on transsexuality highlighted the Court's belief in strict heterosexuality as a requirement for marriage.

A. Has Marriage Always been Heterosexual?

The concern about the heterosexual character of marriage drove the Court to a particular scenario over the consequences of denying the marriage claims of

[50] It is worth mentioning again that the Court found a violation of Art 8 in the case, but it did not impose upon France the obligation to fully recognise Miss B's gender or her right to marry a man. *B v France* (n 43).

[51] ibid, dissenting opinion of Judge Pettiti, 35.

[52] ibid, dissenting opinion of Judge Valticos, joined by Judge Loizou, 37.

transsexual applicants. It is interesting to note a peculiar assertion made in the *Cossey* case, in an attempt to refute Miss Cossey's argument that she was actually forbidden from marrying, as the domestic legislation did not allow her to marry a man. The Court stated that the right to marry had not been impaired, since there was no legal impediment to Miss Cossey marrying a woman.[53] This assertion was made by the Court in order to justify the view that prohibiting a transsexual person from marrying a person of the same sex to that assigned to them at birth was not truly an absolute denial of the right to marry, since transsexual people could still legally marry individuals of their unrecognised gender. Nevertheless, while the Court was refusing the right of heterosexual transsexuals to marry, it was unintentionally confirming its support for the right to marry of gay and lesbian transsexuals. Arguably, it was the Court's strong conviction of the heterosexuality of transsexual individuals which made it believe that forbidding the right to (heterosexually) marry according to their acquired gender would stop transsexual weddings. What the Court did not consider was that the assumed heterosexuality of transsexual people is only part of a medical discourse (as discussed in Chapter 2) and does not have a basis in reality.[54] In any case, the Court confirmed with its ruling in *Cossey* that lesbian and gay transsexuals had the right to marry.

In 2002, in *Goodwin* and *I*, the Court reviewed the right to marry of transsexual individuals. The Court observed that Article 12 secures the fundamental right of a man and woman to marry and to found a family. Nonetheless, it affirmed that founding a family was not a condition of the right to marry, and the inability of any couple to conceive a child cannot be regarded as per se removing their right to enjoy the first part of the provision.[55] The Court stated that even though it was true that the first sentence of Article 12 refers in explicit terms to the right of a man and woman to marry, it should not be assumed that those terms impose a determination of gender by purely biological criteria.[56] Therefore, the Court concluded that post-operative transsexual individuals had been deprived of the right to marry as they had been unable to marry a person of their opposite (acquired) sex.[57]

While the rulings in *Goodwin* and *I* were positive for the applicants, who lived as heterosexual women and wanted to marry heterosexual men, the consequence has been the loss of the right to marry under the Convention for gay and lesbian transsexuals. With these judgments, the Court normalised the gender of transsexual individuals and also their sexuality. From 2002 onwards, only heterosexual transsexual people have acquired the right to marry, while transsexual individuals who desire to marry someone of their same gender have lost the right.

[53] *Cossey v United Kingdom* (n 48) para 45.

[54] Dylan Vade, 'Expanding Gender and Expanding the Law: Toward a Social and Legal Conceptualization of Gender that is More Inclusive of Transgender People' (2005) 11 *Michigan Journal of Gender and Law* 253, at 270.

[55] *Christine Goodwin v United Kingdom* (GC), Application no 28957/95, ECHR 2002-VI, para 98; *I v United Kingdom* (GC), Application no 25680/94, 11 July 2002, para 78.

[56] *Goodwin v United Kingdom* (n 55) para 100; *I v United Kingdom* (n 55) para 80.

[57] *Goodwin v United Kingdom* (n 55) para 101; *I v United Kingdom* (n 55) para 81.

The loss of the right to marry for gay and lesbian transsexual people was confirmed in *L v Lithuania* in a passing paragraph. The applicant in that case was considered by the Court to be a pre-operative transsexual person, and he claimed the right to have his male gender recognised and the right to marry his female partner. However, the Court held that his complaint regarding the right to marry was premature, subordinating the applicant's claim to 'finishing' his gender transition. The Court stated that: 'should he complete full gender-reassignment surgery, his status as a man would be recognised together with the right to marry a woman'.[58] Consequently, only as a heterosexual transsexual person, as recognised by the Court, would he acquire the right to marry a woman.

This amended case law was consistent with the heterosexual matrix. Allowing heterosexual transsexual individuals to get married is a lesser threat to the matrix than continuing to validate the right to marry of gay and lesbian transsexuals, as expressly accepted by the Court in the *Cossey* ruling. In fact, it is possible to argue that the Court believed that heterosexual transsexuals pose no real threat to the heterosexual matrix. Transsexual individuals who have undergone gender transition and demand due recognition of their gender still exist within the strict gender binary.[59] Arguably, a straight transsexual person shows a perfect coherence between their gender and their sexual desire, even greater consistency than a straight cissexual person, since there has been an important element of will and sacrifice in order to achieve heterosexuality for straight transsexuals.

To summarise, within its case law regarding marriage and transsexuality the Court has struggled to confirm the heterosexuality of marriage. However, the driving principle of all these cases has been the dogmatic view that marriage has to be heterosexual. This idea was certainly present when the Court (inadvertently) authorised the marriage of sexually diverse transsexual people in *Cossey*, based on the assumption that it would not happen in reality. Furthermore, the belief in the heterosexuality of marriage was the reason why the Court amended its case law in 2002, authorising only heterosexual transsexual individuals to marry. One of the most extreme dogmatic statements of the heterosexuality of marriage made its appearance in the *Parry* case, as discussed below.

B. A Literal Understanding of Heterosexuality

In the *Parry* case, the applicants, Wena and Anita Parry, were a married couple. The first applicant had undergone a gender affirming process, having been recognised as a woman in certain legal aspects (she was granted a change of name),

[58] *L v Lithuania*, Application no 27527/03, ECHR 2007-IV, para 64.

[59] Surya Monro, 'Transgender: Destabilising Feminisms?' in Vanessa E Munro and Carl F Stychin (eds), *Sexuality and the Law: Feminist Engagements* (Routledge, 2007) 123–48, at 127; Aeyal Gross, 'Gender Outlaws Before the Law: The Courts of the Borderland' (2009) 32 *Harvard Journal of Law and Gender* 165, at 220 and 228.

and was regarded as a woman in all private and public relationships, including by her wife. Both applicants described their relationship as a 'loving and married couple'.[60] However, the first applicant was unable to obtain full legal recognition of her gender unless the couple had their marriage annulled or dissolved, as the legislation did not allow for same-sex marriage. Since both applicants wanted to remain legally married, the first applicant could not have her gender fully recognised. The applicants complained that the domestic legislation imposed an unjustified interference with numerous Convention rights, in particular, their right to respect for private and family life and their right to marry. On the one hand, the first applicant was unable to obtain legal recognition of her gender unless she terminated her marriage to the second applicant; and, on the other, the state required their marriage to be dissolved before recognising the attained gender of the first applicant.

The Court acknowledged that the legislation clearly put the applicants in a quandary; the first applicant had to sacrifice either her gender or their marriage. There was a direct and invasive effect on the applicants' enjoyment of their right to respect for their private and family life. The Court noted that the requirement that the applicants annul their marriage was based on the lack of recognition of same-sex marriage in domestic legislation, but it stated that the applicants could continue their relationship through a civil partnership, which carried the same legal rights and obligations. Therefore, regarding the right to respect for private and family life, the Court affirmed that the effects of the domestic regulation had not been shown to be disproportionate and a fair balance had been struck in the circumstances. Moreover, the Court held that the Convention enshrines the traditional concept of marriage as being between a man and a woman and that same-sex marriage did not flow from an interpretation of the right to marry as laid down by the States Parties in the Convention in 1950. It concluded that the matter of how to regulate the effects of the change of gender in the context of marriage fell within the margin of appreciation of the State Party. The state could not be required to make allowances for the small number of marriages where both partners wished to continue married, notwithstanding the change in gender of one of them. Consequently, the Court rejected the applicants' claim, finding their case to be inadmissible.[61]

It truly requires a strong desire to believe in the heterosexuality of marriage, to consider that the marriage between a cissexual woman and a transsexual woman, who had undergone gender transition and only lacked the recognition of her gender in certain legal aspects, was indeed a heterosexual marriage. In particular, in the case of the applicants, the decision whether to remain married or to divorce became the basis of Wena's sexuality. According to the Court, Mrs Parry needed to choose between being a married heterosexual man or

[60] *Parry v United Kingdom* (Dec), Application no 42971/05, ECHR 2006-XV, 2.
[61] ibid 14.

a divorced homosexual woman. The Court offered the applicants two complex options that position Mrs Parry on either side of three interlinked identity binaries: married/divorced, heterosexual/homosexual, man/woman. All these statuses came together into two mutually exclusive concatenations: either married-heterosexual-man or divorced-homosexual-woman, and the choice between the two depended on a legal document, namely, the one recognising the end of their marriage.

For the Court, the sexual orientation of the applicants, a legal category for protection against discrimination, was going to change as soon as they put an end to their marriage. In other words, any marital sexual practice that the Court considered to be heterosexual was to become homosexual the moment they obtained a legal certificate. Consequently, the Court was protecting only the (legal) fiction of heterosexuality within marriage, an idea completely divorced from the materiality of sexual conduct, and only based on the literality of a label given to it by a legal document. Indeed, the ideology of the heterosexual character of marriage was used *ad absurdum* to justify denying formal recognition to Mrs Parry's gender. A dogmatic conviction that marriage could not be anything but heterosexual was built upon the legal ban on same-sex marriage and became the foundation for understanding the applicants' marriage as heterosexual. In the eyes of the Court, marriage was more important than genitalia for determining heterosexuality.

C. Confirming the Illusion of Heterosexual Marriage

In 2014, the Court rendered its final judgment in *Hämäläinen v Finland*,[62] a case very similar to *Parry*. Ms Hämäläinen was a transsexual woman who was married to another woman, with whom she had a daughter. In 2006, Ms Hämäläinen underwent gender transition and she was able to legally change her name, but the domestic authorities did not allow her to amend her identity number, which continued to identify her as a man. The refusal to modify her identity number was based on the domestic ban on same-sex marriage. In Finland, only different-sex couples had access to marriage, while same-sex couples could only register their relationships in a civil partnership.[63] As a consequence, the legislation regulating the recognition of gender transition established the requirement to be single. In case of an existent marriage or partnership, the consent of the spouse/partner was required, in order to transform a marriage into a partnership and a partnership into a marriage depending upon whether the gender transition made the couple

[62] I have discussed the *Hämäläinen v Finland* case further elsewhere. See Damian A Gonzalez-Salzberg, 'Confirming (The Illusion of) Heterosexual Marriage: *Hämäläinen v Finland*' (2015) 2 *Journal of International and Comparative Law* 173.

[63] After the Court's ruling, the Finnish Parliament has passed a same-sex marriage law. See International Lesbian, Gay, Bisexual, Trans and Intersex Association (ILGA), *State-Sponsored Homophobia: A World Survey of Sexual Orientation Laws: Criminalisation, Protection and Recognition*, 12th edn (May 2017), available at https://ilga.org/state-sponsored-homophobia-report (accessed 1 June 2018).

same-sex or different-sex. As in the *Parry* case, the applicant could not achieve the full recognition of her gender unless she put an end to her marriage.

The case was originally decided by a Section Chamber of the Court, which judged that there had been no violation of the applicant's rights, leading her to request a referral to the Grand Chamber. Before the Grand Chamber, Ms Hämäläinen attempted to differentiate her case from that of a same-sex marriage. She stated that her complaint was not aimed at extending marriage rights to same-sex couples, but only to preserve her pre-existing marriage.[64] She also affirmed that her gender transition did not necessarily transform the couple into a homosexual couple, since her wife 'continued to be heterosexual'.[65] However, the majority ruling rejected her arguments, stating that if the applicant's claim was to be accepted, it 'would in practice lead to a situation in which two persons of the same sex could be married to each other'.[66] The Court recalled that, since 2002, its case law had established that states are under the positive obligation to legally recognise the gender transition undergone by transsexual individuals,[67] but that they were not obliged by the Convention to allow same-sex marriage.[68]

The Court ruled against the applicant, focusing on the fact that the domestic legislation allowed Ms Hämäläinen to obtain full recognition of her gender, as long as her marriage was transformed into a registered partnership. It stated that the difference between marriage and registered partnerships concerned the establishment of paternity, joint adoption, and the regulation of the family name, and considered that those differences would not affect the family life between the applicant, her wife, and their daughter. Ms Hämäläinen's relationship with her wife could continue, and the paternity of her daughter would not suffer any changes. Consequently, the majority judgment found the requirement to transform her marriage into a partnership, in order to obtain recognition of her gender, to be respectful of the applicant's rights under the Convention. The Court also examined the complaint under the prohibition of discriminatory treatment, since the lack of full recognition of her gender forced her to reveal that she was transsexual in diverse circumstances. However, the Court again refused to find a violation, concluding that her situation was not 'sufficiently similar' to that of cissexual individuals.[69]

Judges Sajó, Keller and Lemmens issued a joint dissenting opinion, in which they declared a violation of Ms Hämäläinen's rights. According to them, when an important aspect of an individual's identity is at stake, states should only be given a narrow margin of appreciation for deciding whether a fair balance between

[64] *Hämäläinen v Finland* (GC), Application no 37359/09, 16 July 2014, para 41.
[65] ibid para 44.
[66] ibid para 70.
[67] ibid para 68.
[68] ibid para 71.
[69] ibid para 112.

conflicting interests has been achieved. In the particular case, they found that the state had exceeded this margin when trying to strike a balance between, on the one hand, the applicant's rights to have her gender recognised and to preserve her marriage; and, on the other, the state interest in preserving the heterosexuality of marriage.[70]

In addition, the dissenting judges accepted the applicant's argument that she and her wife did not constitute a same-sex couple. They stated that Ms Hämäläinen (and her wife) had been victims of discrimination, because the domestic authorities failed to differentiate between their situation and that of same-sex couples, by not introducing an exception to the prohibition of same-sex marriage for cases such as theirs. According to these judges, the applicant and her wife had been discriminated against by being treated as a same-sex couple. They affirmed that: 'Even after the applicant's gender reassignment, it is an oversimplification of the situation to treat her relationship as a homosexual one'.[71] Indeed, at several points, the dissenting judges highlighted the heterosexuality of the applicant's wife. They emphasised that: 'the applicant's spouse continues to identify as heterosexual'[72] and they stressed the deep commitment to marriage of the applicant and 'her heterosexual spouse'.[73]

In conclusion, after the *Hämäläinen* case, the Court has widened even further the scope of heterosexual marriage. First, the majority confirmed the decision adopted in *Parry*. Heterosexuality did not necessarily depend on sexuality and genitalia, but could be based on the official label granted to it by legal documents, such as a birth or divorce certificate, or an identity number. Moreover, for the dissenting judges, even those documents were irrelevant. According to them, Ms Hämäläinen's marriage to her wife was heterosexual while the law only partially recognised her as a transsexual woman, and it would continue to be heterosexual if she were to obtain full recognition of her gender. On this view, heterosexuality was not only detached from sexuality and genitalia, but also from the legal recognition of gender. The heterosexuality of the couple was only evidenced by the fact that they were married.[74] The level of dogmatism acquired by the heterosexuality of marriage seemed to have placed the issue beyond any possible challenge.

[70] ibid, joint dissenting opinion of Judges Sajó, Keller and Lemmens, paras 12–14.
[71] ibid, joint dissenting opinion of Judges Sajó, Keller and Lemmens, para 20.
[72] ibid, joint dissenting opinion of Judges Sajó, Keller and Lemmens, para 6.
[73] ibid, joint dissenting opinion of Judges Sajó, Keller and Lemmens, para 8.
[74] When I challenge the understanding given by the Court and the dissenting judges to the heterosexuality of the marriage between Ms Hämäläinen and her wife, it is not my intention to affirm that Ms Hämäläinen's wife should not be considered to be heterosexual, if that is how she identifies herself. As anybody else, she should be completely free to self-identify sexually in any way she feels best reflects her identity. However, I disagree with how the dissenting vote made use of her sexuality, in order to defend the heterosexuality of the institution of marriage. Challenging the validity of the restriction on the exercise of the human right to marry, based on the sexual identities of individuals, would have been a much better path to actually protect the sexual identity of Ms Hämäläinen, her wife, and any other individual who is not allowed to exercise a right based on their sexual identity. As to the importance of

D. The Dogmatic Heterosexuality of Marriage

To recap, the Court's case law (so far) continues to allow states to keep marriage a heterosexual and privileged institution. Marriage can be used as a materialisation of the heterosexual matrix, ensuring that individuals who enter and remain within the institution are opposed and binary gendered (one man and one woman) and heterosexual. Nevertheless, the heterosexuality of marriage within the Court's case law seems to have become a dogmatic issue. According to the Court, marriage was heterosexual when the Court refused the claim of Mr Schalk and Mr Kopf that the ban on same-sex marriage violated their rights.[75] Marriage was also heterosexual when the Court validated Miss Cossey's right to marry someone of her acquired gender, while refusing her right to marry a person of her 'opposite' sex.[76] Nonetheless, marriage remained heterosexual when the *Cossey* ruling was overturned and the Court affirmed Christine Goodwin's right to marry a person of the opposite sex to that acquired after gender transition.

Moreover, marriage continued to be heterosexual when the Court declared inadmissible Mrs Parry's claim to have her gender recognised while remaining married to her wife, validating the heterosexuality of her marriage after gender transition as long as her birth certificate remained unchanged. The Court confirmed this understanding in the *Hämäläinen* case, reaffirming the heterosexuality of the marriage between a transsexual and a cissexual woman, as long as the identity number of the first one remained that of a male. In addition, in a dissenting opinion, a group of judges affirmed that even if Ms Hämäläinen's gender became fully recognised and her marriage officially turned into a marriage between two women, it would still be heterosexual.[77]

In brief, the heterosexuality of marriage has acquired many different manifestations within the Court's case law. There are instances in which the heterosexuality of marriage seems to even become tautological. Marriage remains heterosexual because it has to be heterosexual, and this heterosexuality of marriage cannot be affected by any changes in the gender or sexuality of the spouses. In this way, the Court has continued to validate states' ban on same-sex marriage, safeguarding the heterosexually exclusive character of marriage. However, while the legal exclusion preserved might be real, the prohibition of same-sex marriage seems to have become a (legal) fiction.

research in the area of the partners of trans individuals, see Carey Jean Sojka, 'Partners of Transgender People' in Steven Seidman, Nancy Fischer and Chet Meeks (eds), *Introducing the New Sexuality Studies*, 2nd edn (Routledge, 2011) 236–41.

[75] *Schalk and Kopf v Austria* (n 8).

[76] *Cossey v United Kingdom* (n 48).

[77] In fact, the dissenting judges found discriminatory that the applicant's marriage was treated as if it were a same-sex marriage. *Hämäläinen v Finland* (n 64), joint dissenting opinion of Judges Sajó, Keller and Lemmens, para 20.

E. The Immutable Character of Marriage

In a concurring opinion in *B v France*, Judge Walsh affirmed:

> [M]arriage referred to in Article 12 of the Convention is confined to the intermarriage of two persons one of whom is biologically of the female sex, thus reflecting what has been *universally accepted throughout human history*.[78]

Nevertheless, Judge Walsh was mistaken. Marriage is not a universal truth, as there is no definition of marriage that has been universally held throughout history. The Court itself seems to have accepted that marriage changes, when in the *Goodwin* case it recognised that: 'There have been major social changes in the institution of marriage since the adoption of the Convention'.[79]

Similar to Judge Walsh, in a recent dissenting opinion Judges Pejchal and Wojtyczek affirmed that extending the right to marry under the Convention to same-sex couples was 'conceptually impossible', as this would not only affect the 'denotation' but also substantially change the 'connotation' of the term marriage.[80] They asserted that: 'Marriage in its initial meaning presupposes the community of lives between a man and a woman'.[81] They actually resorted to Roman law to show how: 'The complementariness of the biological sexes of the two spouses is a constitutive element of marriage'.[82] However, what the dissent failed to explain is why Roman law should be considered an adequate tool for treaty interpretation. Even if we assume, for the sake of argument, that Roman law was to be thought as providing appropriate guidance for interpreting current international treaties, it would still remain unclear why they decided to rescue from such legal regime the need for gender binarism, but seemingly forgot other requirements for marriage also established by Roman law, such as the age of consent of 12 years old for girls or the restrictions concerning class and status.[83]

The final argument proposed by Judges Pejchal and Wojtyczek to deny the possibility of same-sex marriage under the Convention was that marriage is by (their) definition: 'a social institution open to procreation'.[84] And even the 'fact that certain married couples may suffer from infertility does not affect its social function'.[85] Thus, according to Judges Pejchal and Wojtyczek, marriage requires being open to procreation, which then leads to restricting the institution to heterosexual couples. However, there are rather obvious objections to their argument. The first one is that the definition of marriage as 'open to procreation'

[78] *B v France* (n 43), concurring opinion of Judge Walsh, para 4 (emphasis added).
[79] *Goodwin v United Kingdom* (n 55) para 100.
[80] *Orlandi and others v Italy* (n 34), dissenting opinion of Judges Pejchal and Wojtyczek, para 6.
[81] ibid, dissenting opinion of Judges Pejchal and Wojtyczek, para 6.
[82] ibid, dissenting opinion of Judges Pejchal and Wojtyczek, para 6.
[83] Judith Evans Grubbs, *Women and the Law in the Roman Empire: A Sourcebook on Marriage, Divorce and Widowhood* (Routledge, 2002) 88, 142–50, and 166; Andrew Riggsby, *Roman Law and the Legal World of the Romans* (Cambridge University Press, 2010) 174–75.
[84] *Orlandi and others v Italy* (n 34), dissenting opinion of Judges Pejchal and Wojtyczek, para 6.
[85] ibid, dissenting opinion of Judges Pejchal and Wojtyczek, para 6.

but inclusive of non-procreative couples, provides scarce support for excluding other non-procreative couples. In addition to this, it can certainly not justify the exclusion of procreative lesbian couples. Therefore, if (some) non-procreative couples cannot be excluded from marriage, but some procreative ones can, this conception of marriage as an institution that requires being 'open to procreation' seems to have little to do with procreation itself and to reflect a much bigger concern about heterosexuality. That is to say, procreation appears as an excuse on which these judges attempted to justify a heteronormative view on marriage they desire to read in the Convention.

It should be acknowledged that marriage is a social construction that differs in time and space. The meaning of marriage and the requirements to enter into a valid marriage are certainly not universal.[86] The rules governing the institution of marriage are not the same in different jurisdictions and have even changed within any given jurisdiction through time. Indeed, the idea of marriage out of romance and decided by the partners is a recent one. Foucault highlighted in the first volume of the *History of Sexuality* that the institution of marriage responded to different rules in pre-Modern times, where the deployment of alliance was the foundation for marriage.[87] There is an abundance of evidence to support that marriage is not a monolithic institution. To mention only some: the introduction of divorce as a general rule for ending a marriage (as an alternative to death); the extension of the institution to allow for same-sex couples;[88] as well as the subsistence of polygamous marriage in different latitudes (although mainly a patriarchal manifestation).[89] Marriage is not the universal truth proclaimed by Judge Walsh, nor the Roman institution desired by Judges Pejchal and Wojtyczek; it is a social construction that has changed though time and, therefore, can certainly be re-signified in the future.

The heterosexually exclusive conception of marriage has been widely criticised by human rights scholars, such as Robert Wintemute and Paul Johnson. Wintemute has persuasively argued that denying same-sex couples access to marriage is a clear case of prohibited discrimination.[90] Johnson has proposed that the European Court of

[86] Martha Albertson Fineman, 'Why Marriage?' (2002) 9 *Virginia Journal of Social Policy and the Law* 239, at 245 and 247; Gayle Rubin, *Deviations: A Gayle Rubin Reader* (Duke University Press, 2011) 197; Nicola Barker, *Not the Marrying Kind: A Feminist Critique of Same-Sex Marriage* (Palgrave Macmillan, 2013) 21 and 38.

[87] Michel Foucault, *The History of Sexuality: An Introduction* (Penguin, 1978) 106. Warner also highlighted the change in the primary function of marriage between modern and pre-modern societies. See Michael Warner, 'Normal and Normaller: Beyond Gay Marriage' (1999) 5 *GLQ: A Journal of Lesbian and Gay Studies* 119, at 145.

[88] To name but a few, this is the case of the Netherlands, Belgium, Spain, Argentina, Uruguay, and the United Kingdom. For a full list of states that allow for same-sex marriage, see ILGA, 'State-Sponsored Homophobia' (n 63).

[89] In fact, the Court seems to have understood that the regulation of polygamy, as it exists in certain states, entails gender discrimination. See *Refah Partisi (the Welfare Party) and others v Turkey* (GC), Application nos 41340/98, 41342/98, 41343/98 and 41344/98, ECHR 2003-II, para 128.

[90] Robert Wintemute, 'Strasbourg to the Rescue? Same-Sex Partners and Parents' in Robert Wintemute and Mads Andenæs (eds), *Legal Recognition of Same-Sex Partnerships: A Study of National, European and International Law* (Hart Publishing, 2001) 713–29, at 728; Robert Wintemute, 'From

Human Rights needs to rethink its position against same-sex marriage by critically assessing the heteronormative assumptions underpinning its understanding of marriage, instead of hiding behind the argument that same-sex marriage is a controversial topic on which no consensus has been reached.[91]

Of course, making use of human rights to claim access to marriage for same-sex couples seems like the iconic example of homonormative strategies. However, even some queer theorists, including Judith Butler herself, have supported the idea that marriage should not be restricted to different-sex couples. In her own words:

> No doubt, marriage and same-sex domestic partnerships should certainly be available as options, but to install either as a model for sexual legitimacy is precisely to constrain the sociality of the body in acceptable ways.[92]

That is to say, marriage should not be kept as the paradigmatic example for sexual legitimacy, but as long as the institution exists, it should be an option open to same-sex couples. My position is that so long as the right to marry continues to be recognised as a human right, access to the institution of marriage should not be denied based on gender or sexuality. This stance can be supported from a human rights perspective and it is not irreconcilable with queer theory. Even Warner, who famously explained *The Trouble with Normal*, acknowledged this point in the context of same-sex marriage:

> It is possible, at least in theory, to imagine a politics in which sex-neutral marriage is seen as a step toward the more fundamental goals of sexual justice: not just formal equality before the law, based on a procedural bar on discrimination, but a substantive justice that would target sexual domination, making possible a democratic cultivation of alternative sexualities.[93]

In fact, marriage could be a site for re-inventing the meaning of domesticity and sexuality. What was discussed in Chapter 4 concerning identity categories can also be applied to institutions: it is possible to ask for access to an institution, while at the same time opening it as a site for contestation.[94] At the end, it would be up to those who opt into marriage to give it its meaning and significance.

Even the European Court of Human Rights can play a role in unsettling the heteronormativity character of marriage, if it decides to abandon the conflation of marriage and heterosexuality. Opening marriage to same-sex couples could be but a first step towards a more queer institution. Nonetheless, the Court has not

"Sex Rights" to "Love Rights": Partnership Rights as Human Rights' in Nicholas Bamforth (ed), *Sex Rights: The Oxford Amnesty Lectures 2002* (Oxford University Press, 2005) 186–224, at 211.

[91] Paul Johnson, 'Challenging the Heteronormativity of Marriage: The Role of Judicial Interpretation and Authority' (2011) 20 *Social and Legal Studies* 349, at 359–62; Paul Johnson, *Homosexuality and the European Court of Human Rights* (Routledge, 2012) 161–62.

[92] Judith Butler, 'On Being Beside Oneself: On the Limits of Sexual Autonomy' in Nicholas Bamforth (ed), *Sex Rights: The Oxford Amnesty Lectures 2002* (Oxford University Press, 2005) 48–78, at 59–60.

[93] Warner, *The Trouble with Normal* (n 3) 90.

[94] See Judith Butler, *Bodies that Matter: On the Discursive Limits of Sex* (Routledge, 1993) 222. See also Carl F Stychin, *Law's Desire: Sexuality and the Limits of Justice* (Routledge, 1995) 155–56.

yet reached this stage. Up to now, same-sex marriage is only an option that states are free to either grant or deny. Thus, marriage can be made to remain as exclusionary and privileged as claimed by Warner.[95] In fact, the Court went so far as to re-define heterosexuality, in order to avoid issuing a judgment stating that the right to marry should be granted free from discrimination based on gender and sexuality. However, as discussed in section II, the time for conceiving marriage as a heterosexually exclusive institution under the Convention is coming to an end, irrespective of the number of Roman law sources salvaged by opposing judges.[96]

IV. LGBT Parenthood

As mentioned in the Introduction to the chapter, together with access to legal recognition for relationships, parenting rights are one the most current claims brought to Strasbourg by LGBT families. This section will analyse five cases in which the Court dealt with parenting rights of LGBT individuals. The first concerned artificial insemination and a transsexual father, while the other four were about adoption by gays and lesbians. The first two cases on adoption dealt with single-parent adoption, while the other two concerned second-parent adoption.[97] Many of the cases demonstrate how the *best interests of the child* test has been deployed to oppose LGBT parenthood. This confrontation between the child's best interests and LGBT parents drew on the idea of LGBT individuals as dangerous and particularly harmful for children.[98] Therefore, before analysing the specific cases, I will briefly discuss both the law's construction of LGBT people as harmful, as well as the content of the best interests of the child principle.

Western law has traditionally constructed the homosexual individual as dangerous and potentially harmful. Wayne Morgan, amongst other scholars, explained how the law has been one of the multiple discourses that demonises sexual

[95] ibid 82.

[96] In addition to the hints in this direction provided by the Court in *Chapin and Charpentier v France* and *Orlandi and others v Italy*, which were discussed in section II.A above, Judges Spano and Bianku expressed their disagreement with the Court's current position concerning the margin of appreciation granted to states when it comes to same-sex marriage, indicating that they considered themselves only bound to such opinion on the basis of the principle of *stare decisis*. *Taddeucci and McCall v Italy*, Application no 51362/09, 30 June 2016, concurring opinion of Judge Spano, joined by Judge Bianku, para 1.

[97] For a brief summary of the Court's case law on adoption by gays and lesbians, see Francesco Crisafulli, 'Same-Sex Couples' Rights (Other than the Right to Marry) Before the ECtHR' in Daniele Gallo, Luca Paladini and Pietro Pustorini (eds), *Same-Sex Couples before National, Supranational and International Jurisdictions* (Springer, 2013) 409–36, at 425–35.

[98] See Judith Butler, *Undoing Gender* (Routledge, 2004) 14; Cheshire Calhoun, *Feminism, the Family, and the Politics of the Closet: Lesbian and Gay Displacement* (Oxford University Press, 2000) 104–5, 122, and 160; Stephen Whittle, 'Sex: Has It Any Place in Modern Marriage' in Robert Wintemute and Mads Andenæs (eds), *Legal Recognition of Same-Sex Partnerships: A Study of National, European and International Law* (Hart Publishing, 2001) 693–712, at 708; Peter Dunne, '"Recognizing Identities, Denying Families": Conditions for the Legal Recognition of Gender Identity in Europe' in Carlo Casonato and Alexander Schuster (eds), *Rights on the Move: Rainbow Families in Europe* (Conference Proceedings, Trento, October 2014) 295–309, at 298.

diversity, presenting the homosexual as a threat to society and especially harmful to the most vulnerable elements of society, such as children.[99] The European Court of Human Rights has mostly avoided making explicit references to the allegedly dangerous character of LGBT individuals, but there are certain notorious exceptions. The earliest appearance of the dangerous homosexual within the Court's case law took place in the *Dudgeon* case. In his dissenting opinion, Judge Matscher presented the homosexual individual as a potential paedophile, claiming that it was well known that relations with minors were a 'widespread tendency in homosexual circles'.[100]

However, probably the most evident depiction of the dangerous homosexual appeared in the case law as recently as 2017, demonstrating that these ideas can still be found within the Court's jurisprudence. Judge Dedov elaborated a strong dissent to the Court's judgment in *Bayev and others v Russia*, which was discussed in Chapter 3. On that occasion, the Court ruled that Russia's legislative ban on the promotion of homosexuality and non-traditional sexual relations among minors not only reinforced stigma and prejudice, encouraging homophobia, but also amounted to a breach of the Convention.[101] Nevertheless, Judge Dedov disagreed with the ruling, which he considered had failed to 'seriously take into account the fact that the private life of children is more important than the freedom of expression of homosexuals'.[102] The representation of the homosexual as a sexually abusive paedophile plagued Judge Dedov's opinion, which counts the terms 'paedophile' and 'abuse' (or related terms) nineteen times. According to the dissent, raising awareness of non-traditional sexualities makes children more vulnerable to sexual abuse. He affirmed that:

> Children may easily become interested in any information or ideas, *especially in homosexual relations*, without understanding their nature. *The idea that same-sex sexual relations are normal indeed creates a situation where they are ready to engage in such relations, just because of the curiosity which is an integral part of a child's mind.*[103]

The irresistible character of homosexuality, denounced decades before by Judge Walsh in *Dudgeon*, reappeared in Judge Dedov's depiction. Children were represented as 'ready to engage' in homosexuality, just because it is presented as normal.

He conceded that his stance on freedom of expression and non-traditional sexuality would be different, if it were not for the problem of paedophilia. Without disclosing any sources, Judge Dedov stated that every year up to 50,000 children in Russia are victims of sexual abuse. He asserted the reliability of such data

[99] Wayne Morgan, 'Queer Law: Identity, Culture, Diversity, Law' (1995) 5 *Australasian Gay and Lesbian Law Journal* 1, at 9–10 and 23.

[100] *Dudgeon v United Kingdom*, Series A no 45, 22 October 1981, dissenting opinion of Judge Matscher, 30.

[101] *Bayev and others v Russia*, Application nos 67667/09, 44092/12 and 56717/12, 20 June 2007.

[102] ibid, dissenting opinion of Judge Dedov, 44.

[103] ibid, dissenting opinion of Judge Dedov, 40 (emphasis added).

based on the fact that a report elaborated in 1994 and focusing on the United States affirmed that almost 150,000 children suffered yearly from such a crime.[104] Following the referenced study, he explained that all perpetrators were men and that the victims were 70 per cent girls and 30 per cent boys. That is to say, the vast majority of paedophiles victimised children of the opposite sex. Half of the cases, he revealed, were instances of family abuse. Based on such data, his conclusion was that 'same-sex violence constitutes a significant part of such cases, so that it deserves to be taken into consideration by making a special reference to same-sex relations in the law'.[105] In other words, given that the majority of the crimes seemed to be committed by male family members against girls, paedophilia was a topic that deserved a lengthy discussion within a judgment dealing with the fundamentally different question of homosexuality and freedom of expression in the public sphere. Some may argue that Judge Dedov's interpretation of the data could reveal a certain degree of discomfort with homosexuality.

The homosexual paedophile is not the only LGBT threat that has appeared in the Court's case law. Transsexual individuals have been presented by certain judges as mischievous and deceitful, a portrayal that can also be found in several domestic jurisdictions.[106] In *B v France*, one of the reasons given by Judges Morenilla and Walsh to oppose the amendment of the applicant's birth certificate was the protection of the rights of those who the transsexual applicant might try to deceive by keeping secret the sex originally stated on her birth certificate.[107] According to Judge Walsh:

> It could be very unfortunate if the law permitted a situation in which a person wishing to marry a person of the other biological sex could not, when a doubt arises, be satisfied as to the true biological sex of the other party save by the admission of that other party.[108]

Paraphrasing, the 'truth' of the sex of transsexual individuals needed to be kept registered by the state in order to protect the potential victims of the deceitful transsexual.

While those were clear examples of the abusive homosexual and the lying transsexual, the harmful character of LGBT individuals continued to resonate in the judgments dealing with LGBT parenthood. In these cases, the gender and the sexuality of the applicants have been used as characteristics that conflicted with the

[104] This is not the only source used by the Judge. He also referred to a 1986 report and a 1998 journal article. Ibid, dissenting opinion of Judge Dedov, 41 and 43.

[105] ibid, dissenting opinion of Judge Dedov, 41.

[106] See Vade, 'Expanding Gender and Expanding the Law' (n 54) 287–88; Emily Grabham, 'Governing Permanence: Trans Subjects, Time, and the Gender Recognition Act' (2010) 19 *Social and Legal Studies* 107, at 109; Alex Sharpe, 'Transgender Marriage and the Legal Obligation to Disclose Gender History' (2012) 75 *Modern Law Review* 33, at 35; Alex Sharpe, 'The Ethicality of the Demand for (Trans)parency in Sexual Relations' (2017) 43 *Australian Feminist Law Journal* 161, at 163–64.

[107] *B v France* (n 43), dissenting opinion of Judge Morenilla, para 2.1 and concurring opinion of Judge Walsh, para 5.

[108] ibid, concurring opinion of Judge Walsh, para 5.

best interests of the child. The principle of the best interests of the child was originally developed in the twentieth century as a gender-neutral legal construction for the judicial determination of child custody.[109] The standard was later adopted by the almost universally ratified Convention on the Rights of the Child,[110] and turned into a general principle for all issues concerning children's rights.[111] This Convention states that:

> In all actions concerning children, whether undertaken by public or private social welfare institutions, courts of law, administrative authorities or legislative bodies, the best interests of the child shall be a primary consideration.[112]

Since the best interests principle became a rule applicable in every legal aspect, and given the fact that the Convention is practically universal, this principle has become a general standard within human rights law, and the case law of the European Court of Human Rights has been no exception.

Notwithstanding the (almost) universal acceptance of this rule, it is important to highlight the vagueness and indeterminate character of the principle.[113] There is neither a general definition of what is, in every situation, the best interests of the child nor clear criteria as to how the best interests should be established. This has allowed the principle to be used for reinforcing heteronormative family models.[114] In fact, in its early case law concerning LGBT parenthood, the Court resorted to the best interests of the child in order to question the parenting rights of the applicants. However, in its later jurisprudence, the focus of the Court shifted from the best interests of the child to the marital status of the parents, as I will discuss below.

A. Transsexuals' Parenting Rights

The first case on LGBT parenthood decided by the Court concerned a state's refusal to recognise a transsexual man as the father of a child. The applicants in the case were a couple, X (a transsexual man) and Y (a cissexual woman), and Z, their first

[109] Helen Chang, 'My Father is a Woman, Oh No! The Failure of the Courts to Uphold Individual Substantive Due Process Rights for Transgender Parents under the Guise of the Best Interest of the Child' (2003) 43 *Santa Clara Law Review* 649, at 656.

[110] Convention on the Rights of the Child (adopted 20 November 1989, entered into force 2 September 1990) 1577 UNTS 3. This Convention has been ratified by all United Nations Member States, with the sole exception of the United States of America, available at https://treaties.un.org/Pages/ViewDetails.aspx?src=TREATY&mtdsg_no=IV-11&chapter=4&lang=en (accessed 1 June 2018).

[111] Philip Alston, 'The Best Interests Principle: Towards a Reconciliation of Culture and Human Rights' (1994) 8 *International Journal of Law and the Family* 1, at 1.

[112] Convention on the Rights of the Child, Art 3.1.

[113] Stephen Parker, 'The Best Interests of the Child: Principles and Problems' (1994) 8 *International Journal of Law and the Family* 26, at 26.

[114] Katherine Arnup and Susan Boyd, 'Familial Disputes? Sperm Donors, Lesbians Mothers and Legal Parenthood' in Carl F Stychin and Didi Herman, *Legal Inversions: Lesbians, Gay Men and the Politics of the Law* (Temple University Press, 1995) 77–101, at 87; Nadine Gartner, 'Lesbian (M)Otherhood: Creating an Alternative Model for Settling Child Custody Disputes' (2007) 16 *Law and Sexuality* 45, at 48.

born child, who had been conceived through artificial insemination. The applicants complained that the lack of legal recognition of the relationship between X and Z entailed a violation of the right to respect for their family life. The Court, by a majority of 14 to 6, acknowledged that the relationship between the applicants amounted to family life,[115] but it held that the state was under no obligation to grant legal recognition to the relationship between X and Z.[116] Only the dissenting judges concluded that there was a violation of the applicants' right to respect for family life, and even discriminatory treatment, since a cissexual man in X's position would have faced no legal inconvenience in being recognised as Z's father.[117]

The majority of the Court stated that the community as a whole had an interest in maintaining a coherent system of family law which places the *best interests of the child* at the forefront.[118] In particular, it stated that it was not clear that an amendment to the law that would allow the recognition of X, a transsexual man, as the father of Z, his child conceived through artificial insemination, would necessarily be to the advantage of the child.[119] In support of this statement, the Court argued that such a reform could be criticised as inconsistent, since the transsexual man would still be treated as a woman in other legal aspects.[120] The Court also affirmed that it was uncertain how the best interests of a child in Z's position could be protected and that it was impossible to predict the extent to which the absence of a legal connection between X and Z would affect the latter's development.[121] However, it seems ironic that the Court expressed its concern about 'consistency' in a case decided a few years after *Cossey* and a year before *Sheffield and Horsham*, in which the Court accepted that transsexual individuals could be treated as men for certain legal purposes and as women for some others.

The concurring opinions rendered by Judge Pettiti and Judge De Meyer made even more explicit the non-familial character attributed to transsexual individuals. Judge Pettiti stated that: 'Studies have shown that not all transsexuals have the same aptitude for family life (after an authorised operation) as a non-transsexual'.[122] However, this statement, and the conclusions drawn from it, are problematic. First, Judge Pettiti seemed to imply that all 'non-transsexuals', which he compared to transsexual individuals, have a similar aptitude for family life, a generalisation lacking any supporting evidence. Secondly, the studies quoted by the Judge (one of them written by the Judge himself)[123] do not seem to provide scientific grounds

[115] *X, Y and Z v United Kingdom*, Reports of Judgments and Decisions 1997-II, 22 April 1997, para 37.
[116] ibid para 52.
[117] ibid, partly dissenting opinion of Judge Casadevall, joined by Judges Russo and Makarczyk, dissenting opinion of Judge Thór Vilhjálmsson, dissenting opinion of Judge Foighel, and dissenting opinion of Judge Gotchev.
[118] ibid para 47.
[119] ibid.
[120] ibid.
[121] ibid para 51.
[122] ibid, concurring opinion of Judge Pettiti, 17.
[123] Louis-Edmond Pettiti, *Les Transsexuels* (Presses Universitaires de France, 1992).

for affirming that transsexuals might not be as adept as cissexuals at family life. Lastly, even if the referred studies were scientifically solid, and some transsexual people were indeed not as suited to be parents as some cissexuals, the Judge at no point found that Mr X was one of the allegedly familially unsuited individuals. In brief, Judge Pettiti's rejection of the applicant's claim to be recognised as the father of his child seemed to be based on reasons other than scientific studies.

Similar to Judge Pettiti, the opinion of Judge De Meyer strongly rejected the applicants' claim. It consisted of only a few paragraphs, in which he affirmed that X did not enjoy family life with either his partner or his child, but only the 'appearance' of family ties. He then went on to express: 'Indeed, it is self-evident that a person who is manifestly not the father of a child has no right to be recognised as her father'.[124] However, it was certainly not self-evident that a person who was raising a child and who was referred to as 'father' by the child is indeed not the father. Judge De Meyer might have been alluding to the fact that X was not genetically linked to his child, but that is to be expected in any case of artificial insemination by donor or, for that matter, in any case of adoption. Would Judge De Meyer have referred to such fathers as 'manifestly' not the father as well? It might be the case that the 'manifest' lack of father-child link between X and Z highlighted by the Judge was merely covering his personal opinion of transsexual individuals as non-familial people.

In conclusion, in the *X, Y and Z* case, the Court made use of the best interests principle to cast doubts on whether it would be best for a child to have a legal bond with her father, who lived with her and who was raising her. The only basis for the Court's doubts was that her father was transsexual, as the question would have never been raised if X was a cissexual man. That is to say, the best interests standard was used by the Court to reinforce the idea that LGBT individuals are potentially harmful and children should be protected from them.

B. (LGBT) Individual Adoption

The topic of adoption by LGBT individuals has been analysed by the Court in a small number of cases. The Court has highlighted that there are three types of adoption, which raise different kinds of concerns: individual adoption, second-parent adoption and joint adoption.[125] By the end of 2017, the Court had decided cases concerning individual adoption by LGBT people (*Fretté* and *EB*) and also cases regarding second-parent adoption by LGBT couples (*Gas and Dubois* and *X and others*). It has not yet issued a judgment regarding joint adoption by LGBT couples, but it has rendered *obiter dictum* a clear opinion on the matter. In the

[124] *X, Y and Z v United Kingdom* (n 115), concurring opinion of Judge De Meyer, 19.
[125] *X and others v Austria* (GC), Application no 19010/07, 19 February 2013, para 100.

Alekseyev ruling, it affirmed that joint adoption by same-sex couples was a topic that lacked European consensus. Consequently, the Court seemed to have anticipated its position on the topic, granting states a wide margin of appreciation to legislate on the issue.[126]

Regarding LGBT individual adoption, the Court first ruled on the topic in the *Fretté* case in 2002, but this opinion was later overruled in the *EB* case in 2008.[127] The *Fretté* case concerned the refusal of an individual's application for authorisation to adopt as a single parent, which the applicant claimed was based on his sexual orientation and was, therefore, discriminatory. The Court analysed the case under the prohibition of discrimination, following the four-tier system discussed in Chapter 4. The first step was for the Court to decide whether Article 14 of the Convention was applicable, which required the facts of the case to fall 'within the ambit' of a Convention right. This does not require the actual violation of a human right, but it does require the factual basis of the case to be covered by the scope of a Convention right. In the particular case of adoption, the Court noted that the Convention does not guarantee a right to adopt. Nevertheless, the judgment stated that the facts of the case fell within the ambit of the right to respect for private and family life.[128]

After having established that the case passed the 'within the ambit' test, the Court should have proceeded to the second step, the 'analogous situation' analysis. However, no express reference was made concerning how similar or dissimilar the situation of the applicant was to that of a heterosexual applicant. The Court continued with step three, concerning whether there was a legitimate aim pursued in the rejection of the application (the 'legitimate aim' test). In the Court's view, there was no doubt that the decision to reject the application for authorisation to adopt pursued a legitimate aim, namely, to protect the health and rights of children who could be involved in an adoption procedure.[129]

What then remained to be decided was whether there existed a justification for the difference in treatment. The reasoning of the Court in this last step (the 'proportionality' test), which led it to grant the state a wide margin of appreciation, was peculiar. It first held that sexual orientation was a concept undoubtedly covered by the prohibition on discrimination. Nonetheless, the Court ignored its previous case law, which stated that issues dealing with sexual orientation required very

[126] *Alekseyev v Russia*, Application nos 4916/07, 25924/08 and 14599/09, 21 October 2010, para 83.

[127] In *X and others*, the Court recognised that the *EB* judgment had indeed overruled its previous *Fretté* decision. *X and others v Austria* (n 125) para 103.

[128] *Fretté v France*, Application no 36515/97, ECHR 2002-I, paras 31–32. It was actually the dissenting judges who provided a more in-depth justification as to why the right to adopt fell within the broad right to respect for family life. Conversely, the concurring judges actually disagreed with the applicability of Art 14, considering the facts of the case to fall outside the ambit of the Convention. See *Fretté v France*, joint partly dissenting opinion of Judges Nicolas Bratza, Fuhrmann and Tulkens, and partly concurring opinion of Judge Costa joined by Judges Jungwiert and Traja.

[129] ibid para 38.

weighty reasons by way of justification.[130] Instead, it opted to widen the margin of appreciation of the state by affirming that single parent adoption by homosexual individuals was a topic lacking consensus within European states.[131] In order to justify the claim that there was no consensus on the topic, the Court seemingly examined the legislation of the states of the Council of Europe, concluding that:

> Although most of the Contracting States do not expressly prohibit homosexuals from adopting where single persons may adopt, it is not possible to find in the legal and social orders of the Contracting States uniform principles on these social issues on which opinions within a democratic society may reasonably differ widely.[132]

That is to say, the Court seemed to have checked the domestic legislation, observed that most states did not prohibit adoptions by homosexual individuals, but still concluded that there was little common ground amongst European states. It used this curious finding to conclude that, given the lack of consensus, the state should enjoy a wide margin of appreciation to regulate the issue.[133]

The Court then proceeded to evaluate whether the authorities remained within this margin when denying the authorisation to adopt. It offered a rationale for adoption: 'providing a child with a family, not a family with a child',[134] and highlighted the importance of the best interests of the child principle. In order to analyse the best interests standard, the Court affirmed:

> It must be observed that the scientific community – particularly experts on childhood, psychiatrists and psychologists – is divided over the possible consequences of a child being adopted by one or more homosexual parents, especially bearing in mind the limited number of scientific studies conducted on the subject to date.[135]

In the same paragraph, the Court also stated: 'In addition, there are wide differences in national and international opinion, not to mention the fact that there are not enough children to adopt to satisfy demand'.[136]

Therefore, the Court resorted to unspecified scientific research in order to question the ability of a homosexual parent to raise a child.[137] In other words, even

[130] *Salgueiro da Silva Mouta v Portugal*, Application no 33290/96, ECHR 1999-IX, para 36; *Smith and Grady v United Kingdom*, Application nos 33985/96 and 33986/96, ECHR 1999-VI, para 105; *Lustig-Prean and Beckett v United Kingdom*, Application nos 31417/96 and 32377/96, September 1999, para 98.

[131] *Fretté v France* (n 128) paras 40–41.

[132] ibid para 41.

[133] ibid.

[134] ibid para 42.

[135] ibid.

[136] ibid.

[137] It is worth highlighting that studies on gay and lesbian parenting have found no significant difference between children raised by heterosexual parents and those raised by gays and lesbians. Nonetheless, as affirmed by Currah and Zanghellini, even positive comparative studies can be seen as problematic, since are often also grounded in different heteronormative assumptions. See Ellen C Perrin and others, 'Technical Report: Coparent or Second-Parent Adoption by Same-Sex Parents' (2002) 109 *Pediatrics* 341; Jenni Millbank, 'From Here to Maternity: A Review of the Research on Lesbian and Gay Families' (2003) 38 *Australian Journal of Social Issues* 541; James G Pawelski and others, 'The Effects of Marriage,

though it did not have any evidence of the dangerous character of 'homosexual parents', it used this lack of evidence to raise suspicions about the potentially dangerous homosexual. Consequently, it curiously inverted the burden of proof: since science seemed to be uncertain, it was up to the potentially dangerous homosexual to prove his harmless character.[138] Thus, the potential harmful character of homosexuality was used against the applicant, who needed to prove his innocence. Moreover, the added comment concerning the lack of enough children to satisfy demand seems to contradict the Court's own reasoning. If the problem with allowing adoption by homosexual parents was their (unproven) dangerousness, why would the number of adoptable children be relevant? In this way, the Court constructed the assumed dangerous character of the homosexual as a characteristic dependent on the increase in the offer of adoptable children or the decrease on adoption demand. That is to say, the harmful/harmless character of homosexuality varied according to the law of supply and demand.

To summarise, the Court found that it was in the best interests of children to allow the national authorities the ability to refuse homosexual individuals' right to adopt. This conclusion was based on the inconclusive scientific evidence that could not disprove the presumption of the harmful character attached to LGBT individuals.[139] As happened in the *X, Y and Z* case, the Court constructed a confrontation between the best interests principle and an allegedly dangerous character of LGBT parents. The Court then used this constructed struggle to justify the decision of the domestic authorities as a measure protected by the broad margin of appreciation left to the state.[140]

Conversely, the dissenting judges, Judges Bratza, Fuhrmann and Tulkens, found that the refusal of the authorisation to adopt suffered by the applicant was discriminatory. These judges held that the refusal of the authorisation was because of the applicant's sexuality, based on the view that to be brought up by gay or lesbian parents was harmful to a child.[141] They concluded that, since the decision was solely based on sexual orientation and no very weighty reasons were offered by way of justification, it amounted to discrimination according to the Court's own case law.[142] This conclusion was to be later adopted by the Court, when it revisited the topic in the *EB* case.

Civil Union, and Domestic Partnership Laws on the Health and Well-Being of Children' (2006) 118 *Pediatrics* 349; Paisley Currah, 'Defending Genders: Sex and Gender Non-Conformity in the Civil Rights Strategies of Sexual Minorities' (1997) 48 *Hastings Law Journal* 1363, at 1380 and 1385; Aleardo Zanghellini, 'Scientific Positivism and the Controversy over Research into Lesbian and Gay Parenting' (2007) 4 *Sexuality Research and Social Policy* 100, at 100 and 109.

[138] On the contrary, the Court has been adamant that the burden of proof rests upon the state which aims at justifying a difference in treatment. See *EB v France* (GC), Application no 43546/02, 22 January 2008, para 74; *X and others v Austria* (n 125) para 141.

[139] *Fretté v France* (n 128) paras 42–43.

[140] ibid para 42.

[141] ibid, joint partly dissenting opinion of Judges Nicolas Bratza, Fuhrmann and Tulkens.

[142] ibid, joint partly dissenting opinion of Judges Nicolas Bratza, Fuhrmann and Tulkens.

C. Revisiting the Dangerous Homosexual Parent

Six years after the decision in *Fretté*, the Court overturned this ruling.[143] It decided the *EB* case and held that a restriction on the right to adopt based on the sexuality of the applicant was indeed discriminatory treatment.[144] The facts were similar to *Fretté*. A single woman was refused authorisation to adopt based on two grounds: the lack of a paternal reference in her household and the indifference of the applicant's partner towards the adoption. Nonetheless, according to the Court, the sexuality of the applicant was a determining factor that featured overall in the decision of the domestic authorities. Consequently, the Court framed the case as it did in *Fretté*, stating that what needed to be decided was whether a refusal of the right to adopt based on the sexuality of the applicant amounted to discriminatory treatment.

This time, the Court affirmed that when sexual orientation was at stake there is a need for particularly convincing and weighty reasons to justify a difference in treatment.[145] Moreover, contrary to the reasoning in *Fretté*, the Court held that the burden of proof rested on the state.[146] In order to decide the case, the Court did not resort to the margin of appreciation of the state. Rather, it stated that if the reasons advanced for a difference in treatment were based solely on considerations regarding sexual orientation, that would amount to discrimination under the Convention.[147] The Court concluded that the domestic authorities' decision had been based on the applicant's sexual orientation, which was not acceptable under the Convention.[148]

On this occasion, the Court did not resort to the best interests standard in order to portray an incompatibility between the dangerous sexuality of a prospective parent and the wellbeing of a child. In fact, reference to this principle in the majority judgment was very limited. The ruling merely highlighted that the national authorities, when evaluating the application for adoption, considered that the applicant displayed personal qualities that would be in the prospective child's best interest.[149] By contrast, the only judge who showed a negative view regarding the possibility of adoption by gays and lesbians, Judge Loucaides, did make wide use of the best interests principle to support his position. He argued that in order to decide what was in the best interests of the child, the domestic authorities

[143] As acknowledged by the Court itself in the *X and others* judgment. *X and others v Austria* (n 125) para 93.
[144] *EB v France* (n 138) para 96.
[145] ibid para 91.
[146] ibid para 74.
[147] ibid para 93.
[148] ibid para 96.
[149] ibid para 95.

could take into account the sexual orientation of the applicant and the fact that she cohabited with her same-sex partner. In his own words:

> I believe that the erotic relationship with its inevitable manifestations and the couple's conduct towards each other in the home could legitimately be taken into account as a negative factor in the environment in which the adopted child was expected to live. Indeed there was, in these circumstances, a real risk that the model and image of a family in the context of which the child would have to live and develop his/her personality would be distorted.[150]

In this way, Judge Loucaides presented the sexuality of a lesbian couple as harmful for a child's development. Same-sex couples were portrayed not only as a distorted model of family, highlighting the idea of the non-familial homosexual, but also as a dangerous role model, capable of disrupting the healthy upbringing of children.

Judge Loucaides went on to affirm that homosexuality was actually incompatible with adoptive parenthood. He stated:

> Homosexuals, like anybody else, have a right to be themselves and should not be the target of discrimination or any other adverse treatment because of their sexual orientation. However, they must, like any other persons with some peculiarity, accept that they may not qualify for certain activities which, by their nature and under certain circumstances, are incompatible with their lifestyle or peculiarity.[151]

In sum, Judge Loucaides considered that homosexuality was a 'peculiarity' that clashed with the ability to adopt and raise a child. Therefore, he not only disagreed with a potential right to adopt by these peculiar people, but he also considered that homosexual individuals must accept his personal opinion as fact. It is worth highlighting that it is not easy to find such an explicit position against LGBT family rights within the Court's case law as the one sustained by Judge Loucaides in his judgment. According to him, adoption can only be thought of as belonging to the realm of the heterosexual matrix.

D. A Second Lesbian Mother (Wasn't One Enough?)

As mentioned above, the Court has issued two judgments on the topic of second-parent adoption: *Gas and Dubois v France* and *X and others v Austria*. In the first case, it examined the French prohibition on second-parent adoption for same-sex couples. Two women in a civil partnership (PACS) had a child through assisted reproduction, but only the biological mother was recognised as a parent of the child. While the domestic legislation allowed married couples to share parental responsibility through second-parent adoption, it denied the same right to

[150] ibid, dissenting opinion of Judge Loucaides, 39.
[151] ibid, dissenting opinion of Judge Loucaides, 39.

unmarried couples. Since the applicants were unable to marry under French law, which did not provide for same-sex marriage at the time, they were also prevented from sharing parental responsibility of their child.

The Court analysed the case using its four-tier approach to discrimination. As to the first step, it affirmed that the facts clearly fell 'within the ambit' of the right to respect for family life.[152] Consequently, it continued to the second step, concerning the existence of differential treatment in an 'analogous situation'. It first stated that, for the purpose of second-parent adoption, the applicants' legal situation could not be said to be comparable to that of married couples.[153] On the contrary, the Court held that the applicants' situation was comparable to that of cohabitating different-sex couples, and that these couples would also be unable to share parental responsibility through second-parent adoption.[154] Therefore, it concluded the analysis regarding discrimination in the second step, affirming that the applicants had not been victims of discriminatory treatment.[155]

For the Court, the fact that different-sex couples would be able to share parental responsibility by getting married, a possibility that was prohibited to the applicants, had no relevance.[156] The Court recalled that in the *Schalk and Kopf* case, it held that the Convention did not impose an obligation on states to grant same-sex couples access to marriage and that when a state chooses to provide same-sex couples with an alternative means of recognition, it enjoys a certain margin of appreciation with regard to the exact status conferred.[157] The Court again confirmed the privileged and exclusionary character of marriage, but this time it allowed the validated privileged status to have consequences for individuals other than the unmarried couple. On this occasion, the Court permitted the privileged institution of marriage to impact on the rights of the child of the couple.

In contrast to previous cases on LGBT parenthood, the Court did not construct the best interests of the child as being in conflict with the potentially harmful homosexual parent. The best interests standard was actually absent from the majority ruling. However, echoes of the notion of the dangerous homosexual parent could still be found in the majority's dismissal of the applicants' and the interveners' claims that it was in the child's best interests to have two LGBT parents. Importantly, for the first time, the best interests principle was presented as compatible with the homosexuality of parents in the only dissenting opinion in the judgment. Dissenting Judge Villiger argued that joint parental custody undoubtedly would be in the best interests of the child.[158] He found discriminatory the fact that, in

[152] *Gas and Dubois v France*, Application no 25951/07, ECHR 2012, para 37.
[153] ibid para 68.
[154] ibid para 69.
[155] ibid para 73.
[156] ibid paras 70–71.
[157] ibid para 66.
[158] This position has also been persuasively defended by Loveday Hodson. Loveday Hodson, 'Ties that Bind: Towards a Child-Centred Approach to Lesbian, Gay, Bi-Sexual and Transgender Families under the ECHR' (2012) 20 *International Journal of Children's Rights* 501, at 516 and 520.

France, the children of a heterosexual couple could benefit from joint parental responsibility, if the couple marries, while children of same-sex couples could not. Therefore, he concluded that in this case there was discrimination in respect of the best interests of the child.

This ruling marked the end of the use of the best interests of the child as an argument to object to parenting by LGBT individuals. Nonetheless, the abandonment of the confrontation between the best interests of the child and LGBT parenting rights came hand in hand with the Court's belief in the importance of heterosexual marriage for parenthood. Marriage became the new argument for opposing LGBT parenthood.

E. Confirming the Privileged Character of the Children of Marriage

The topic of second-parent adoption was revisited by the Court in *X and others v Austria*. The legal background of this case was different from *Gas and Dubois*, since the legislation in Austria allowed second-parent adoption for both married and unmarried different-sex couples, while this type of adoption was forbidden to same-sex couples,who were also legally unable to marry. The applicants submitted that it was discriminatory to allow the adoption of one partner's child by the other partner where heterosexual couples, either married or unmarried, were concerned, while prohibiting the adoption of one partner's child by the other partner in the case of same-sex couples.

The Court followed its four-step system for deciding discriminatory treatment, but it divided the analysis into two parts. First, it compared the situation of the applicants with that of a married (different-sex) couple, and then with an unmarried different-sex couple. When comparing the applicants' situation to that of a married couple, the Court made specific reference to its ruling in *Gas and Dubois*, where it had stated that the circumstances of a same-sex couple could not be considered to be similar to that of a married couple.[159] Hence, according to the Court, it was not discriminatory to treat the applicants detrimentally, since they did not pass the 'analogous situation' test.[160]

Nonetheless, the Court found the applicants' situation to be comparable to that of an unmarried cohabitating different-sex couple.[161] It affirmed that there was no doubt that the applicable legislation led to a distinction between unmarried different-sex and same-sex couples in respect of second-parent adoption.[162] That difference was inseparably linked to the fact that the first and third applicants

[159] *X and others v Austria* (n 125) paras 106 and 109.
[160] ibid para 110.
[161] ibid para 112.
[162] ibid para 116.

formed a same-sex couple, and was thus based on their sexual orientation.[163] Therefore, the Court held that the case was distinguishable from *Gas and Dubois*, in which unmarried couples were treated equally regardless of their being same-sex or different-sex couples.[164]

The analysis proceeded to the examination of whether allowing second-parent adoption to unmarried different-sex couples, but refusing that right to same-sex couples, served a legitimate aim and was proportionate to that aim. As to the 'legitimate aim' test, the Court accepted the state's claim that the distinction in treatment was aimed at both protecting the family in the traditional sense and securing the best interests of the child, and it considered these objectives to be legitimate.[165] Consequently, it continued to the fourth step of the discrimination analysis, the 'proportionality test'. The Court stated that when there was a difference in treatment based on sexual orientation, the margin of appreciation left to the state was narrow. It affirmed that, in these cases, the principle of proportionality did not merely require the measure chosen to be suitable for achieving the aim. It must be shown to be necessary, in order to achieve the aim, to exclude certain categories of people from the scope of the provisions at issue.[166] Moreover, applying its own case law, the Court noted that the burden of proof rested upon the state. It was for the state to show that the aims pursued required the exclusion of same-sex couples from second-parent adoption.[167] However, the Court noted that the state did not offer any evidence to suggest that a family with two parents of the same sex could not adequately provide for a child's needs.[168] Therefore, given the failure of the state to adduce weighty and convincing reasons for the differential treatment, the Court found the distinction established by the legislation to be discriminatory.[169] Nonetheless, the Court made it clear that the discriminatory character of the legislation was only due to the fact that unmarried different-sex couples were treated more favourably than same-sex couples, since it did not consider discriminatory the privileged treatment of married couples and, consequently, of their children.[170]

On the one hand, with this judgment the Court seemed to confirm the abandonment of the presumption of dangerousness of the homosexual parent. The judgment did not pit the best interests of the child against the (peculiar) sexuality of their parents. In fact, the Court confirmed that the burden of proof rested on the state, which meant that the homosexual parent was no longer assumed to be dangerous, but it was up to the state to prove that the homosexuality of a parent was a danger for the development of children. Furthermore, the Court affirmed that very weighty reasons were needed for proving this harmful character.

[163] ibid para 130.
[164] ibid para 131.
[165] ibid paras 76 and 138.
[166] ibid para 140.
[167] ibid para 141.
[168] ibid para 142.
[169] ibid para 153.
[170] ibid paras 151 and 153.

On the other hand, the judgment reaffirmed the privileged character given by the Court to marriage. The true reason why homosexual parents were not seen as dangerous in the case was because they were compared to other unmarried parents: to voluntarily unmarried parents. In other words, homosexual parents were presumed to be as dangerous/harmless as heterosexual parents that reject marriage. Nevertheless, when homosexual parents were compared to married heterosexuals, the opinion of the Court was different. The married heterosexual couple was the ideal, allowing states to consider it as a certainly more suitable model for parenthood. With this ruling, the Court confirmed that the privileged character of marriage is not restricted to the area of economic benefits, but it also extends to parenting rights.

The Court's judgment in *Taddeucci and McCall*, discussed in Chapter 4, could have raised expectations as to a significant change in the case law: specifically, as to whether states were no longer allowed to treat differently married heterosexual couples and same-sex couples, when marriage is not open to both. Certainly, dissenting Judge Sicilianos expressed his concern about this.[171] However, as I argued in Chapter 4, this was not the case. Rather, *Taddeucci and McCall* should be read as a sanction against a state that was not providing any form of legal recognition for same-sex couples. The clear consequence flowing from it is that states that do not provide legal means of registration for same-sex couples can be forced by the Court to extend certain marital privileges to different-sex couples, such as residence permits for family reasons. Unfortunately, the criteria adopted in that judgment did not imply the extension of parenting rights to same-sex couples in equal terms to those enjoyed by heterosexual married couples. In fact, as recently as October 2017, the Court has asserted the lack of European consensus when it comes to the parenting rights of the two mothers of a child conceived through assisted insemination.[172] Thus, it ratified that the topic of second-parent adoption by same-sex couples can still be regarded as falling within the margin of appreciation of states.

F. Parenting from beyond the Heterosexual Matrix

The Court has never explicitly stated that being raised by LGBT parents is against the best interests of the child. Only some dissenting judges, such as Judge Pettiti and Judge Loucaides, went as far as arguing that such a conflict existed. Nonetheless, in the first two cases discussed in this section, the Court constructed such a potential confrontation, based on its own fear (in *X, Y and Z*) and on inconclusive scientific research (in *Fretté*), in order to cast doubts upon the ability of LGBT individuals to raise a child. Those decisions were later overruled. The Court clearly

[171] *Taddeucci and McCall v Italy* (n 96), partly dissenting opinion of Judge Sicilianos, para 10.
[172] *D and B v Austria* (Dec), Application no 40597/17, 31 October 2017, para 24.

overturned the *Fretté* judgment with its ruling in *EB*. Regarding *X, Y and Z*, even though the Court has not yet ruled again on the right of transsexual individuals to be recognised as parents,[173] since *Goodwin* and *I*, the case law of the Court on transsexuality is clear regarding the full recognition of the gender of transsexual individuals. My view is that this amended jurisprudence has implicitly overturned *X, Y and Z*, as a person in X's situation should face no restrictions in having his gender and his paternity fully recognised.[174] Moreover, the recent ruling in *AP, Garçon and Nicot v France*, discussed in Chapter 2, showed the Court's willingness to acknowledge the familial character of trans individuals, when it confirmed that sterility cannot be demanded as a requirement for gender recognition.[175]

However, the doubts of the Court as to whether having an LGBT parent could be contrary to the bests interests of the child did not disappear. In *Gas and Dubois*, the Court dismissed the applicants' claim that it was in the best interests of their child to have a legal bond with both lesbian mothers, rather than just with one. In the cases on second-parent adoption, the Court shifted the main focus of attention from the best interests of the child to the institution of marriage. If the sexuality of the parents was less relevant, their marital status became of extreme importance. With the judgments in *Gas and Dubois* and in *X and others*, heterosexual marriage was constructed as an accepted reason for denying LGBT parenthood. The concern about the potential harmful character of LGBT parents was replaced with a new ground for refusing parenting rights: not belonging to the heterosexual institution of marriage. This raises the question as to whether the validation of parenting rights based on marriage is just a new way to allow for restrictions on LGBT parenthood.

V. Conclusion

As discussed in the last two chapters of this book, the Court continues to conceive family rights through the heterosexual matrix. While LGBT families have gained inclusion within the legal understanding of kinship, in the eyes of the Court, the traditional nuclear family remains the ideal social unit. In its recent jurisprudence, the Court has selected marriage as the institution that states are allowed to use in order to privilege the traditional family. That is to say, the Court has

[173] It is worth noting that in *PV v Spain*, what was at stake was not parental recognition, but the contact arrangement after the separation of the couple. *PV v Spain*, Application no 35159/09, 30 November 2010.

[174] By contrast, both Sabatello and Edel hold less optimistic views as to whether the Court's stance on this situation might have changed. See Maya Sabatello, 'Advancing Transgender Family Rights Through Science: A Proposal for an Alternative Framework' (2011) 33 *Human Rights Quarterly* 43, at 59; Frédéric Edel, *Case Law of the European Court of Human Rights Relating to Discrimination on Grounds of Sexual Orientation or Gender Identity* (Council of Europe, 2015) 124.

[175] *AP, Garçon and Nicot v France*, Application nos 79885/12, 52471/13 and 52596/13, 6 April 2017.

validated the use of the institution of marriage to deny the enjoyment of human rights based on the sexuality of individuals, as long as this restriction is formally performed through the preferential treatment of married people. In the Court's current case law, a distinction based on sexuality or gender identity is formally prohibited. However, a distinction based on marital status (which, in turn, can be made dependent on sexuality through the prohibition of same-sex marriage) is perfectly valid.

The Court continues to affirm that those who are married are in a situation that is not analogous to those who are not married and this dissimilar situation allows states to treat married people in a more favourable manner. The Court has validated different economic privileges granted to married people, such as tax exemptions and survivor pensions, and more recently, the prerogatives of marriage confirmed by the Court have included parenting rights. Second-parent adoption became a new accepted privilege for married couples and their children.[176] In other words, within the Court's case law, marriage remains exclusionary (as confirmed in *Schalk and Kopf* and *Parry*), economically favoured (as stated in *Manenc*, *MW* and *Courten*), and also the preferred site for parenting (as established in *Gas and Dubois* and *X and others*). Marriage has become the validated path to grant family rights based on heterosexuality and gender conformity. Personally, I am unsure whether the Court continues to believe in the extreme importance of the institution of marriage, granting privileges (both economic and family ones) to those who enter this institution. Alternatively, by securing the heterosexual character of marriage and the benefits attached to it, the Court may be merely offering states a safe path for privileging heterosexuality. Whichever is the case, heterosexual marriage (or at least the illusion of heterosexual marriage) remains central for the enjoyment of all human rights. The heterosexual matrix, this ideological net that preserves binary genders and heterosexual desire, continues to be in place within the Council of Europe.

Moreover, it is not just marriage and heterosexuality that appear privileged within the Court's case law, but also heteronormative ideals, such as couplehood, stability and domesticity. In 2016, with its judgment in *Taddeucci and McCall*, the Court decided that homosexual couples who are willing but legally banned from registering their couplehood status should actually be treated better than heterosexual couples who reject the opportunity to legally sanction theirs.[177] In fact, the adoption of heteronormative standards is rewarded by the Court. As discussed in section II.A above, the Court has developed an obligation under the Convention for states to make available alternative means of recognition for same-sex couples, even if these do not need to provide couples with identical rights to those enjoyed by married heterosexual couples.

[176] *Mata Estevez v Spain* (n 2); *Courten v United Kingdom* (n 2); *Manenc v France* (Dec), Application no 66686/09, 21 September 2010; *Gas and Dubois v France* (n 152); *X and others v Austria* (n 125).

[177] The applicants in the *Taddeucci and McCall* case actually married in the Netherlands, shortly after leaving Italy. *Taddeucci and McCall v Italy* (n 96) para 25.

As to parenting rights, adoption is still a contentious topic for the Court. Not only has it allowed states to have in place different rules for second-parent adoption for married and unmarried couples, but it has also (implicitly) advanced its position regarding joint adoption by same-sex couples as a topic lacking European consensus.[178] Nevertheless, I believe that it is possible to foresee that clear (even if slow) progress in the fulfilment of LGBT family rights will continue to take place through litigation in Strasbourg. Of course, it is a topic open to debate whether wider access to marriage and parenthood should provide reasons for celebration or for (homonormative) concern. On the one hand, a broader inclusion into familial structures can certainly lead to further reinforcing heteronormative ideals, such as domesticity and *repronormativity*.[179] On the other hand, this can also lead to continue changing the meaning of the institutions of the family, marriage and parenthood.

The present chapter has been centred on the case law of the Court and how the construction of family rights as gendered and sexualised has impacted on the enjoyment of human rights by LGBT individuals. The next chapter will focus on how the Court's jurisprudence can be amended through the use of insights from queer theory. Queer theory will be presented as more than a useful tool for performing a deconstructive analysis of human rights law. It will be used to propose a change of direction in the Court's jurisprudence that can transform our understanding of human rights and the individuals entitled to them.

[178] *Alekseyev v Russia*, Application nos 4916/07, 25924/08 and 14599/09, 21 October 2010, para 83.

[179] The term is used to refer to the normative discourses that present reproduction as an irresistible natural drive. It was discussed in Chapters 1 and 4 as a component of the broad regime of heteronormativity.

6

A Queer(er) Human Rights Jurisprudence

I. Introduction

In the previous five chapters of this book I have made use of queer theory as a methodological tool for deconstructing human rights discourse. This deconstructive analysis started with the sex/gender and sexuality of the applicants that appeared before the European Court of Human Rights in Chapters 2 and 3. I went on to use queer theory to examine the institution of the family under human rights law in Chapter 4 and to explore the two main familial bonds, that of marriage/partnerships and parenthood in Chapter 5. Chapter 6 will be about revisiting some of the cases deconstructed in previous chapters. The method of this chapter will consist of drafting imaginary queer dissents for some key cases brought before the Court. The aim is to show that insights from queer theory can also have a normative purpose and that they could have been used to decide these cases so as to do justice to the needs and interests of LGBT applicants. I will focus on four cases in which the Court has denied the enjoyment of human rights based on the sexual or gender identity of the applicants. Drawing on the construction of the notions of gender and sexuality, as they have been analysed in Chapters 2 and 3, the queer dissenting judgments will illustrate an alternative understanding of the cases.

The re-writing of judgments as a method of critical study of law is becoming more popular and accepted with legal scholars. For instance, in 2012, a group of legal academics published a book in which they critically rewrote different judgments of the European Court of Human Rights making use of diverse theoretical perspectives.[1] Similarly, in 2010, feminist legal scholars undertook the Feminist Judgments Project, in which they rewrote an array of rulings from different courts making use of feminist theories as their common methodological approach. The well-known book *Feminist Judgments* is the main outcome of that endeavour.[2] That project was inspired by a similar venture that took place in Canada in 2006,

[1] Eva Brems (ed), *Diversity and European Human Rights: Rewriting Judgments of the ECHR* (Cambridge University Press, 2013).

[2] Rosemary Hunter, Clare McGlynn and Erika Rackley (eds), *Feminist Judgments: From Theory to Practice* (Hart Publishing, 2010).

the Women's Court of Canada.[3] Also, in 2002, a group of legal scholars wrote different judicial opinions of one of the most important constitutional cases concerning discrimination, the United States Supreme Court decision in *Brown v Board of Education*.[4] The main inspirations for the method I chose for this chapter are the 2010 and 2012 books mentioned above, together with the oldest 'imaginary' judgment I have read, and probably one of the most controversial of them all, the one written by Hannah Arendt in the last pages of the Epilogue of *Eichmann in Jerusalem*.[5] While I do not share the outcome of Arendt's imaginary ruling, I believe that it was her judgment that best illustrates how judicial decisions can be grounded in theoretical insights from beyond the traditional legal world.

The method selected for this chapter offers many advantages. One of them is that it shows that queer theory is not only a tool for critique. Rather, queer theory can also be used prescriptively.[6] Another advantage of this method is that it demonstrates that human rights law can benefit from an engagement with queer theory. In particular, I propose that insights from queer theory can be reclaimed by human rights law in order to further develop the enjoyment of human rights by LGBT individuals. In other words, I claim that queer judgments of the kind developed in this chapter could be the outcome of a productive dynamic beyond the obvious tension between (liberal) human rights and (postmodern) queer theory.

The aim of the chapter is to show how the use of queer theory could have radically changed some of the decisions adopted by the Court. The main focus will be on four cases discussed in Chapters 4 and 5, in which the Court ruled against the applicants' claims due to a restrictive interpretation of LGBT rights. The first of these cases is about same-sex marriage, as it was denied to same-sex couples in the *Schalk and Kopf* judgment.[7] The second case concerns trans marriage and, in particular, the requirement to end a valid marriage in order to obtain full legal recognition of gender transition. The Court originally dealt with this topic in its decision on admissibility in the *Parry* case.[8] The focus then shifts to the economic privileges granted to married heterosexual couples, which are denied to same-sex couples, as happened in *MW v United Kingdom*.[9] Finally, insights from queer theory will be used to re-think second-parent adoption by same-sex couples, as denied to the applicants in the *Gas and Dubois* ruling.[10]

[3] ibid 3.

[4] Jack M Balkin (ed), *What Brown v. Board of Education Should Have Said: The Nation's Top Legal Experts Rewrite America's Landmark Civil Rights Decision* (New York University Press, 2001).

[5] Hannah Arendt, *Eichmann in Jerusalem: A Report on the Banality of Evil* (Viking Press, 1964).

[6] Graeme W Austin, 'Queering Family Law' (1999) 8 *Australasian Gay and Lesbian Law Journal* 39, at 51; Lisa Gotell, 'Queering Law: Not by Vriend' (2002) 17 *Canadian Journal of Law and Society* 89, at 92; Aleardo Zanghellini, 'Queer, Antinormativity, Counter-normativity and Abjection' (2009) 18 *Griffith Law Review* 1, at 9.

[7] *Schalk and Kopf v Austria*, Application no 30141/04, ECHR 2010.

[8] *Parry v United Kingdom* (Dec), Application no 42971/05, ECHR 2006-XV.

[9] *MW v United Kingdom* (Dec), Application no 11313/02, 23 June 2009.

[10] *Gas and Dubois v France*, Application no 25951/07, ECHR 2012.

II. Same-Sex Marriage before the Court

The *Schalk and Kopf* judgment was the first time the Court dealt with same-sex marriage as the central question of a case. As discussed in Chapter 5, in its ruling the Court opted for *heterosexualising* the subject of human rights instead of *queering* the institution of marriage. The Court's decision was that access to same-sex marriage was not a right protected by the Convention, but an option that might be open to individuals, depending on the discretion of states. The following queer judgment is aimed in the exact opposite direction.[11]

A. A Queer Twist on *Schalk and Kopf v Austria*

1. The case originated in an application against Austria lodged by Mr Horst Michael Schalk and Mr Johan Franz Kopf on 5 August 2004.[12] The applicants alleged that they were discriminated against by the state, since they were denied the possibility of marrying each other or having their relationship legally recognised by law due to the fact that they were a same-sex couple.

2. Mr Schalk and Mr Kopf submitted an application to this Court after their request to marry was unsuccessful within the Austrian domestic jurisdiction. An original rejection from the Vienna Municipal Office was confirmed by the Regional Governor. Both local authorities agreed that it was an impediment to marriage if the two persons concerned were of the same sex. Faced with the rejection from the local authorities, the applicants lodged a constitutional complaint, which was dismissed by the Constitutional Court.

3. When the case reached our Court, the Registered Partnership Act of 2010 had entered into force, providing an alternative means of legal recognition to same-sex couples. The legal provision establishes: 'A registered partnership may be formed only by two persons of the same sex (registered partners). They thereby commit themselves to a lasting relationship with mutual rights and obligations'.

4. The new institution is similar to marriage but carries some significant differences, as the majority of the Court recognises. In addition to the rules regarding the procedure to enter the institution and those that regulate the partners' last names, the most important difference concerns parenting rights. Registered

[11] The structure of the queer judgments mirrors the actual structure of the judgments of the Court. In particular, within the queer judgments, the references to academic and legal sources appear within the text of the judgment, rather than in footnotes, as this is the usual practice of the Court. The only few footnotes in the following sections are used to bring attention to sources or ideas that are not used by the imaginary queer judge, but by the author of this book (despite both being the same person).

[12] A different rewriting of *Schalk and Kopf* was performed by Holning Lau. See Holning Lau, 'Rewriting *Schalk and Kopf*: Shifting the Locus of Deference' in Eva Brems (ed), *Diversity and European Human Rights: Rewriting Judgments of the ECHR* (Cambridge University Press, 2012) 243–64.

partners are not allowed to adopt a child, neither have they the right to access artificial insemination techniques.

5. I concur with the majority that this new legislation has not put an end to the case. The applicants' complaint regards the lack of access to the institution of marriage; the right to marry being a human right protected by the Convention. While the new legislation has granted same-sex couples the possibility to access an array of rights and privileges that only married couples used to enjoy, it still does not grant access to the right to marry. For that reason, the case of the applicants is still unresolved and needs to be decided by this Court.

6. The facts of the case are not in dispute: only different-sex couples can marry in Austria. Therefore, the question before the Court is clear: Does the European Convention on Human Rights allow states to restrict the right to marry to different-sex couples?

7. The majority judgment highlights that this was the first opportunity the Court has had to examine same-sex marriage. For this purpose, attention was drawn to the wording of Article 12 which states: 'Men and women of marriageable age have the right to marry and to found a family, according to the national laws governing the exercise of this right'.

8. While I agree with the majority that attention needs to be paid to the wording of Article 12, I disagree with the statement that this is the first time the Court has dealt with same-sex marriage. While this might be the first occasion on which same-sex marriage is the main focus of a case, the Court has shown in the past an unproblematic acceptance of the domestic prohibition of same-sex marriage. Clear examples of this are early cases of the Court dealing with transsexuality, such as *Rees* (*Rees v United Kingdom*, Application no 9532/81, Series A no 106), or more recent cases, such as *Parry* (*Parry v United Kingdom* (Dec), Application no 42971/05, ECHR 2006-XV). In particular, in the *Parry* case the Court affirmed that the right to marry, as laid down in the Convention in 1950, did not include same-sex marriage (*Parry v United Kingdom* (Dec), cited above, para 12).

9. As to the wording of the Convention, the majority agrees that the language of Article 12 itself does not exclude same-sex marriage, as it reads: 'Men and women of marriageable age have the right to marry and to found a family' without stating that the only possibility is for a man to marry a woman. However, they affirm that taking into consideration the rest of the Convention, this article is the only one that instead of granting a right to 'everyone' does so to 'men and women'. For that reason, the majority holds that the choice of wording in this article has to be regarded as deliberate. In addition, the majority reinforces their opinion by affirming that in the 1950s, when the Convention was adopted, marriage was understood as a union between partners of different sex.

10. I disagree on this point with the majority ruling. In particular, I consider that there are a number of problems with the interpretation of Article 12, as I will highlight. According to the rules of treaty interpretation, the Convention's provisions should be interpreted 'in good faith in accordance with the ordinary meaning to be given to the terms of the treaty in their context and in the light of its object

and purpose' (Article 31 of the Vienna Convention on the Law of Treaties). This means that the interpretation of the scope of the rights should consist of a textual reading, attributing to the terms their ordinary meaning within their (textual) context, and this should be complemented with a teleological interpretation that pays special attention to the object and purpose of the treaty under analysis (see A Aust, *Modern Treaty Law and Practice* (Cambridge University Press, 2000) 188; A Orakhelashvili, *The Interpretation of Acts and Rules in Public International Law* (Oxford University Press, 2008) 318–54). Consequently, the majority's search for the 'deliberate' intention of the wording of the article, or the 'historical' meaning of marriage, was not allowed under the applicable rules of international law.

11. The recourse to supplementary methods of interpretation, such as the circumstances of the conclusion of the treaty or its preparatory work, can only take place after an interpretation that is literal, systemic and teleological is carried out and under very specific circumstances. These circumstances were absent in this case.

12. The first situation in which supplementary methods are allowed is to confirm the meaning of the provision that results from its textual and teleological reading (Vienna Convention on the Law of Treaties, Article 32). This was not the case. The understanding reached by the majority following a textual reading is that 'the wording of Article 12 might be interpreted so as not to exclude the marriage between two men or two women' (see paragraph 55 of the majority judgment). However, the conclusion they reach through the use of supplementary methods does not confirm such an interpretation, but allegedly disproves it.[13]

13. The second circumstance that would have allowed the Court to make use of supplementary methods is when the textual and teleological approaches left the meaning of the provision ambiguous or obscure, or led to a result which is manifestly absurd or unreasonable (Vienna Convention on the Law of Treaties, Article 32). Once again, this requirement was clearly absent. As highlighted above, the textual interpretation led the majority to affirm that: 'the wording of Article 12 might be interpreted so as not to exclude the marriage between two men or two women'. This textual interpretation needed to be complemented with a teleological reading, before it was permissible to proceed to other means of interpretation, which the majority failed to do.

14. My position is that a combined textual and teleological interpretation of Article 12 should have led the Court to the conclusion that there was a violation of the right to marry. As the Court has held in the past, the object and purpose of the Convention is the protection of human rights, which requires its provisions

[13] Even if the Court would have been allowed under international law to make use of the preparatory work of the Convention, Paul Johnson has argued that the *travaux préparatoires* showed no intention of the drafters to restrict marriage to different-sex couples. Johnson proposed that the use of the preparatory work should have been allowed in order to confirm the interpretation that same-sex marriage is permitted under Art 12. Paul Johnson, '"The Choice of Wording Must be Regarded as Deliberate": Same-Sex Marriage and Article 12 of the European Convention on Human Rights' (2015) 40 *European Law Review* 207.

be interpreted so as to make them practical and effective (*Soering v United Kingdom*, Application no 14038/88, Series A no 161, para 87). This teleological method of interpretation is applied by the Court under the 'living instrument' doctrine (*Mamatkulov and Askarov v Turkey* (GC), Application nos 46827/99 and 46951/99, para 121 and joint partly dissenting opinion of Judges Caflisch, Türmen and Kovler, ECHR 2005-I, para 154), which mandates the reading of the Convention to be undertaken in the light of present-day conditions. In fact, the International Court of Justice itself has stated that in treaties that are of continuing duration, such as the European Convention on Human Rights, the generic terms used thereby, such as 'marry', should be interpreted to have an evolving meaning (ICJ, *Dispute Regarding Navigational and Related Rights, Costa Rica v Nicaragua*, 13 July 2009, para 66).

15. In order to read Article 12 in present-day conditions, giving an evolving meaning to its terms, I will make use of queer theory to further substantiate my dissent. It might seem at odds with queer theory to issue a judgment in favour of same-sex marriage (M Warner, *The Trouble with Normal* (Harvard University Press, 1999) 66; J Halley, 'Recognition, Rights, Regulation, Normalisation' in *Legal Recognition of Same-Sex Partnerships* (Hart Publishing, 2001) 100). However, the objective of this opinion is not to support the rejection of queer lives in favour of a 'banalized respectability', as feared by Warner. This opinion is not aimed at promoting same-sex marriage, but at denouncing the heteronormative character of exclusively heterosexual marriage, which should be understood as a breach of the correct interpretation of Article 12.

16. Marriage is one of the institutions the state uses to legitimise relationships (Warner, cited above, 82). Marriage traditionally has been utilised as the paradigmatic case of official recognition for intimate relationships, which means that relationships that are not marriage lack this level of recognition. In other words, other intimate relationships have a taint of inferiority when compared to marriage.

17. This understanding of marriage can be clearly seen in the Court's case law. Indeed, the majority judgment highlights that the right to marry is a fundamental right and that the exercise of this right gives rise to personal, social and legal consequences (see paragraph 49 of the majority judgment). Therefore, the Court is of the opinion that there is something special about the institution of marriage, which is not shared by other intimate relationships.

18. Moreover, the majority ruling is also saying that there is something special about heterosexuality, as it is allowing states to deny access to the special institution of marriage to those who do not form a different-sex couple. That is to say, the majority ruling reinforces the existence of a hierarchy of both intimate relationships and sexualities. As long as marriage remains heterosexual, the Court is validating the inferiority of same-sex sexuality, since only heterosexuality holds the key to access the special institution of marriage.

19. It is fair to remember that this Court has opposed on many occasions the legal hierarchies of sexualities created by many States Parties to the Convention.

It made states stop the criminalisation of same-sex sexuality (*Dudgeon v United Kingdom*, Series A no 45, 22 October 1981; *Norris v Ireland*, Series A no 142, 26 October 1988; *Modinos v Cyprus*, Series A no 259, 22 April 1993). It opposed the existence of different ages of consent for same-sex sexuality and different-sex sexuality (*L and V v Austria*, Application nos 39392/98 and 39829/98, ECHR 2003-I; *SL v Austria*, Application no 45330/99, ECHR 2003-I). And it did not allow state restrictions on the public defence of different sexualities (*Bączkowski and others v Poland*, Application no 1543/06, 3 May 2007). Nonetheless, the Court is still allowing states to delegitimise same-sex sexuality by restricting the enjoyment of a human right to heterosexual couples. Through the denial of the right to marry, the majority judgment seems to support the idea that heterosexuality deserves to be placed higher in a hierarchy. This is certainly inconsistent with the Court's constant jurisprudence.

20. As highlighted by Janet Halley, opening marriage to same-sex couples would erase the heterosexual/homosexual distinction currently drawn at the borders of marriage (Halley, cited above, 100). Halley expressed her concern about this, arguing that same-sex marriage would make the married/unmarried distinction become more powerful, and unmarried adults and their sex lives would become 'weirder'. Nonetheless, there is another possible outcome of the erasure of the heterosexual/homosexual difference at the limit of marriage. Nowadays, the ban on same-sex marriage allows the use of the institution of marriage to stabilise heterosexuality. Since same-sex sexuality can be institutionally banned from marriage, heterosexuality can be comfortably consolidated within. That is to say, marriage can be used to establish a clear boundary for heterosexuality. Those within the institution can have their heterosexuality certified by the state. However, extending marriage to same-sex sexuality also means opening to question the sexuality of those within the institution.

21. In addition to this, Halley's argument that same-sex marriage will make unmarried sex 'weirder' ignores that opening marriage to same-sex couples can actually make marriage more *queer*, diversifying sexuality within marriage and providing a site for re-imagining conjugality (C Stychin, *A Nation by Rights* (Temple University Press, 1998) 198). The argument also discounts queer's own project of embracing and celebrating weirdness – a project that same-sex marriage can enable and facilitate. If same-sex marriage becomes an option for individuals, staying away from the institution and its 'banalized respectability' will become more clearly a matter of choice, instead of being seen as the only possible alternative. This may well give more visibility to the queer lives and politics of those who refuse to assimilate (Warner, cited above, 66).

22. I want to be clear that with this judgment I do not intend to validate the privileged character of marriage. In fact, I would like to highlight that states are free to amend the Convention and deprive marriage of the character of a fundamental human right. However, as long as marriage remains a human right, it cannot be kept exclusively heterosexual (J Butler, 'On Being Beside Oneself' in *Sex Rights* (Oxford University Press, 2005) 59–60). Such an interpretation is not consistent with the rules of treaty interpretation, as I stated above.

23. The Court should not allow States to use the institution of marriage to make judgments about same-sex sexuality. It should no longer be an institution that legitimises heterosexuality by excluding and de-legitimising same-sex sexuality. Indeed, the Court should not allow human rights to be used as a tool of heteronormativity.

24. The subject of human rights law, the individual entitled to the rights recognised by this Convention and other human rights treaties, is not only the heterosexual man/woman. The subject of human rights can also be an LGBT individual, as was recognised by this Court when prohibiting discrimination based on an individual's sexuality (*Salgueiro da Silva Mouta v Portugal*, Application no 33290/96, ECHR 1999-IX; *Karner v Austria*, Application no 40016/98, ECHR 2003-IX; *EB v France* (GC), Application no 43546/02, 22 January 2008).

25. The individuals entitled to rights can be heterosexual, but can also be asexual, homosexual or bisexual. They are free to identify with a specific sexuality, if that is how they feel, but they should not be required to fix their sexuality in order to obtain protection of their human rights. They should be free to experience their sexuality in as many consensual ways as they want to without being deprived of human rights for this reason. Ultimately, the intensity of pleasures matters more than sexual identities and labels (M Foucault, *Herculine Barbin* (Harvester Press, 1980) vii).

26. Austria, together with other States Parties that still consider marriage to be a privileged and exclusionary heterosexual institution, is depriving individuals of what is currently recognised as a human right, based on their sexuality. This means the establishment of a hierarchy of sexualities, devaluing those sexualities that differ from the heterosexual model. States should not be allowed to accord legitimacy to some kinds of consensual sexualities but not to others (Warner, cited above, 82), or to grant them different degrees of legitimacy.

27. Consequently, by restricting the enjoyment of the right to marry based on sexuality, the state has breached Article 12. As there has been a violation of the right to marry (Article 12), there is no need to analyse the case under different provisions.

III. Revisiting Transsexual Marriage after *Goodwin*

The *Parry* case was not a final judgment of the Court, but a decision on admissibility in which the Court found the claim of the applicants to be manifestly ill-founded. As a consequence, the application was declared inadmissible.[14] The same day, the Court declared inadmissible an almost identical application in the *R and F* case, also against the United Kingdom.[15] The outcome of these decisions was that states can force individuals to choose between preserving their marriage

[14] *Parry v United Kingdom* (n 8) 14.
[15] *R and F v United Kingdom* (Dec), Application no 35748/05, 28 November 2006.

and obtaining full recognition of their gender identity. Conversely, this dissenting opinion offers a queer alternative to that situation.

A. *Parry v United Kingdom*: An Already Queer Decision without a Queer Outcome

1. The applicants are a married couple, Mrs Wena Parry and Mrs Anita Parry, who have been married since 1960 and have three children. Wena started undergoing gender transition in 1998, paid for by the National Health Service, and legally adopted her current name that same year. She has completed all the surgical interventions she desired to undergo and now continues to receive hormone treatment. Her wife Anita has stood by her side during her transition and they remain together as a loving and married couple.

2. Following the entry into force of the Gender Recognition Act in 2004, Wena made an application to obtain a 'Gender Recognition Certificate', a formal and full legal recognition of her gender by the state. However, according to the domestic law, a full 'Gender Recognition Certificate' can only be issued to unmarried individuals. Therefore, only a provisional certificate was granted to Wena, which would allow her to annul her marriage and only then would she be issued a full 'Gender Recognition Certificate'. The problem is that neither Wena nor Anita wants to annul their marriage. Thus, Wena remains unable to have her gender fully recognised by the state.

3. Given this situation, the applicants' main complaint is clear. They argue that the requirement imposed by the domestic legislation that a marriage needs to be terminated in order to obtain full recognition of a person's gender amounts to a violation of the right to respect for their family and private life (Article 8), because for no cogent reason it obliges a person to choose between their gender and their marriage. They also argue that this situation causes a violation of other human rights, such as the right to marry; their religious beliefs, to which marriage is central (indeed, Wena is an ordained church minister); the peaceful enjoyment of possessions; the prohibition of discrimination in conjunction with all the human rights mentioned; and the right to access an effective remedy.

4. The majority's assessment of the case takes place mostly within the framework of Article 8 and Article 12, while the claims relating to the remaining rights are all broadly dismissed. Nevertheless, before proceeding to the assessment of the case, the Court rejected a preliminary objection interposed by the state of a procedural character, regarding the lack of exhaustion of domestic remedies, and it also highlights the relevant domestic legislation applicable to the case, the Gender Recognition Act 2004, the Matrimonial Causes Act 1973, and the Civil Partnership Act 2004.

5. Concerning the Gender Recognition Act, the majority ruling emphasises that this norm 'provides a mechanism whereby transsexuals may have their [new] gender recognised'. The majority describes how the transsexual individual

is pathologised, by requiring a medical diagnosis of 'gender dysphoria' as one of the main requirements for granting recognition of their gender. Other requirements include 'having lived' in the acquired gender throughout the two years immediately preceding the application, and the intention to continue to live in the acquired gender until death. When an application to obtain gender recognition is successful, a full Gender Recognition Certificate is issued and the person's gender becomes recognised in all legal aspects. The exception to this rule is that only an interim Gender Recognition Certificate is issued if the applicant is married. This certificate can be used to dissolve the existing marriage, after which a full certificate is issued.

6. Regarding the meaning and scope of marriage within English law, the majority decision mentions that the domestic courts continue to affirm that marriage is the union of a man and a woman and that the gender of a person is established at birth. Nonetheless, the House of Lords in a ruling of 2003 highlighted that not allowing transsexual individuals to marry heterosexually was a violation of their rights to marry and to respect for their private and family life. The majority also highlights that the Civil Partnership Act came into force in December 2005, allowing same-sex couples to register their relationship and to acquire an array of rights and responsibilities akin to marriage.

7. As to the parties in the case, the government argues that when the Court ruled in *Goodwin*, it specifically stated that the effect of gender transition on past marriages was left within the margin of appreciation of states (*Christine Goodwin v United Kingdom* (GC), Application no 28957/95, ECHR 2002-VI, para 103). It also affirms that, when passing the Gender Recognition Act, Parliament established the requirement of bringing existing marriages to an end in order to preserve the heterosexuality of the institution of marriage. The government claims that those couples that resort to the dissolution of a marriage in order to obtain recognition of the gender transition of one of the partners can enter into a civil partnership that same day. In addition, the government intends to sustain its position by putting a monetary cost to the proceedings from gender recognition to civil partnership in the amount of £570.

8. The applicants argue that they have been married for about 40 years and have brought up children together. They emphasise their will to continue to be married, stating that a civil partnership does not provide them with the equivalent of marriage, as they believe this new institution lacks the historic, social and religious contexts of marriage, which they consider to be a cornerstone of social organisation.

9. The majority recognises that the legislation put the applicants in a quandary, as Wena is required to sacrifice either her gender or their marriage. Therefore, there is a direct and invasive effect on the applicants' enjoyment of their right to respect for private and family life. The majority understands that the origin of the requirement to dissolve a marriage in order to obtain gender recognition is the position that marriage has to be a heterosexual institution. Nonetheless, it considers that the possibility of continuing the relationship through a civil partnership,

which carries with it almost the same legal rights and obligations, is not a disproportionate outcome towards the protection of the right to respect for family life. Consequently, the majority concludes that the application should be rejected as manifestly ill-founded concerning Article 8.

10. Concerning the violation of the right to marry, the government's submission is that requiring the dissolution of the marriage for the recognition of Wena's gender is not a violation of Article 12, since the applicants are not being forced to end their marriage, but are free to choose between their marriage and Wena's gender recognition.

11. In opposition to this, the applicants submit that the right to marry must include the right to ongoing recognition of a marriage. They affirm that there are 'no other circumstances in which the State purports to be able to cease to recognise a marriage that it accepts was lawfully entered into' and they deny there is 'any element of choice involved in deciding whether to terminate their marriage, as it could not be said that the first applicant could by an act of will stop following her identity' (see page 11 of the majority decision).

12. The majority decision states that the regulation of marriage in national law cannot be left entirely to the states. However, it affirms that given the 'sensitive moral choices concerned and the importance to be attached in particular to the protection of children and the fostering of secure family environments, this Court must not rush to substitute its own judgment in place of the authorities who are best placed to assess and respond to the needs of society' (see page 12 of the majority decision). The majority then observes that when the British Parliament adopted the Gender Recognition Act, it was aware that a number of transsexual individuals were married, but deliberately made no provision for the subsistence of such marriages in the event that one of the partners requested a Gender Recognition Certificate.

13. The majority ruling holds that Article 12 of the Convention enshrines the traditional concept of marriage between one man and one woman. In fact, the majority decision asserts that same-sex marriage as it exists in a number of states does not 'flow from an interpretation of the fundamental right as laid down by the Contracting States in the Convention in 1950' (see page 12 of the majority decision).

14. Consequently, the majority concludes that the regulation of the effects of gender recognition is an issue that falls within the discretion of the state and that the state cannot be required to make allowances for the small number of marriages where the partners wish to continue to be married after the gender transition of one of them. Hence, this part of the application is also declared inadmissible.

15. I disagree with the majority decision. I understand that there has been a violation of both Article 8 and Article 12 with regards to the situation Wena and Anita were put in by the application of the Gender Recognition Act. The majority acknowledges that the Gender Recognition Act put the applicants in a quandary, as Wena was required to sacrifice either her gender or their marriage. I believe that this quandary is in itself a violation of the applicants' human rights.

16. I will begin with the analysis of Article 8 and Wena's right to respect for her private life. The Gender Recognition Act approved by the British Parliament was a clear improvement for the rights of trans individuals who want to have their gender recognised by law. However, the requirements imposed by the legislation in order to obtain a Gender Recognition Certificate established the pathologisation of the transsexual person. The first requirement that a transsexual individual needs to prove is a medical diagnosis of 'gender dysphoria'. Therefore, only by identifying as clinically ill can a transsexual person obtain recognition of their gender.[16]

17. The second requirement established is also problematic and refers to 'having lived' in the gender for two years. Ironically, it seems as if Judith Butler herself might have drafted the requirement. On the one hand, the state recognises that gender is nothing but a performance. Even more, it has established the exact period of time the repetitive performance is needed in order to create the appearance of a permanent gender: two years. On the other hand, Butler's idea pursued the deconstruction of gender as a constraining technique from which liberation can be imagined, since Butler understood gender performativity as the consequence of a regulatory regime (J Butler, 'Critically Queer' in *Playing with Fire* (Routledge, 1997) 16–17). This piece of legislation pursued the exact opposite idea. Understanding gender as a social performance, it imposes on transsexual individuals the requirement to perform consistently one specific gender during a two-year period.

18. The third requirement continues a similar path of suspicion and constraining impositions. In order to obtain gender recognition the transsexual person has to evidence the intention to continue to live in their gender until death. On the one hand, the legislation is appealing in the sense that it clearly reflects the mutability of gender. The 'until death' requirement is based on the suspicion that a person can change their mind and decide to once again cross the gender binary. On the other hand, this realisation is to be limited by law. As the legislation understands sex to be mutable, it feels the need to put a stop to it. If transsexual people want their gender recognised they have to commit to it for life. However, who can commit to anything for life? Marriage is no longer 'so long as … both [spouses] shall live', and sexuality is certainly mutable (as this judgment also shows and I will discuss further below); why should gender be for life? What would be the problem if a person decides to change their sex more than once?

[16] While even nowadays the Court continues to validate domestic legislation that pathologises transsexuality, other human rights monitoring bodies have held that it is no longer viable to conceive of transsexuality as a mental disorder. *AP, Garçon and Nicot v France*, Application nos 79885/12, 52471/13 and 52596/13, 6 April 2017; Commissioner for Human Rights of the Council of Europe, *Issue Paper on Human Rights and Gender Identity*, CommDH/IssuePaper(2009)2 (29 July 2009) para 3.3; Committee on Economic, Social and Cultural Rights, *Concluding Observations of the Committee on Economic, Social and Cultural Rights on Germany*, E/C.12/DEU/CO/5 (20 May 2011) para 26; Inter-American Commission on Human Rights, *Violence Against LGBTI Persons in the Americas*, OAS/Ser.L/V/II.rev.1 (12 November 2015) para 419 and recommendations 26; Inter-American Court of Human Rights, Advisory Opinion OC-24/17, Gender Identity, and Equality and Non-discrimination with regard to Same-Sex Couples, Series A No 24 (24 November 2017) para 130 and opinion para 3.

19. I understand that the requirements imposed by the Gender Recognition Act are already problematic enough to find multiple violations of the right to respect for private life as protected by the Convention. Nonetheless, in its applicability to the case of Wena Parry there is an additional element that justifies my dissent with the majority decision. A final intriguing aspect of the application, with regard to Article 8, is that because Wena was married, she was issued with an 'interim Gender Recognition Certificate'. The most obvious question concerning this point is: What is an 'interim Gender Recognition Certificate'?

20. According to the analysis in the majority ruling, this certificate is issued when all the requirements are fulfilled for obtaining the full legal recognition of the person's gender, but the person is married. Consequently, this certificate would only be an 'interim' recognition of the person's gender. That is to say, the individual's gender is recognised temporarily. Once again, the legislation could have been inspired by Butler's *Gender Trouble* (J Butler, *Gender Trouble* (Routledge, 1999)), as it clearly emphasises the mutability and temporality of individuals' gender. However, the legislation does so as a means of denying the possibility of a married transsexual person who is not heterosexual. It provides recognition of the desired gender only in a provisional manner. The recognition is subject to the transsexual individual putting an end to their marriage so the state can continue to avoid recognising same-sex marriage.

21. A final question remains: if the state is actually acknowledging the gender of the transsexual individual (as the name of the certificate indicates), but the applicant fails to fulfil the last requirement to transition from an interim recognition into a full recognition (dissolution of marriage), is their gender taken away from them again? In the present case, Wena has obtained provisional recognition of being a woman. If she continues to be married to Anita, is the state going to consider her a man? Certainly, this situation of recognising a gender that might stop being recognised, if the conditions are not complied with, is a clear violation of Wena's right to respect for her private life. Therefore, on this basis, the application should be declared admissible and the Court should rule that there is a clear violation of Article 8.

22. As to the analysis of Article 12, I agree with the applicants that the right to marry refers not only to the right to enter into a marriage, but also to the right to continue an existing marriage. It is worth remembering that with the *Goodwin* judgment (*Christine Goodwin v United Kingdom* (GC), cited above), the Court did not just protect the right of transsexual individuals to marry, but it imposed on the state the obligation to allow transsexual individuals to marry heterosexually.

23. In the case law preceding *Goodwin* (specifically in *Cossey*, see *Cossey v United Kingdom*, Series A no 184, 27 September 1990), the Court argued that transsexual individuals could still marry, since they could marry individuals of the same gender to that acquired (but not officially recognised). This means that the Gender Recognition Act, which allows transsexual individuals to have their gender recognised and to marry individuals of the 'opposite' gender, also meant changing one prohibition for another. While marrying individuals of the opposite

gender to that which is legally attained is now possible, it became legally impossible to marry individuals of the same sex to that recognised. In other words, the Gender Recognition Act did not just enable the exercise of a right (for heterosexual transsexuals), but it also imposed a restriction on the same right. In fact, believing that a right was created means ignoring that transsexual individuals may not be heterosexual.

24. As the majority affirms, Parliament contemplated the fact that some marriages were going to be ended due to the requirement of the Gender Recognition Act (and not due to the desire of the spouses), but it decided not to make any exceptions for these cases. The majority then reaches the conclusion that the state 'cannot be required to make allowances for the small number of marriages where both partners wish to continue notwithstanding the change in gender of one of them' (see pages 12 and 13 of the majority decision).

25. The fact that the number of marriages that would be dissolved might be small should not be reason enough to allow the restriction of a human right. In any event, the assumption that this number is small is certainly problematic. The majority seems to be assuming the immutability of individual's sexuality, in a case in which it is taking into consideration the actual mutability of sexuality. That is to say, the majority is suggesting that many marriages will be brought to an end because one of the partners changes their gender (assumption of the immutability of sexuality) and then recognising that some of them might not be dissolved following gender transition (accepting the mutability of sexuality). Consequently, the majority decides to deny the right to continue an ongoing marriage based on the immutability of sexuality, but did so after acknowledging that sexuality might actually not be immutable.

26. I cannot agree with the majority that the quandary into which Wena was put, as she had to choose between her gender and her marriage, can be an acceptable restriction on the right to continue a marriage. As argued above, having her gender fully recognised by the state is a right to which Wena is entitled. The applicants also have a right to continue their ongoing marriage, as this is their wish. Subjecting this right to the sacrifice of another right is an unreasonable restriction. It is a situation that comes as a sad consequence of taking the conviction in the heterosexuality of marriage to an unacceptable extreme. This is a restriction on the right to marry that exceeds the margin of discretion states are allowed. Hence, the 'quandary' in which Wena and Anita have been placed by the state amounts to a breach of Articles 8 and 12.

27. Furthermore, I believe that the Gender Recognition Act does not allow for continuation of a marriage in another possible scenario, which might have not been considered by Parliament, showing another restriction imposed by the Gender Recognition Act on the right to marry. What would happen to a marriage in which both partners decide to transition their assigned gender? The procedure stipulates that they need to dissolve their marriage, as this is a requirement for the legal recognition of gender. However, the marriage of these partners would continue to be heterosexual. Therefore, the restriction on the right to marry

imposed by the legislation goes beyond the prohibition of same-sex marriage. It actually seems to be aimed at scrutinising the sexuality of all transsexual applicants who want to obtain full recognition of their gender.

28. As a closing note, I would like to highlight that *Parry* has possibly been one of the *queerest* cases ever decided by the Court. In this case the Court was faced with the clear lack of fixity of both gender and sexuality. Indeed, the majority has accepted the mutability of Wena's gender and assumed the mutability of her sexuality (from a heterosexual husband to a lesbian wife), but did this by assuming her sexuality has not truly changed, conceiving her as always attracted to a woman, both as a man and as a woman.[17] However, it was the inability to accept the possible mutability of Anita's sexuality that made the majority allow the United Kingdom to restrict the human rights of both applicants. The idea of the potential mutability of the sexuality of a cissexual woman, who had not been pathologised, was a step that the Court did not seem to be willing to validate.

IV. Que(e)rying the Privileged Character of Marriage

The *MW v United Kingdom* decision was adopted in one of the different cases in which the Court has analysed whether granting certain economic benefits to heterosexual married couples, while denying them to same-sex couples, amounted to discrimination. As discussed in Chapter 4, the Court declared the applicant's claim to be inadmissible, validating the differential treatment carried out by the state. The present queer opinion will offer reasons to disagree with the Court's decision on many different levels.

A. Questioning the Privileges of the Heterosexual Married Couple in *MW v United Kingdom*

1. The application against the United Kingdom was lodged by Mr MW, who had lived with his same-sex partner for 23 years until the latter's death in 2001. From the late 1980s onwards, they resided in jointly-owned properties and were financially interdependent; also they each had designated the other as their heir. According to Mr MW, their degree of mutual commitment was such that 'had they been a heterosexual couple they would have married'.

2. As to the facts of the case, after his partner's death, Mr MW asked a social worker whether he was entitled to claim Bereavement Payment, a lump sum of £2,000, to which survivors of a married couple were entitled. However, the social

[17] In an interview for the book *Going to Strasbourg*, Wena actually asserted that following her gender transition she became attracted to men. Paul Johnson, *Going to Strasbourg: An Oral History of Sexual Orientation Discrimination and the European Convention on Human Rights* (Oxford University Press, 2016) 138.

worker advised him that he was ineligible, since he had not been married to his partner.

3. In December 2005, the Civil Partnership Act entered into force, broadening eligibility for Bereavement Payment. From that moment, people who had entered into a civil partnership were eligible to apply for Bereavement Payment under the same conditions as married people. Nevertheless, this did not apply retroactively; hence, it did not benefit Mr MW.

4. The applicant complains that as a survivor of a same-sex couple, who had no means to achieve formal recognition of their relationship, he had been denied a benefit available to a survivor of a married (heterosexual) couple. He asserts that this situation amounts to discrimination based on sexual orientation under Article 14 of the Convention in conjunction with the right to respect for private and family life (Article 8) and also in conjunction with the right to the peaceful enjoyment of possessions (Article 1 of Protocol No 1).

5. The government opposes the applicant's complaint first on a procedural basis, as it considers that Mr MW had not exhausted domestic remedies before complaining to the Court. In addition, the government submits that there has not been a violation of the prohibition of discrimination, since the applicant and his partner were not in a situation analogous to that of a married couple. In order to further sustain this position, the government points out the similarities between this case and the *Courten* case, in which same-sex partners were denied a tax benefit based on the lack of marriage bonds, and requests this Court to reiterate that legal interpretation.

6. As to the ruling of the case, the majority first decided that the preliminary objection interposed by the state should be rejected, since there was no effective remedy available to the applicant within the domestic jurisdiction (see page 6 of the majority decision). I agree with this decision. Nonetheless, concerning the substance of the case, the majority then proceeds to declare the application inadmissible, finding the applicant's claim to be manifestly ill-founded (see page 7 of the majority decision). It is on this point in which I disagree with the majority ruling and will, therefore, issue the present dissenting opinion.

7. When this Court has been faced with privileges granted to married couples and denied to same-sex couples, such as pensions (*Mata Estevez v Spain* (Dec), Application no 56501/00, ECHR 2001-VI) or tax exemptions (*Courten v United Kingdom* (Dec) Application no 4479/06, 4 November 2008), the answer has always been the same: it is not discriminatory treatment. The arguments followed by the Court in such cases have changed slightly and the decision to find that there was no violation of the Convention has been adopted at two different stages of the analysis under Article 14. In the *Courten* ruling and in the present case, the Court has resorted to the idea that same-sex couples are not 'analogous' to heterosexual married couples, finishing the analysis in that step.

8. Since same-sex couples who are unable to marry are (apparently) different to married different-sex couples, the majority understands that the difference in treatment between them (granting privileges to one and denying the same

privileges to the other) does not amount to discrimination. I disagree with the rationale behind these decisions. I believe that the arguments offered by the Court on these occasions are flawed due to a variety of reasons. In particular, there are problems when the Court considers individuals to be in dissimilar situations based on their sexuality.

9. In order to decide this case, the majority affirms that the differential treatment between the applicant and the survivor of a heterosexual married couple is based on the 'objective' fact that the applicant was not married. Thus, according to the majority, the married/unmarried difference positioned the applicant in a situation that is 'not analogous' to the survivor of a heterosexual married couple. In other words, the Court is not saying that people are not similar enough due to their sexuality, but because of their marital status.

10. However, according to the applicant, the married/unmarried difference is a consequence of the heterosexual/homosexual binary, since he and his partner were not allowed to get married in the United Kingdom only because of their sexuality. Therefore, it is only a superficial analysis of the majority that allows them to hide away from the fact that, in the present circumstances, saying that married/unmarried couples are not similar enough to each other means actually stating that same-sex/different-sex couples are not similar enough.

11. Following the Foucauldian idea that sexuality is discursively produced (M Foucault, *The History of Sexuality* (Penguin, 1978) 105–6), this Court should acknowledge its role in the construction of the homosexual subject. Indeed, each decision this Court adopts regarding human rights and sexuality not only plays a role in the production of sexualities, but also establishes notions of sexuality that are performed by applicants in subsequent cases when they appear before the Court, reinforcing the constructions originally sketched by the Court (then reiterated by other sitting judges). That is to say, this Court cannot ignore the fact that it has become an important player in the continuing performative construction of homosexuality within the Council of Europe.[18]

12. When this Court states that same-sex couples are 'not analogous' to heterosexual married couples, it is discursively constructing the homosexual applicant as different to the heterosexual individual. This difference is used to justify denying access to marriage based on the heterosexual/homosexual binary, and the denied access is then utilised as an 'objective fact' (they are actually not married) on which to base the privileges granted to the heterosexual married couple and denied to same-sex couples.

[18] I have developed this argument further elsewhere. See Damian A Gonzalez-Salzberg, 'The Making of the Court's Homosexual: A Queer Reading of the European Court of Human Rights' Case Law on Same-Sex Sexuality' (2014) 65 *Northern Ireland Legal Quarterly* 371. On this specific point, see also Paul Johnson, *Homosexuality and the European Court of Human Rights* (Routledge, 2012) 41–43. As to the role played by courts of law regarding the construction of the meaning of sexual identities, see Aeyal Gross, 'Challenges to Compulsory Heterosexuality: Recognition and Non-Recognition of Same-Sex Couples in Israeli Law' in Robert Wintemute and Mads Andenæs (eds), *Legal Recognition of Same-Sex Partnerships: A Study of National, European and International Law* (Hart Publishing, 2001) 391–414.

13. Therefore, the 'objective fact' of the existence/non-existence of a marriage certificate is only a pretext used for making a biased construction the grounds for denying benefits. This is certainly not good enough reason to declare the application inadmissible.

14. This becomes even clearer when the majority attempts to justify why heterosexual married couples are entitled to economic privileges. In just two sentences, the majority highlights the reasons why married couples are privileged over unmarried ones. First, it identifies marriage as a legally binding agreement. Then, it distinguishes marriage from 'informal personal relationships, however permanent and supportive' (see page 6 of the majority decision). Consequently, the relevance of marriage does not lie in its permanent or its supportive character, since that is not the reason for economic privileges. This has been confirmed by the Grand Chamber in the *Burden* case, when it validated the refusal to extend tax exemptions to cohabiting sisters (*Burden v United Kingdom* (GC), Application no 13378/05, ECHR 2008). The privileged character of marriage seems to follow from it being a formal and binding agreement, one that can only be celebrated by those belonging to one side of the heterosexual/homosexual binary.

15. While the applicant was not in the same situation to that of the survivor of a married couple, this was because the state did not allow him to be in such a position. The reason behind this impediment was the sexuality of the applicant. However, differential treatment based on sexuality is not acceptable under the Convention (*EB v. France* (GC), Application no 43546/02, 22 January 2008). Therefore, denying the applicant the benefit he requested amounted to discriminatory treatment based on his sexuality. As a consequence, as long as the ban on same-sex marriage subsists, the state should be under the obligation to allow unmarried same-sex couples to access the benefits granted to married heterosexual couples, since the opposite will entail discriminatory treatment based on the prohibited category of sexuality.

16. However, extending benefits to same-sex couples would only put an end to the discriminatory treatment against them. As this Court has affirmed in the past: 'Although the primary purpose of the Convention system is to provide individual relief, its mission is also to determine issues on public-policy grounds in the common interest, thereby raising the general standards of protection of human rights' (*Karner v Austria*, Application no 40016/98, ECHR 2003-IX, para 26). The subject matter of the present application involves an important question of general interest for all States Parties to the Convention, namely: Are states entitled under the Convention to use economic benefits to promote certain types of intimate relationships? I will discuss this topic, presenting an alternative (and more queer) approach to the case.

17. As affirmed by Ruthann Robson, economic privileges are the most obvious forces that reinforce the institution of marriage (R Robson, 'Compulsory Matrimony' in *Feminist and Queer Legal Theory* (Ashgate, 2009) 314). In fact, the privileges most states grant exclusively to married couples can be seen either as

an incentive to choose or as a reward for having chosen heterosexual marriage – and may even show a certain degree of concern that people might opt out of heterosexual marriage altogether, if it is not accompanied by economic benefits. The concession of these economic incentives points at the state having decided that heterosexuality, marriage and couplehood are the right options for individuals. Nevertheless, since these three constructions (heterosexuality, marriage and couplehood) are means for regulating sexual life, granting privileges on the basis of any of them means encouraging a specific way of regulation.

18. The construction and regulation of sexuality through the homosexual/heterosexual binary responds to the idea of both terms existing in an oppositional order in which one is presented as normal while the other is constructed as deviant (see E Kosofsky Sedgwick, *Epistemology of the Closet* (California University Press, 1990) 9–10; D Fuss, *Inside/Out* (Routledge, 1991) 2; D Halperin, *Saint Foucault* (Oxford University Press, 1997) 44–45). Similarly, the fact that marriage is an institution that regulates sexuality is not a secret. A paradigmatic example of the norms marriage carry over sexuality is the legally imposed duty of fidelity through the traditional regulation of adultery either as a criminal offence or as grounds for divorce.[19]

19. Lastly, the couple, as the exemplary form of intimate relationship is also regulatory in the sense that it has been established in the Western world as the only intimate relationship that can obtain legal recognition. In fact, bigamy remains a crime within the Council of Europe and this Court has clearly expressed its negative view regarding polygamy, when presenting it as a manifestation of gender discrimination (*Refah Partisi (the Welfare Party) and others v Turkey* (GC), Application nos 41340/98, 41342/98, 41343/98 and 41344/98, ECHR 2003-II, para 128), a comment criticised by Judge Kovler, although probably accurately made by the majority. Therefore, the couple appears as the ideal type of relationship, establishing a clear cap on the number of people who can share a legally recognised intimate relationship.

20. This Court should have questioned the fact that privileges come attached to these regulatory regimes, and that just extending them to other couples that can be assimilated to the heterosexual married couple was not an appropriate solution. Indeed, maybe the answer to the differential treatment of same-sex couples is not to be found in the extension of economic privileges to all couples, regardless of sexuality, but through uncoupling couples and privileges (A Gross, 'Sex, Love, and Marriage' (2008) *Leiden Journal of International Law* 246, 247 and 252).

21. As highlighted by Carl Stychin, the law has so far been unwilling to think beyond the couple, ignoring the complexities of queer lives in which companionship, care and kinship exist beyond the partnership paradigm (C Stychin, 'Family Friendly? Rights, Responsibilities and Relationship Recognition' in

[19] The Court has actually accepted that adultery can have legal effects in the *Obst v Germany* judgment. *Obst v Germany*, Application no 425/03, 23 September 2010.

Feminist Perspectives on Family Law (Routledge, 2006) 34). In fact, a lesson that the Court can learn from queer theory is that relationships that do not parallel the married heterosexual couple should not be subordinated (S Roseneil, 'Why We Should Care About Friends' (2004) *Social Policy and Society* 411). Other relationships should not be treated detrimentally due to an alleged failure to reach a heteronormative ideal.

22. Discrimination based on sexuality does not only take place when explicit reference is made to homosexuality, but also when individuals are required to achieve heteronormative ideals,[20] such as marriage and couplehood. It is imperative that this Court contributes to ending these forms of discrimination as well. While extending economic privileges to same-sex couples would have meant putting an end to discrimination against them, thinking beyond the privileged couple is the appropriate path to fight against discrimination based on sexuality more broadly.

23. In conclusion, the Court should not declare this application inadmissible. This is the narrowest possible approach to the case, which confirms the view that married heterosexual couples can be rewarded for their sexuality. The applicant's situation certainly amounts to a violation of Article 14 of the Convention in conjunction with the right to respect for private and family life (Article 8) and the right to the peaceful enjoyment of possessions (Article 1 of Protocol No 1).

24. Nonetheless, the answer the Court should give to this claim is not merely the extension of privileges to more couples, through the recognition that the denial of privileges based on sexuality is clearly discriminatory. The answer to the case should be guided by a more queer understanding of kinship, which refuses to think of the couple as the main unit entitled to economic privileges. Rewarding the achievement of other heteronormative ideals, such as marriage or couplehood, still perpetuates discrimination against every person opting out of these regulatory regimes. Economic incentives should be linked to economic need and not to encouraging those who choose the 'right' sexuality framework, whether it be heterosexuality, marriage or couplehood.

V. Re-thinking Second-Parent Adoption

The *Gas and Dubois* judgment was the first case in which the Court dealt with the issue of second-parent adoption by same-sex couples. French law prohibited second-parent adoption by same-sex couples, while allowing it for heterosexual married couples. However, the Court refused to find France's adoption norms to be discriminatory. In order to substantiate its decision, the Court resorted to

[20] This idea was further developed by Paul Johnson. See Paul Johnson, 'Heteronormativity and the European Court of Human Rights' (2012) 23 *Law and Critique* 43, at 58.

emphasising the importance of heterosexual marriage. The following dissenting judgment draws on insights from queer theory to argue that the Court should reconsider its jurisprudence, on the basis that it reinforces heteronormative conceptions of parenting and the family.

A. The Heterosexual Dyad as the Only Form of Co-Parenting: Dissenting from *Gas and Dubois v France*

1. The case originated in an application against the French Republic lodged with the Court by Ms Valérie Gas and Ms Nathalie Dubois on 15 June 2007. The applicants claim that they have been discriminated against, compared to different-sex couples, since there are no legal means in France for allowing same-sex couples to have access to second-parent adoption. They argue that this situation amounts to discriminatory treatment based on their sexual orientation, in breach of their right to respect for private and family life.

2. The applicants have lived together for over 20 years and had a daughter in 2000 via anonymous donor insemination (which took place in Belgium). Nevertheless, the domestic legislation did not allow for both applicants to be recognised as mothers of their daughter; only Ms Dubois (the biological mother) is legally considered to be the mother. In order to establish a legal bond between Ms Gas and her daughter, she applied for 'simple adoption' of their child, with the express consent of her partner. According to the domestic legislation, simple adoption does not sever the ties between the child and the biological mother, but creates an additional legal parent-child relationship. However, simple adoption results in the transference of all the rights associated with parental responsibility from the biological parent to the adoptive parent, unless the adopting parent is married to the biological parent.

3. Ms Gas and Ms Dubois are not married, since the domestic legislation only allows for different-sex marriage. They entered into a French civil partnership (PACS) in 2002. This civil partnership entails a number of obligations for those who enter into it, such as the obligation to live as a couple and to lend each other support. While partners are treated as a married couple in many ways, the partnership does not give rise to any kinship or inheritance ties between them. In particular, the PACS has no implications regarding adoptive relationships and parental responsibility. Therefore, the exception benefiting married couples in simple adoption does not apply to civil partners.

4. On 3 March 2006, Ms Gas applied to the Nanterre tribunal for a simple adoption order in respect of her daughter (although legally only her partner's daughter), with the express consent of Ms Dubois. The tribunal observed that the legal requirements for adoption were met and that both applicants were jointly involved in the upbringing of their daughter. Nevertheless, the court rejected the application on the grounds that it was against the best interests of the child, since the adoption would transfer parental responsibility to Ms Gas, depriving

Ms Dubois of her own rights in relation to their child. The applicants appealed the decision to the Versailles Court, arguing that the loss of parental responsibility on the part of Ms Dubois could be remedied through a delegation of parental responsibility. However, the Appeal tribunal confirmed the refusal of their application. The applicants then lodged an appeal before the Court of Cassation, but they did not pursue the proceedings up to the end, considering that it had no prospect of success in view of a contemporaneous judgment issued by that court in which it ruled out the possibility of simple adoption for same-sex couples (see *Gas and Dubois v France* (Dec), Application no 25951/07, 31 August 2010, 9).

5. Ms Gas and Ms Dubois then complained before this Court. The government objected to the admissibility of the case by the Court on two procedural grounds, but the Court rejected both objections in a decision of admissibility issued on 31 August 2010 (*Gas and Dubois v France* (Dec), cited above). We are now on 15 March 2012 delivering this judgment on the merits of the case. The question this Court has to answer is clear: Does allowing for second-parent adoption for heterosexual married couples, while denying it for same-sex couples in a civil partnership, amount to a discriminatory infringement of the right to respect for family life?

6. The applicants argue that they have been discriminated against in the enjoyment of the right to respect for their family life. A different-sex couple in the same circumstances would have been able to marry and subsequently obtain a single adoption order, both partners becoming legally recognised as parents of their child. Conversely, this was not allowed to them, due to the combined effect of marriage being the only possibility for second-parent adoption and this institution being reserved for different-sex couples.

7. The government presents two main arguments for opposing the applicants' claim. The first one is that the distinction between married heterosexual couples and same-sex couples (who are not allowed to marry under French law) is not discriminatory. The second one is that the parenting model adopted by the government is based on the idea of sexual difference and this is a decision that should be considered within the political discretion of the state.

8. The majority of the Court is ruling in favour of the government, finding no violation of the Convention (see paragraph 73 of the majority judgment). According to the majority, there is no discrimination in the case because, when comparing the applicants to a different-sex couple in a civil partnership, they would have been denied the possibility of second-parent adoption as well (therefore, there is equality in treatment). And as to the comparison of the applicants to a married different-sex couple, the differential treatment is justified due to the different circumstances of both couples, one being married and the other one not (see paragraphs 68 and 69 of the majority judgment). Lastly, regarding the issue of 'indirect' discrimination, based on the fact that the applicants could not become a married couple because of the domestic ban on same-sex marriage, the majority rejects this argument as well.

9. I disagree with the majority decision. In particular, while the use of the 'endless loop' argument in order to negate the existence of discrimination based on

sexual orientation is not a novelty within the Court's case law (see *Courten v United Kingdom* (Dec) Application no 4479/06, 4 November 2008; *MW v United Kingdom* (Dec) Application no 11313/02, 23 June 2009), the Court has never before been so explicit in the use of a reasoning suffering from epistemic circularity.

10. The reasoning of the majority is as follows: In paragraph 65, the majority recognises that the applicants cannot benefit from the only situation in which second-parent adoption is allowed – marriage – since France prohibits same-sex marriage. In paragraph 66, the majority reiterates that the prohibition of same-sex marriage is compatible with the Convention and that it does not amount to discrimination based on sexual orientation. In paragraph 68, the majority emphasises that marriage gives rise to important legal consequences and, therefore, the applicants are not in a similar situation to married couples. In paragraph 69, the majority expresses how 'equal' the treatment given to the applicants has been, since heterosexual couples who are unmarried do not benefit from the possibility of second-parent adoption either, highlighting that the difference in treatment is clearly based on marriage and has nothing to do with the sexuality of the applicants.

11. However, in paragraph 70, the majority faces the challenge posed by the applicants that unmarried heterosexual couples can actually benefit from second-parent adoption by marrying, while this alternative is forbidden to them. In paragraph 71, the reply of the majority is: 'in that connection the Court can only refer to its previous findings (see paragraphs 66–68)'.

12. In other words, the majority itself recognises that the differential treatment was clearly based on the sexuality of the applicants. However, they avoid expressly saying so by referring to the 'objective' fact that the deciding factor was (technically) marital status.

13. In this case, I am not the only dissenting voice in the Court, Judge Villiger is also issuing a dissenting opinion. Judge Villiger's compelling opinion is based on the understanding that it would be in the best interests of the applicants' daughter to have two legally recognised mothers, rather than just one. He considers that the blanket prohibition of joint parental custody over the children of same-sex couples is discriminatory against the children. And he adds that attempting to justify this discriminatory treatment against the children on the basis of the special status marriage has in society is plainly unconvincing. Therefore, he affirms that there has been a violation of the Convention, as the applicants' daughter has been deprived of two legal mothers, due to the sexuality of her parents (see dissenting opinion of Judge Villiger).

14. I concur with the dissenting opinion of Judge Villiger. However, I would like to express further reasons why denying the possibility of second-parent adoption for same-sex couples amounts to a discriminatory infringement of the right to respect for family life. First, I would like to highlight that this decision of the Court seems to be a step backwards in the case law regarding discrimination based on sexuality. In *EB v France*, this Court established that the sexuality of the parents should not be a deciding factor to grant an adoption (*EB v France* (GC),

Application no 43546/02, 22 January 2008). That is to say, when determining parenting rights, the parents' sexual orientation should be irrelevant.

15. Nonetheless, after having established the irrelevance of the parent's sexual orientation for the adoption of a child, the majority now decides in this case the relevance of sexuality. As mentioned before, the majority does so by validating a restriction for second-parent adoption beyond married couples, knowing that married couples equal heterosexual couples, given the ban on same-sex marriage.

16. In other words, the Court seems to be affirming two contradictory positions. On the one hand, when it comes to individual adoption, it is discriminatory to forbid adoption based on the sexuality of the adopter (as established in *EB v. France* (GC), cited above), but concerning second-parent adoption, it becomes legitimate to forbid adoption based on the sexuality of the adopter (an adopter who is, in addition, already the mother of the child).[21] This reason alone should have been sufficient for this Court to find that the domestic legislation amounted to discrimination based on sexuality.

17. Furthermore, I believe that the problems with this judgment are far greater than a lack of legal coherence, and I will make use of insights from queer theory to put into question the ideological basis of this judgment: the validation of a parenting model that idealises the heterosexual parenting dyad (see paragraph 52 of the majority judgment). The 'model of sexual difference', as labelled by the government, predicates the heteronormative belief that the ideal parents are those in a long-term committed heterosexual couple (P Johnson, 'Heteronormativity and the European Court of Human Rights' (2012) *Law and Critique* 49), regardless of the personal characteristics of the individuals.

18. The ideology of the heterosexual parenting dyad, based on the belief in the superior value of the heterosexual family, professes that children should better be raised by one man and one woman, rather than two men or two women. This is what happened to Ms Gas and Ms Dubois in the present case. On the assumption that children can only have one father and one mother, the ideology of the heterosexual parenting dyad establishes the need to sever parenting ties in order to create new ones. Therefore, the idealised model imposed that Ms Gas could not legally be the mother of her daughter, because the place of the mother is already filled, and since her gender inhibits her from being the father, she cannot have a legal parent-child bond with her own daughter.

19. Moreover, the heterosexual parenting dyad not only requires that parents should be of different gender, but also establishes a cap on the number of parents a child can have. Each child can only have a maximum of two parents, even though the reasons for the restriction on the number of parents do not seem to be obvious. A traditional argument for limiting the number of parents to two is that this is the number of biological parents a child has, since a person is conceived by one man and one woman.

[21] I have developed this idea further elsewhere. See Gonzalez-Salzberg, 'The Making of the Court's Homosexual' (n 18).

20. Nonetheless, there are actually no reasons why the upbringing of children needs to involve the same number of participants as their conception. In fact, the use of the 'biological' argument tries to present ideology as biology.[22] The idea that a child cannot be raised either by a same-sex couple or by more than two people has nothing to do with biology, and everything to do with the belief in the superior value of the heterosexual family (D Cornell, *At the Heart of Freedom* (Princeton University Press, 1998) 127).

21. I agree with Nanci Clarence when she affirmed that: 'the premise that exactly two and only two people can claim parental rights is as arbitrary and unreflective of social reality as the requirement in two parent families, that parents must be different genders' (N Clarence, cited in K Arnup and S Boyd, 'Familial Disputes? Sperm Donors, Lesbians Mothers and Legal Parenthood' in *Legal Inversions* (Temple University Press, 1995) 91). Consequently, the French model of parenting, which establishes the heteronormative family as ideal, restricts the different possibilities that family ties can adopt. There is a maximum of two parents per child and, in addition, those can only be two individuals of different sex.

22. Nevertheless, reality shows that children are raised by a variety of family forms, including two-parent families, one-parent families, other relatives, or foster families. While the law continues to assume that each child only has one father and one mother, the complexities of family life in our century demonstrates that some children actually have more than one father and/or one mother (E Jackson, 'What is a Parent?' in *Feminist Perspectives on Family Law* (Routledge, 2006) 59, 60 and 73). In fact, in some respects, even the applicant's daughter has at least three parents: a biological mother (Ms Dubois), a second mother (Ms Gas) and a genetic father (the anonymous donor).

23. However, only one of these parents is legally recognised as a parent by the law, even though two of them are performing that role. The domestic legislation and its obsession with the heterosexual parenting dyad have already established who can be the parents of the applicants' daughter and the actual family bonds need to adapt to this decision.

24. The question that seems appropriate to pose is: Why does the domestic legislation continue to insist on an idealised family that fails to accommodate the diverse reality of kinship? As affirmed by Emily Jackson: 'people no longer reproduce and raise children within the conventional biological nuclear family, the law should stop pretending that the answer to the question "What is a parent?" is a fact waiting to be discovered' (Jackson, cited above, 74).

25. I would like to emphasise that the limitation of legal parenthood upon two individuals is only a legal fiction that can be challenged, since it is based on the

[22] Indeed, in *X and others v Austria*, both the state and a third-party intervener (a Christian organisation) raised the issue of 'biology'. In particular, the state argued that 'recreating the biological family' was a legitimate aim of adoption. See *X and others v Austria* (GC), Application no. 19010/07, 19 February 2013, para 76.

heteronormative ideology of the heterosexual couple as the family norm (Cornell, cited above, 96). As Eve Kosofsky Sedgwick has proposed, it is time to start thinking of a more 'elastic' definition of the family. A definition that will be comprehensive not only of same-sex bonds, but also of non-marital and non-procreative bonds, of non-dyad bonds, of bonds not defined by genitality and of 'step'-bonds, among others (E Kosofsky Sedgwick, *Tendencies* (Routledge, 1994) 69–71).

26. To conclude, I would suggest that it is time for this Court to stop thinking of the reproductive heterosexual couple as the ideal to be achieved and to start considering the human rights of those individuals with families that exist beyond heteronormative standards. In this case, in particular, the Court should find the parenting model adopted by France, which is based on the idea of gender difference, discriminatory towards the applicants due to their sexuality and, therefore, in breach of Article 14 of the Convention in conjunction with Article 8.

VI. Conclusion

In this chapter I have raised my disagreement with certain judgments of the Court that denied the enjoyment of human rights based on the sexual and gender identities of individuals. However, the criticisms were proposed in a constructive manner, showing that the Court could (and should) have found a way to overcome clear heteronormative assumptions underpinning its judgments. In particular, the chapter has proposed that insights from queer theory, as expressed in the queer dissenting judgments, can help the Court to re-imagine a jurisprudence that does not deny human rights based on individuals' genders or sexualities.

The Court needs to be mindful that its understanding of marriage as an institution that can be made to remain exclusively heterosexual, according to the *Schalk and Kopf* judgment, shows an overly restrictive view. It was mentioned in Chapter 5 that human rights proponents, such as Robert Wintemute, have argued that denying the right to marry to same-sex couples is actually discriminatory treatment which contravenes the Convention itself. While reaching the same conclusion, the queer judgment I penned has also raised a general critique of marriage as an institution and, in particular, a criticism regarding its use to reinforce the privileged character of heterosexuality. In fact, the judgment rendered in the case has been criticised for the array of heteronormative assumptions underlying the Court's reading of the Convention, and the dissent was aimed at putting an end to such an interpretation.

The second case dealt with the requirement that certain states are imposing on married transsexual individuals to choose between continuing their marriage and having their gender transition fully acknowledged by law. As discussed in Chapter 5, this was the case in *Parry v United Kingdom*, and more recently in the *Hämäläinen v Finland* judgment issued by the Grand Chamber. The problems raised by the 'quandary' in which married trans people are placed should be considered a violation of human rights. The queer judgment discussed the idea that the decision of the Court in *Parry* was already based on postmodern notions about the mutability of gender and sexuality. However, those findings were used against the applicant, validating the requirement of ending a marriage to fully transcend her legally recognised gender. The Court could actually rescue those very queer insights developed in the case and, in the future, use them to reverse the restrictive understanding of gender and sexuality expressed in *Parry* and *Hämäläinen*.

The issue evaluated in the third judgment was the economic benefits that many states grant to married couples. These privileges vary depending on the domestic legislation of the state, but tend to include tax advantages, community property, inheritance rights, immigration benefits, and privileges in hospital visitations. Queer theorists have supported the idea that most of these benefits could be extended to other kinds of households and intimate relations, uncoupling them from the institution of marriage,[23] or could even be completely detached from couplehood.[24] The queer dissenting opinion in the decision on admissibility on *MW* was aimed in this direction. Human rights can make use of the critical view held by queer theorists of the privileges associated with marriage. Indeed, it is possible to think that those benefits currently granted to the heterosexual married couple could be extended to other couples who do not take part in the institution of marriage (either out of choice or due to prohibitions existing in domestic legislations), or they could be conceived of as being beyond conjugality, an idea that would certainly be consistent with the universality of human rights.

Lastly, the fourth judgment concerned the topic of second-parent adoption for same-sex couples. As discussed in Chapter 5, this issue was decided by the Court in its rulings in *Gas and Dubois v France* and *X and others v Austria*. On both occasions, the Court confirmed that states were allowed to restrict second-parent adoption to married couples, since this did not amount to discrimination under the Convention. The queer judgment drafted for *Gas and Dubois* disagreed with this position. It highlighted that the idealisation of the heterosexual married couple as the most appropriate environment for raising a child is a restrictive idea, since this parenting model imposes that only two individuals can be recognised as the parents of a child and establishes that these people need to be of different gender. However, reality is much more complex than just heterosexual couples raising children and the Court should realise that restricting the rights of those outside the traditional nuclear family amounts to a denial of human rights.

To conclude, this chapter was aimed at showing that human rights law does not need to be antagonistic towards queer theory, even if queer theory, with its

[23] Michael Warner, *The Trouble with Normal: Sex, Politics, and the Ethics of Queer Life* (Harvard University Press, 2000) 108 and 117–18.

[24] Aeyal M Gross, 'Sex, Love, and Marriage: Questioning Gender and Sexuality Rights in International Law' (2008) 21 *Leiden Journal of International Law* 235, at 246–47 and 252; Aeyal Gross 'The Burden of Conjugality' in Eva Brems (ed), *Diversity and European Human Rights: Rewriting Judgments of the ECHR* (Cambridge University Press, 2013) 265–92, at 281.

relentless critical and anti-normative commitments, frequently adopts a hostile posture towards human rights law. The dissenting judgments in all four cases showed that queer insights can certainly help the Court to overcome heteronormative assumptions currently supported by its jurisprudence. My claim is that queer insights can provide a perspective for interpreting human rights law that can enable the Court to find alternative solutions in cases in which the gender and sexuality of individuals are still considered to be legally relevant. As mentioned above, in certain cases the Court has already (perhaps inadvertently) resorted to understandings of gender and sexuality that look very similar to postmodern interpretations. I believe that, in the future, the Court can reclaim those queer ideas that already exist in its case law and deploy them in order to put an end to legal restrictions on the enjoyment of rights for LGBT applicants; hence, allowing human rights to approach its aspiration to universality.

7

Conclusion

The purpose of this book has been to make use of queer theory as a methodological approach to analyse how the European Court of Human Rights has constructed the gendered and sexual subject of human rights through its case law. Working within the tension between queer theory and human rights law, I have argued that, on the one hand, human rights law can make use of insights from queer theory in order to further approach its ideal of universality. On the other hand, I have proposed that queer activism can also take advantage of human rights strategies with an aim to *queering* the law, without abandoning its critical awareness of the regulatory power of rights.

Throughout the book I have made use of various strands of queer theory in different ways. Chapter 1 provided an initial approach to the topics of the book: human rights law, queer theory, and the work of the European Court of Human Rights. I discussed a (working) definition of queer theory and how this theoretical approach can guide us into challenging naturalised views on the genders and sexualities of individuals, which are (unsurprisingly) upheld and reproduced by human rights law. Nonetheless, my position has been that this regulatory power of rights should not lead us to discarding human rights as a strategy to better people's lives. Rather, acknowledging this aspect of human rights demands that we give greater critical reflection to the deployment of rights-based strategies.

The remaining chapters focused specifically on the case law of the European Court of Human Rights, the world-leading authority concerning the legal regulation of gender and sexuality through human rights. Chapter 2 discussed the Court's construction (and re-construction) of the notion of sex within its jurisprudence. The chapter showed how the Court's use of the combined force of the law and medicine, and their powerful claims to speak the truth,[1] seemingly reinforces the two-sex system within human rights law. Nevertheless, one key finding has been that the Court had (inadvertently) acknowledged that the binary gender system is not sufficient to comprehend the identity of every individual who requests the protection of human rights. From its earliest jurisprudence on transsexuality, the Court has actually validated the possibility of existing in-between the sexes, since trans individuals have been considered to belong to one sex for certain legal purposes and to the 'opposite' one in other legal aspects. Until 2002, the

[1] See Carol Smart, *Feminism and the Power of Law* (Routledge, 1989) 11.

'in-between' existence was the realm of the (post-operative) transsexual person, which came to an end when the Court embraced genital surgery as the basis for establishing the gender of trans individuals in the *Goodwin v United Kingdom* and *I v United Kingdom* judgments. From 2002 onwards, it was trans individuals who had not undergone genital surgery who were considered to remain in the 'intermediate position' between the sexes, as confirmed by the Court's rulings in *L v Lithuania* and *Nunez v France*.

A new jurisprudential shift in 2017 meant that surgery has now lost its position as the deciding criteria for establishing gender, but medical diagnosis came to occupy this place. While states can no longer require the surgical modification of genitalia for crossing the border between genders, they can request a diagnosis of suffering from a mental disorder, as established in *AP, Garçon and Nicot v France*. However, the sanctification of any legal requirement for allowing gender recognition (eg biology, surgery, diagnosis) also means that trans individuals who refuse to comply with such a requisite might be made to remain indeterminately in the domain of the gender in-between. My position is that the validation of the gender in-between should be *queerly* recuperated from these rulings. The Court has offered gender non-conforming individuals the possibility of existing in-between binary genders, in an intermediate position of intermittently moving across the sex boundary. This option might not be sufficiently queer for some, in the sense that it does not yet materialise a complete rejection of a sex attribution, but it provides a clear starting point from which to question the binary understanding of gender. If this 'intermediate' position is re-claimed by queer activism as a desired means by which to challenge an imposed binary existence, it could become a powerful tool to queer stable gender identities. Indeed, it might be one of the only tools available, as long as human rights law continues to request from its subject the performative construction of one of the two validated genders.

Chapter 3 focused on the notion of sexuality, with special emphasis on the construction of homosexuality by the Court. While the Court has affirmed the heterosexuality of the subject of the European Convention on Human Rights, it also decided to extend the protection of human rights to homosexual individuals. I argued that the grounds for offering that protection can be found in the Court's conception of homosexuality as an accepted sexual identity. This claim clearly distinguished my analysis from that of most of the academic scholarship on the topic, which tends to affirm that the basis for the Court's protection of homosexuality is its assumed private character.

The chapter also offered a discussion of the Court's construction of homosexuality through the lens of queer theory. The salient elements of the Court's conception of homosexuality (which are not necessarily internally coherent) can be summarised as follows: a categorical understanding of individuals' sexuality through the heterosexual/homosexual binary; the view of homosexuality as a characteristic that is not wilfully adopted, but instead is a predisposition of individuals; an unstable belief in homosexuality as a characteristic that is (most likely) innate, but could even be acquired, depending on the judgment; and an emphasis on sexual identity as an immutable quality. Regarding the mutability/immutability of sexuality, I highlighted that the Court's conviction in immutability seems to go as far as to understand that even in cases of gender transition, the sexuality of individuals remains unchanged. This applies both to those who undergo gender transition, as well as to the intimate partners of those who transition gender.

I argued that the Court's understanding of homosexuality as an immutable identity within a binary conception of sexualities (heterosexual/homosexual) has a likely explanation in the fact that the mutability of homosexuality would also mean the mutability of heterosexuality. The reliance upon immutability thus may well be because the Court is not prepared to question the stability of the sexuality of the true subject of human rights. Moreover, this understanding of homosexuality as a fixed identity of some individuals came to support the Foucauldian conception of the homosexual as a type of person who is defined by their sexuality. In fact, in the Court's case law, the homosexuality of individuals has had various consequences regarding the enjoyment of rights in areas that have no relationship of any kind with sexual practices, such as tax exemptions or parenting rights. Nevertheless, I suggested that the Court might have left open a possible path for challenging the categorical construction of sexuality. The relevance of first-person narratives within the Court's procedure can be the key for introducing into human rights discourse the materiality of sexual identities that exist beyond the inflexible heterosexual/homosexual binary.

Following the discussion in Chapters 2 and 3 about how the Court has constructed the notions of gender and sexualities, Chapters 4 and 5 dealt with the consequences of such constructions in terms of the enjoyment of human rights. The focus was on family rights, as this is the main area in which the Court has validated states' refusal of rights based on the sexual and gender identities of individuals. Making use of insights from queer theory, Chapter 4 reflected on the notion of the family within human rights law. It also provided an in-depth engagement with the prohibition of discrimination under the Convention, as this has been the legal strategy most frequently used to bring claims regarding LGBT family rights to Strasbourg. I raised concerns as to the (homonormative) dangers of LGBT families pursuing strategies grounded on assimilation to the traditional nuclear family. However, my position is that these fears should not lead to forsaking potential queer engagements with human rights law.

To request access into familial structures does not need to equate to embracing them as they stand. Inclusion can (and should) be coupled with interrogation and demands for change.[2] In fact, the inclusion of queer lives into traditional institutions entails, by itself, changes in the institution's own meaning and scope. I proposed two main strategies that should be considered with an aim to *queer* the current human rights protection against discrimination. The first one concerns challenging the fixed gender and sexual categories currently being required to

[2] See Judith Butler, *Bodies that Matter: On the Discursive Limits of Sex* (Routledge, 1993) 222; Carl F Stychin, *Law's Desire: Sexuality and the Limits of Justice* (Routledge, 1995) 155–56.

benefit from the prohibition of discrimination. The second one focuses on the demand to have access to the rights and benefits granted to the traditional family, while refusing to accept heteronormative criteria for determining kinship; hence, resisting the seeming neutrality of current (heteronormative) standards for establishing family ties.

Chapter 5 focused on the two most fundamental pillars of the family as currently conceived by human rights law: marriage and parenthood. I discussed the unstable construction (and re-construction) of marriage as a heterosexual institution. On the one hand, the Court has validated states' ability to impose a domestic ban on same-sex marriage in *Schalk and Kopf v Austria*, which reinforces the heterosexuality of marriage. On the other hand, the Court's position on the right of trans individuals to marry and to remain married has potentially jeopardised the assumed heterosexuality of marriage. The fact that the Court's case law has, at different times, validated the right of transsexual individuals to marry individuals of their own sex and of the 'opposite' sex, demonstrates that, either marriage has not always been heterosexual, or that the meaning of heterosexuality is rather unstable.

The alternative I proposed, that heterosexuality has become a fluid legal fiction, might seem counter-intuitive, but it nevertheless is a logical consequence of the Court's case law. Within the Court's jurisprudence on marriage, the meaning of heterosexuality has become detached from the genitalia of those who are party to it. The heterosexuality of marriage has been validated in the possible marriage of a transsexual woman and a cissexual woman (*Cossey v United Kingdom*), in the potential marriage of a transsexual woman and a man (*Goodwin v United Kingdom*), and in the marriage of a transsexual woman and a cissexual woman (once again), so long as the former did not change her identity number (*Hämäläinen v Finland*). This shows that the Court has constructed the heterosexuality of marriage tautologically, in that it can be defined as heterosexual regardless of sexual acts and genitalia.

Nonetheless, I concluded the chapter by affirming that within the Court's case law the heterosexual matrix continues to permeate the conception of family rights. The Court has actually adopted (heterosexual) marriage as the professed grounds for denying family rights, with LGBT parenting being the paradigmatic example of this phenomenon. While science's claim to truth had an important place in the Court's earlier jurisprudence that denied LGBT individuals the possibility of becoming parents (*X, Y, and Z v United Kingdom* and *Fretté v France*), 'scientific truth' was later replaced by the overarching importance of marriage as the grounds to deny LGBT individuals parenting rights. Parenting rights can be refused to same-sex couples and their children when the parents are not married, even if marriage is only made available by the state to different-sex couples.

Chapter 6 made use of queer theory to reconstruct four of the most controversial judgments in the field of family rights that were analysed in Chapters 4 and 5. The main aims of the chapter were to offer a productive dynamic beyond the obvious tension between (liberal) human rights law and (postmodern) queer theory, as well as to demonstrate that queer theory can also be normative rather than simply a tool for deconstruction. The judgments were not produced with the ambition that the Court would actually adopt them in the future, but in order to demonstrate how insights from queer theory can be reclaimed by human rights law.

The first re-written judgment was *Schalk and Kopf v Austria*, in which I developed the idea that queer's consistent opposition to marriage does not mean that the outcome of the judgment should be against same-sex marriage. On the contrary, I illustrated that insights from queer theory could also lead the way to finding that the prohibition of same-sex marriage is actually a violation of human rights. The second ruling I re-wrote was the Court's decision in *Parry v United Kingdom*. My judgment stated that making the applicant choose between the legal recognition of her gender and the continuation of her existing marriage was a clear violation of human rights. It also emphasised the different, and rather post-modern, assumptions concerning both gender and sexuality that shine through in the Court's own examination of the case. The third queer judgment offered in the chapter was *MW v United Kingdom*. In the original case, the Court confirmed that economic privileges could be attached to heteronormative ideals, such as marriage and couplehood. Conversely, the re-imagined ruling argued that such a decision not only failed to have any consideration for queer ideas, but that it was inconsistent even with the basic liberal principles of human rights law. Lastly, the fourth re-written judgment was *Gas and Dubois v France*. My queer decision highlighted the Court's own use of circular arguments in order to elaborate an unconvincing justification for differential treatment, which could not be truly reconciled with the universality of human rights. Moreover, the alternative judgment drew attention to how the Court accepted as unproblematic ideological assumptions that were disguised as biology. My claim at the end of the chapter was that queer theory can show the Court a possible path for overcoming heteronormative assumptions that underpin some aspects of its jurisprudence.

A Queer(er) Way Forward?

As affirmed in the first chapter of the book, queer theory focuses both on the 'deviant' cases (ie those genders and sexualities that contest the idea of neat identity categories), as well as on the categories themselves, by emphasising how even normalised identities might not truly fit within the idealised binaries.[3] Before reaching my final conclusions, I will adopt this queer approach to highlight again

[3] David M Halperin, 'The Normalization of Queer Theory' (2003) 45 *Journal of Homosexuality* 339, at 341; Stephen Valocchi, 'Not Yet Queer Enough: The Lessons of Queer Theory for the Sociology of Gender and Sexuality' (2005) 19 *Gender and Society* 750, at 753.

how the Court has (inadvertently) already performed this type of queer reading through some of the reasoning in its case law.

With regard to sexuality, the Court has elaborated some queer views on heterosexuality itself. In particular, a certain elasticity of the heterosexual category can be seen within the Court's jurisprudence. The paradigmatic example of this queer conception of heterosexuality is the opinion of Judge Walsh in *Dudgeon v United Kingdom*, which was discussed in Chapter 3. According to this Judge: 'It is known that many male persons who are heterosexual or pansexual indulge in these activities not because of any incurable tendency but for sexual excitement'.[4] The activities that Judge Walsh was referring to were homosexual acts. His reasoning suggested that even heterosexuals might enjoy some same-sex sexual acts every so often, for the purpose of sexual excitement. Thus, since the very first judgment regarding homosexuality, it is possible to see a conception of heterosexuality that is quite elastic, in the sense that includes homosexual desire, without apparently undermining the coherence of heterosexuality as an identity. Indeed, this is a very queer view of heterosexuality, in that it does not require that sexual desire and sexual activity be exclusively directed towards the 'opposite' sex. As a consequence, heterosexuals can have sex with those of their own sex without unsettling the meaning of heterosexuality.

A similar view on heterosexuality exists within the Court's jurisprudence concerning transsexual marriage. The most evident example of this appeared in the judgment in *Hämäläinen v Finland*. As discussed in Chapter 5, Ms Hämäläinen was forced to choose between the legal recognition of her gender transition and the continuation of her marriage, because the Court validated the domestic ban on same-sex marriage. In that case, both the majority ruling and the dissenting opinion accepted that Ms Hämäläinen's wife was heterosexual.[5] They held that she was heterosexual when she married her husband, and continued to be heterosexual even though she desired to maintain her marriage to her transsexual wife. Once again, it is possible to see a very flexible conception of heterosexuality, which includes the heterosexual cissexual woman who is married to a transsexual woman.

Most likely, it has been the anxiety about the potential destabilisation of heterosexuality which led to the elasticity of the category. Whatever the reason, the adaptability of heterosexuality should be celebrated. This understanding of heterosexuality serves to highlight that the Court has adopted certain queer insights within its jurisprudence. In turn, this can open up possibilities for obtaining further recognition and protection of fluid and non-binary sexualities within the realm of international human rights law, which can begin by highlighting the fact

[4] *Dudgeon v United Kingdom*, Series A no 45, 22 October 1981, partially dissenting opinion of Judge Walsh, para 13.

[5] *Hämäläinen v Finland* (GC), Application no 37359/09, 16 July 2014, para 44 and joint dissenting opinion of Judges Sajó, Keller and Lemmens, para 6.

that some queer sexualities, but not others, have already found a place within the judgments of the Court.

With regard to a queer perspective on gender, I discussed in Chapter 2 that while the Court remains a firm believer in the binary gender system, it has simultaneously validated the existence of some trans individuals as both man and woman, depending on the legal topic. In the Court's earliest jurisprudence, a group of judges who supported an applicant's claim for gender recognition, following her sex affirming surgery, stated: 'biologically she is considered not to be a woman. But neither is she a man, after the medical treatment and surgery. *She falls somewhere between the sexes*'.[6] Similarly, concerning a (pre-operative) transsexual applicant, the Court concluded in 2007:

> [T]he applicant finds himself in the intermediate position of a pre-operative transsexual, having undergone partial surgery, with certain important civil-status documents having been changed. However, until he undergoes the full surgery, his personal code will not be amended and, therefore, *in certain significant situations in his private life*, such as his employment opportunities or travel abroad, *he remains a woman*.[7]

As discussed above, this in-between space that was reserved for post-operative transsexual individuals until 2002, and then for pre-operative transsexual people up to 2017, is now the possible legal location of the undiagnosed trans person, following the Court's ruling in *AP, Garçon and Nicot v France*.

Nonetheless, this existence as both a man and a woman has not been the only queer recognition of gender beyond rigid binary categories. In a very controversial dissenting opinion, Judge Valticos claimed to have found a person who belonged to neither gender:

> In the present case we are faced with a voluntary action by the applicant, who, wishing to change sex (for he was originally of male sex, at least in essence, and had performed his military service), underwent an operation in conditions which appear dubious and afforded no guarantee, following which *he found himself in a position where he was no longer completely a man, nor indeed truly a woman*, but to a certain extent had some of the characteristics of both sexes.[8]

To clarify this statement, he later added that the applicant's sex had become 'indeterminate'.[9] While I have already criticised the opinion of Judge Valticos and the reasons that underpinned his judgment, it is nevertheless interesting that he declared himself to be in the presence of a sex beyond the man/woman binary.

It is certainly problematic that this gender existence either in-between or beyond the man/woman binary has been imposed upon individuals that were

[6] *Cossey v United Kingdom*, Series A no. 184, 27 September 1990, joint dissenting opinion of Judges Palm, Foighel and Pekkanen, para 5 (emphasis added).

[7] *L v Lithuania*, Application no 27527/03, ECHR 2007-IV, para 57 (emphasis added).

[8] *B v France*, Series A no 232-C, 25 March 1992, dissenting opinion of Judge Valticos, joined by Judge Loizou, 36–37 (emphasis added).

[9] ibid 37.

requesting due recognition of their gender. Despite this fact, the potential embrace of bi-gender and non-gendered belongings before the Court can open very appealing queer possibilities for human rights law. One of this has been materialised in *AP, Garçon and Nicot v France*, when the Court established the possibility of belonging to a specific (binary) gender category despite one's genitalia. By opposing that genital surgery could be made a requirement for gender recognition, the Court confirmed that gender can no longer be made dependent on genitalia. Unfortunately, at the same time, the Court validated the ongoing pathologisation of trans identities by confirming that medical diagnosis of mental disorder can still be a condition for gender recognition. However, as I affirmed elsewhere,[10] with this ruling the Court drew attention to that which will likely become the site of the next struggle for queer activism within human rights law.

Furthermore, it is possible to affirm that those persons gendered in non-binary ways and those with binary genders not grounded on their genitalia will not be the only queerly gendered people before the Court. Following the *AP, Garçon and Nicot v France* judgment, neither sterilising surgery nor medical treatments likely to lead to sterility, can be made conditions for obtaining gender recognition under the Convention. This means that the Court has acknowledged that the pregnant (trans) man is not a mythological creature, but a person that will eventually appear in Strasbourg, requesting due protection of his human rights. The Court should start looking for a place for the pregnant man within its conception of gender and, perhaps, this search should begin in the queer insights appearing in the jurisprudence concerning trans people.

These queer insights with jurisprudential approval also call attention to areas that are deserving of further reflection. New domestic legislation and judicial decisions in jurisdictions as diverse as Germany, Australia and India, are explicitly acknowledging that the man/woman binary is insufficient to cover the diverse reality of individuals' genders.[11] How these changes will impact on the reconstruction of the gendered subject of human rights law is a question that will need to be explored in the non-distant future. Other international monitoring bodies have already started to recognise that traditional conceptions of gender are insufficient to understand social reality. Almost a decade ago, Martin Scheinin, a then United Nations Special Rapporteur, affirmed in a Report to the General Assembly that gender was not a biological and fixed characteristic, but a social construct,

[10] Damian A Gonzalez-Salzberg, 'An Improved Protection for the (Mentally Ill) Trans Parent: A Queer Reading of *AP, Garçon and Nicot v France*' (2018) 81 *Modern Law Review* 526, at 538.

[11] German legislation started allowing for a third gender option for intersex newborn babies (following which, the German Constitutional Court also ruled on the topic); the judiciary of Australia decided in the *Norrie* case that an individual belonged to a 'non-specific' gender; and the Supreme Court of India recognised trans individuals as belonging to a third gender. See German Civil Status Act (Personenstandsgesetz), s 22 para 3 (amended on 7 May 2013) and German Federal Constitutional Court, Decision of 10 October 2017, Application no 1 BvR 2019/16; *NSW Registrar of Births, Deaths and Marriages v Norrie* [2014] HCA 11 (2 April 2014); *National Legal Service Authority v Union of India* (Writ Petition (Civil) No 400 of 2012) (15 April 2014).

and that this understanding meant that 'gender is not static; it is changeable over time and across contexts'.[12] Likewise, the Inter-American Commission of Human Rights in its 2015 Thematic Report, *Violence Against LGBTI Persons in the Americas*, made reference to 'sex' as a socially constructed concept.[13] These recognitions of sex/gender as a mutable social construct evidences that it can continue to be re-imagined in ways that challenge the binary gender system.[14] In fact, both the Inter-American Commission and the Inter-American Court of Human Rights have expressly acknowledged the existence of genders beyond the binary, actually using the term 'queer' as a possible gender identity category.[15] It is true that these initial references to non-binary genders by human rights bodies have not had any legal consequences so far, in terms of state obligations to provide recognition of non-binary identities. In particular, the Inter-American Court carefully clarified that the discussion it provided in 2017 concerning terminology used to refer to unconventional genders and sexualities only had illustrative purposes and 'insisted' that it had not adopted such terms as its own.[16] However, the mere naming of queer identities can be taken as an initial invitation that the Inter-American Commission and Court have offered to non-binary individuals to appear before them to claim the protection of their human rights.

A final point that I will address concerns the denial of certain family rights that has been validated by the jurisprudence of the European Court of Human Rights based on the genders and sexualities of individuals. As discussed in Chapters 4 and 5, all the rejections are now purportedly based on the validated ban on same-sex marriage. This applies to the right to marry itself, to economic benefits granted to married couples, and to the use of marriage as the basis for the denial of second-parent adoption. I am convinced that, in the future, the Court will reverse its position regarding the compatibility of the prohibition of same-sex marriage and human rights. As has happened with the legal recognition of gender transition, the Court might not even wait for the majority of the states of the Council of Europe to repeal their bans on same-sex marriage. A clear international trend could end up being sufficient for the Court to decide that the lack of recognition of same-sex marriage amounts to a violation of the Convention.[17]

[12] Martin Scheinin, Special Rapporteur on the Promotion and Protection of Human Rights and Fundamental Freedoms While Countering Terrorism, *GA Report on a Gender Perspective on Countering Terrorism*, A/64/211 (3 August 2009) para 20.

[13] Inter-American Commission on Human Rights, *Violence Against LGBTI Persons in the Americas*, OAS/Ser.L/V/II.rev.1 (12 November 2015) para 16.

[14] Judith Butler, *Gender Trouble: Feminism and the Subversion of Identity* (Routledge, 1990) 10–11.

[15] Inter-American Commission on Human Rights, *Violence Against LGBTI Persons in the Americas* (n 13) para 23; Inter-American Court of Human Rights, Advisory Opinion OC-24/17, *Gender Identity, and Equality and Non-discrimination with Regard to Same-Sex Couples*, Series A No 24 (24 November 2017) para 32.h and 32.v.

[16] Advisory Opinion OC-24/17 (n 15) para 32.

[17] See *Christine Goodwin v United Kingdom* (GC), Application no 28957/95, ECHR 2002-VI, para 85; *YY v Turkey*, Application no 14793/08, 10 March 2015, para 108; *Oliari and others v Italy*, Application nos 18766/11 and 36030/11, 21 July 2015, para 178.

An important step in this direction will be the Court overcoming its fear regarding the potential consequences of imposing this view upon a number of states that continue to reject same-sex marriage. For this reason, it is essential to remember that the catastrophic predictions about the almost confirmed arrival of the Four Horsemen of the Apocalypse in case of advancement on LGBT rights by the Court have (so far) proved mistaken. For example, when the Court found that the criminalisation of homosexuality amounted to a violation of human rights, Judge Zekia's prophesied:

> I may be considered to be in a better position in forecasting the *public outcry and the turmoil which would ensue if such laws are repealed or amended in favour of homosexuals either in Cyprus or in Northern Ireland*. Both countries are religious-minded and adhere to moral standards which are centuries' old.[18]

Similarly, Judge Pettiti's warned his fellow judges of the disastrous consequences of a Court's ruling in favour of Miss B, a transsexual woman. According to Judge Pettiti, if Miss B became entitled to the rectification of her gender in official documents: '[t]he whole of civil law and inheritance law could be thrown into confusion'. Nonetheless, the Court ignored the cautionary warnings issued by these judges, and the legal systems of Northern Ireland, Cyprus and France have remained in place. Likewise, I predict that nothing untoward will happen when the Court finally decides to rule that domestic bans on same-sex marriage amount to a violation of human rights.

Nevertheless, it is crucial to highlight that the acknowledgment of same-sex marriage as a human right, and the consequential extension of both economic benefits and the possibility of second-parent adoption to married same-sex couples, is far from being the end of the struggle for LGBT rights before the Court. As discussed throughout the book, the fact that these rights might become available to same-sex couples does not put an end to the heteronormative ideas which underpin the denial of rights in these cases. The problem with granting economic privileges to married couples is not only that it means excluding other couples from them. It is also the fact that the intimate couple is confirmed as the ideal type of relationship to be achieved. Queer theory highlights that the idealisation of the couple as the prescribed model for intimacy should not be considered unproblematic. It actually reinforces the assumption that everyone desires to be part of a couple;[19] and that it is, therefore, a failure not taking part in a coupled relationship. However, this understanding of the couple as the ideal to be reached reproduces a rather limited view of intimate life.[20] The expansion of economic benefits to same-sex couples would continue to reify the intimate couple as the ideal and will only improve the enjoyment of human rights for those within this type of relationship.

[18] *Dudgeon v United Kingdom* (n 4), dissenting opinion of Judge Zekia, para 2 (emphasis added).

[19] Eleanor Wilkinson, 'Single People's Geographies of Home: Intimacy and Friendship Beyond "the Family"' (2014) 46 *Environment and Planning A: Economy and Space* 2452, at 2455.

[20] ibid 2464.

Moreover, it would likely improve the lives of those who are economically privileged already.

The same holds true for extending second-parent adoption (and also joint adoption, of course) to same-sex couples. This would not challenge the idealised two-parent model. Extending parenting rights to other couples, while consistent with universalising rights, also serves to limit the possible ways in which parenting can be reconfigured. Support for legislation that contemplates parenting beyond the two-parent model should be the focus of future (queer) political strategies. In fact, the legal recognition of parenthood to multiple people is a legal phenomenon in current expansion.[21] Different domestic jurisdictions are amending their legislation to allow children to have more than just two legal parents.[22] This type of political struggle that can enable us to re-think the most commonly assumed configurations of kinship is the kind of politics that queer activism can lead within the field of human rights law, as well in other arenas.

In conclusion, this book has made an original and significant contribution to the field of law, in particular, to the areas of human rights law and queer legal theory. It represents the first comprehensive study that has applied queer theory to the analysis of the construction of gender and sexual identities under the European Convention of Human Rights. Approaching the field of human rights law from a perspective grounded in queer theory, I have illustrated that the tension between queer theory and human rights law might not be insurmountable. On the one hand, I hope that queer activism might desire to strategically reconsider its extreme antagonism towards rights tactics. On the other hand, I am certain that human rights law can take advantage of insights from queer theory in order to further approach its ideal of universality. At the end, whether any of the claims made throughout will be drawn upon by the European Court of Human Rights in the future is well beyond my power of prediction, and must be left for the Court to decide.

[21] Haim Abraham, 'A Family Is What You Make It? Legal Recognition and Regulation of Multiple Parents' (2017) 25 *American University Journal of Gender, Social Policy and the Law* 405, at 443.

[22] For instance, this is the case of the 2011 Family Law Act of British Columbia (Canada), in force since 2013, as well as of the 2016 All Families are Equal Act (Parentage and Related Registrations Statute Law Amendment) of Ontario (Canada). Family Law Act (SBC 2011) Chapter 25, Part 3 – Parentage, available at www.bclaws.ca/civix/document/id/lc/statreg/11025_00 (accessed 1 June 2018); All Families Are Equal Act (SO 2016) Chapter 23, Part 1 – Rules of Parentage, available at www.ontario.ca/laws/statute/S16023 (accessed 1 June 2018).

BIBLIOGRAPHY

International Documents

Commissioner for Human Rights of the Council of Europe, *Issue Paper on Human Rights and Gender Identity*, CommDH/IssuePaper(2009)2 (29 July 2009)

Committee on Economic, Social and Cultural Rights, *Concluding Observations of the Committee on Economic, Social and Cultural Rights on Germany*, E/C.12/DEU/CO/5 (20 May 2011)

European Court of Human Rights, *Overview 1959–2017* (March 2018)

High Commissioner for Human Rights, *Discriminatory Laws and Practices and Acts of Violence Against Individuals Based on Their Sexual Orientation and Gender Identity*, A/HRC/19/41 (17 November 2011)

Inter-American Commission on Human Rights, *Violence Against LGBTI Persons in the Americas*, OAS/Ser.L/V/II.rev.1 (12 November 2015)

Parliamentary Assembly of the Council of Europe, *Discrimination on the Basis of Sexual Orientation and Gender Identity*, Resolution 1728 (2010)

Scheinin, Martin, Special Rapporteur on the Promotion and Protection of Human Rights and Fundamental Freedoms While Countering Terrorism, *GA Report on a Gender Perspective on Countering Terrorism*, A/64/211 (3 August 2009)

Books

Anzaldúa, G, *Borderlands / La Frontera: The New Mestiza* (Aunt Lute Books, 1999)

Arendt, H, *Eichmann in Jerusalem: A Report on the Banality of Evil* (Viking Press, 1964)

Aristotle, *Nicomachean Ethics* (Roger Crisp ed and tr, Cambridge University Press, 2004)

Aust, A, *Modern Treaty Law and Practice* (Cambridge University Press, 2000)

Balkin, JM (ed), *What Brown v. Board of Education Should Have Said: The Nation's Top Legal Experts Rewrite America's Landmark Civil Rights Decision* (New York University Press, 2001)

Bamforth, N, *Sexuality, Morals and Justice: A Theory of Lesbian and Gay Rights Law* (Cassell, 1997)

Bamforth, N, Malik, M and O'Cinneide, C, *Discrimination Law: Theory and Context* (Sweet & Maxwell, 2008)

Barker, N, *Not the Marrying Kind: A Feminist Critique of Same-Sex Marriage* (Palgrave Macmillan, 2013)

Bates, E, *The Evolution of the European Convention on Human Rights: From Its Inception to the Creation of a Permanent Court of Human Rights* (Oxford University Press, 2010)

Baxi, U, *The Future of Human Rights*, 2nd edn (Oxford University Press, 2008)

Beger, NJ, *Tensions in the Struggle for Sexual Minority Rights in Europe: Que(e)rying Political Practices* (Manchester University Press, 2009)

Bell, V, *Interrogating Incest: Feminism, Foucault and the Law* (Routledge, 1993)

Bornstein, K, *Gender Outlaw: On Men, Women, and the Rest of Us* (Vintage Books, 1995)

Brems, E (ed), *Diversity and European Human Rights: Rewriting Judgments of the ECHR* (Cambridge University Press, 2013)

Buist, C and Lenning, E, *Queer Criminology* (Routledge, 2015)

Butler, J, *Gender Trouble: Feminism and the Subversion of Identity* (Routledge, 1990)

—— *Bodies that Matter: On the Discursive Limits of Sex* (Routledge, 1993)

—— *Gender Trouble: Feminism and the Subversion of Identity*, 2nd edn (Routledge, 1999)

—— *Antigone's Claim: Kinship Between Life and Death* (Columbia University Press, 2000)
—— *Undoing Gender* (Routledge, 2004)
Calhoun, C, *Feminism, the Family, and the Politics of the Closet: Lesbian and Gay Displacement* (Oxford University Press, 2000)
Chandler, D (ed), *Rethinking Human Rights: Critical Approaches to International Politics* (Palgrave Macmillan, 2003)
Collier, R, *Masculinity, Law and the Family* (Routledge, 1995)
Connolly, W, *Identity/Difference: Democratic Negotiations of Political Paradox* (Cornell University Press, 1991)
Cornell, D, *At the Heart of Freedom: Feminism, Sex and Equality* (Princeton University Press, 1998)
Corrêa, S, Petchesky, R and Parker, R, *Sexuality, Health and Human Rights* (Routledge, 2008)
Cryer, R, Hervey, T and Sokhi-Bulley, B, *Research Methodologies in EU and International Law* (Hart Publishing, 2011)
Delphy, C, *Close to Home: A Materialist Analysis of Women's Oppression* (Hutchinson, 1984)
Dembour, M, *Who Believes in Human Rights? Reflections on the European Convention* (Cambridge University Press, 2006)
Derrida, J, *Psyche: Invention of Other* (Stanford University Press, 2007)
Douzinas, C, *Human Rights and Empire: The Political Philosophy of Cosmopolitanism* (Routledge-Cavendish, 2007)
Duggan, L, *The Twilight of Equality: Neoliberalism, Cultural Politics, and the Attack on Democracy* (Beacon Press, 2003)
Edel, F, *Case Law of the European Court of Human Rights Relating to Discrimination on Grounds of Sexual Orientation or Gender Identity* (Council of Europe, 2015)
Fausto-Sterling, A, *Sexing the Body: Gender Politics and the Construction of Sexuality* (Basic Books, 2000)
Fineman, MA, *The Neutered Mother, the Sexual Family and Other Twentieth Century Tragedies* (Routledge, 1995)
Firestone, S, *The Dialectic of Sex: The Case for Feminist Revolution* (Bantam Books, 1972)
Foucault, M, *The History of Sexuality: An Introduction* (Penguin, 1978)
—— *Herculine Barbin: Being the Recently Discovered Memoirs of a Nineteenth-Century French Hermaphrodite* (Harvester Press, 1980)
Fuss, D (ed), *Inside/Out: Lesbian Theories, Gay Theories* (Routledge, 1991)
Greenberg, DF, *The Construction of Homosexuality* (University of Chicago Press, 1990)
Grubbs, JE, *Women and the Law in the Roman Empire: A Sourcebook on Marriage, Divorce and Widowhood* (Routledge, 2002)
Halley, J, *Split Decisions: How and Why to Take a Break from Feminism* (Princeton University Press, 2006)
Halperin, D, *One Hundred Years of Homosexuality: And Other Essays on Greek Love* (Routledge, 1990)
—— *Saint Foucault: Towards a Gay Hagiography* (Oxford University Press, 1997)
Harris, DJ, O'Boyle, M, Bates, E and Buckley, C, *Law of the European Convention on Human Rights*, 2nd edn (Oxford University Press, 2009)
—— *Law of the European Convention on Human Rights*, 3rd edn (Oxford University Press, 2014)
Hausman, B, *Changing Sex: Transsexualism, Technology, and the Idea of Gender* (Duke University Press, 1995)
Heinze, E, *Sexual Orientation: A Human Right: An Essay on International Human Rights Law* (Martinus Nijhoff, 1995)
Henkin, L, *The Age of Rights* (Columbia University Press, 1990)
Herman, D, *Rights of Passage: Struggles for Lesbian and Gay Legal Equality* (University of Toronto Press, 1994)
Hunt, L, *Inventing Human Rights: A History* (Norton and Company Press, 2007)
Hunter, R, McGlynn, C and Rackley, E (eds), *Feminist Judgments: From Theory to Practice* (Hart Publishing, 2010)

Ishay, MR, *The History of Human Rights: From Ancient Times to the Globalization Era* (University of California Press, 2004)
Jagose, A, *Queer Theory: An Introduction* (Melbourne University Press, 1996)
Johnson, P, *Homosexuality and the European Court of Human Rights* (Routledge, 2012)
—— *Going to Strasbourg: An Oral History of Sexual Orientation Discrimination and the European Convention on Human Rights* (Oxford University Press, 2016)
Katz, J, *The Invention of Heterosexuality* (Dutton, 1995)
Keating, A (ed), *The Gloria Anzaldúa Reader* (Duke University Press, 2009)
Kessler, SJ and McKenna, W, *Gender: An Ethnomethodological Approach* (University of Chicago Press, 1978)
Kosofsky Sedgwick, E, *Epistemology of the Closet* (California University Press, 1990)
—— *Tendencies* (Routledge, 1994)
Laqueur, T, *Making Sex: Body and Gender from the Greeks to Freud* (Harvard University Press, 1990)
Lerner, G, *The Creation of Patriarchy* (Oxford University Press, 1986)
Lyotard, J-F, *The Postmodern Condition: A Report on Knowledge* (Geoff Bennington and Brian Massumi tr, University of Minnesota Press, 1984)
McGhee, D, *Homosexuality, Law and Resistance* (Routledge, 2001)
Moran, L, *The Homosexual(ity) of Law* (Routledge, 1996)
Mutua, M, *Human Rights Standards: Hegemony, Law and Politics* (State University of New York Press, 2016)
Nino, CS, *The Ethics of Human Rights* (Clarendon Press, 1993)
Oakley, A, *Sex, Gender and Society* (Temple Smith, 1972)
O'Donovan, K, *Sexual Divisions in Law* (Weidenfeld and Nicolson, 1985)
—— *Family Law Matters* (Pluto Press, 1993)
Orakhelashvili, A, *The Interpretation of Acts and Rules in Public International Law* (Oxford University Press, 2008)
Otto, D (ed), *Queering International Law: Possibilities, Alliances, Complicities, Risks* (Routledge, 2017)
Ovey, C and White, RCA, *The European Convention on Human Rights*, 4th edn (Oxford University Press, 2006)
Pettiti, LE, *Les Transsexuels* (Presses Universitaires de France, 1992)
Rainey, B, Wicks, E and Ovey, C, *The European Convention on Human Rights*, 6th edn (Oxford University Press, 2014)
Riggsby, A, *Roman Law and the Legal World of the Romans* (Cambridge University Press, 2010)
Rubin, G, *Deviations: A Gayle Rubin Reader* (Duke University Press, 2011)
Schabas, WA, *The European Convention on Human Rights: A Commentary* (Oxford University Press, 2017)
Seidman, S, *The Social Construction of Sexuality* (Norton & Company, 2003)
Sharpe, A, *Transgender Jurisprudence: Dysphoric Bodies of Law* (Cavendish, 2002)
—— *Foucault's Monsters and the Challenge of the Law* (Routledge, 2010)
Smart, C, *Feminism and the Power of Law* (Routledge, 1989)
Spade, D, *Normal Life: Administrative Violence, Critical Trans Politics, and the Limits of Law*, 2nd edn (Duke University Press, 2015)
Steans, J, Pettiford, L, Diez, T and El-Anis, I, *An Introduction to International Relations Theory*, 3rd edn (Pearson, 2010)
Stryker, S and Aizura, A (eds), *The Transgender Studies Reader 2* (Routledge, 2013)
Stychin, CF, *Law's Desire: Sexuality and the Limits of Justice* (Routledge, 1995)
—— *A Nation by Rights: National Cultures, Sexual Identity Politics, and the Discourse of Rights* (Temple University Press, 1998)
—— *Governing Sexuality: The Changing Politics of Citizenship and Law Reform* (Hart Publishing, 2003)
Sullivan, N, *A Critical Introduction to Queer Theory* (New York University Press, 2003)
Van Dijk, P and others, *Theory and Practice of the European Convention on Human Rights*, 4th edn (Intersentia, 2006)

Warner, M (ed), *Fear of a Queer Planet: Queer Politics and Social Theory* (University of Minnesota Press, 1993)
—— *The Trouble with Normal: Sex, Politics, and the Ethics of Queer Life* (Harvard University Press, 2000)
Weber, C, *Queer International Relations: Sovereignty, Sexuality and the Will to Knowledge* (Oxford University Press, 2016)
Weeks, J, *Sexuality* (Tavistock Publications, 1986)
—— *The Languages of Sexuality* (Routledge, 2011)
White, RCA and Ovey, C, *The European Convention on Human Rights*, 5th edn (Oxford University Press, 2010)
Whittle, S, *Respect and Equality: Transsexual and Transgender Rights* (Routledge, 2002)
Whitty, N, Murphy, T and Livingstone, S, *Civil Liberties Law: The Human Rights Act Era* (Oxford University Press, 2001)
Wilchins, R, *Queer Theory, Gender Theory: An Instant Primer* (Alyson Books, 2004)
Wintemute, R, *Sexual Orientation and Human Rights: The United States Constitution, the European Convention, and the Canadian Charter* (Oxford University Press, 1995)
Wittig, M, *The Straight Mind and Other Essays* (Beacon Press, 1992)

Book Chapters

Anzaldúa, G, 'Let Us Be the Healing of the Wound: The Coyolxauhqui Imperative – La sombra y el sueño' in AnaLouise Keating (ed), *The Gloria Anzaldúa Reader* (Duke University Press, 2009) 303–17
Arnup, K and Boyd, S, 'Familial Disputes? Sperm Donors, Lesbians Mothers and Legal Parenthood' in Carl F Stychin and Didi Herman (eds), *Legal Inversions: Lesbians, Gay Men and the Politics of the Law* (Temple University Press, 1995) 77–101
Backer, LC, 'Queering Theory: An Essay on the Conceit of Revolution in Law' in Leslie Moran, Daniel Monk and Sarah Beresford (eds), *Legal Queeries: Lesbian, Gay and Transgender Legal Studies* (Cassell, 1998) 185–203
Bauer, R, 'Non-Monogamy in Queer BDSM Communities: Putting the Sex Back into Alternative Relationship Practices and Discourse' in Meg Barker and Darren Langdridge (eds), *Understanding Non-Monogamies* (Routledge, 2010) 142–53
Butler, J, 'Imitation and Gender Insubordination' in Diana Fuss (ed), *Inside/Out: Lesbian Theories, Gay Theories* (Routledge, 1991) 13–31
—— 'Critically Queer' in Shane Phelan (ed), *Playing with Fire: Queer Politics, Queer Theories* (Routledge, 1997) 11–29
—— 'On Being Beside Oneself: On the Limits of Sexual Autonomy' in Nicholas Bamforth (ed), *Sex Rights: The Oxford Amnesty Lectures 2002* (Oxford University Press, 2005) 48–78
Califia, P, 'Gay Men, Lesbians, and Sex: Do It Together' in Iain Morland and Anabelle Willox (eds), *Queer Theory* (Palgrave Macmillan, 2005) 22–27
Clucas, R and Whittle, S, 'Law' in Christina Richards, Walter Pierre Bouman and Meg-John Barker (eds), *Genderqueer and Non-Binary Genders* (Palgrave Macmillan, 2017) 73–99
Crisafulli, F, 'Same-Sex Couples' Rights (Other than the Right to Marry) Before the ECtHR' in Daniele Gallo, Luca Paladini and Pietro Pustorini (eds), *Same-Sex Couples Before National, Supranational and International Jurisdictions* (Springer, 2013) 409–36
Delphy, C, 'Rethinking Sex and Gender' in Stevi Jackson and Sue Scott (eds), *Gender: A Sociological Reader* (Routledge, 2001) 51–58
Dembour, M, 'Why Should Biological Sex Be Decisive? Transsexualism Before the European Court of Human Rights' in Alison Shaw and Shirley Ardener (eds), *Changing Sex and Bending Gender* (Berghahn, 2005) 39–59
Dhawan, N, 'Homonationalism and State-Phobia: The Postcolonial Predicament of Queering Modernities' in María Amelia Viteri, and Manuela Lavinas Picq (eds), *Queering Paradigms V: Queering Narratives of Modernity* (Peter Lang, 2015) 51–68

Epstein, S, 'Gay Politics, Ethnic Identity: The Limits of Social Constructionism' in Edward Stein (ed), *Forms of Desire: Sexual Orientation and the Social Constructionist Controversy* (Routledge, 1990) 239–93

Filax, G and others, 'Queer Theory/Lesbian and Gay Approaches' in Bridget Somekh and Cathy Lewin (eds), *Research Methods in the Social Sciences* (Sage, 2004) 81–88

Fineman, MA, 'The Sexual Family' in Martha Albertson Fineman, Jack E Jackson and Adam P Romero (eds), *Feminist and Queer Legal Theory: Intimate Encounters, Uncomfortable Conversations* (Ashgate, 2009) 45–63

Foucault, M, 'Sex, Power, and the Politics of Identity' in Paul Rabinow (ed), *Ethics: Essential Works of Michel Foucault 1954–1984* (Penguin, 2000) 163–73

Franke, K, 'Theorizing Yes: An Essay on Feminism, Law, and Desire' in Martha Albertson Fineman, Jack E Jackson and Adam P Romero (eds), *Feminist and Queer Legal Theory: Intimate Encounters, Uncomfortable Conversations* (Ashgate, 2009) 29–44

Gross, A, 'Challenges to Compulsory Heterosexuality: Recognition and Non-Recognition of Same-Sex Couples in Israeli Law' in Robert Wintemute and Mads Andenæs (eds), *Legal Recognition of Same-Sex Partnerships: A Study of National, European and International Law* (Hart Publishing, 2001) 391–414

—— 'The *Burden* of Conjugality' in Eva Brems (ed), *Diversity and European Human Rights: Rewriting Judgments of the ECHR* (Cambridge University Press, 2013) 265–92

Halley, J, 'Misreading Sodomy: A Critique of the Classification of "Homosexual" in Federal Equal Protection Law' in Julia Epstein and Kristina Straub (eds), *Body Guards: The Cultural Politics of Gender Ambiguity* (Routledge, 1991) 351–78

—— 'Recognition, Rights, Regulation, Normalisation: Rhetorics of Justification in the Same-Sex Marriage Debate' in Robert Wintemute and Mads Andenæs (eds), *Legal Recognition of Same-Sex Partnerships: A Study of National, European and International Law* (Hart Publishing, 2001) 97–111

—— 'Queer Theory by Men' in Martha Albertson Fineman, Jack E Jackson and Adam P Romero (eds), *Feminist and Queer Legal Theory: Intimate Encounters, Uncomfortable Conversations* (Ashgate, 2009) 9–28

Iantaffi, A, 'Future Directions' in Christina Richards, Walter Pierre Bouman and Meg-John Barker (eds), *Genderqueer and Non-Binary Genders* (Palgrave Macmillan, 2017) 283–96

Jackson, E, 'What is a Parent?' in Alison Diduck and Katherine O'Donovan (eds), *Feminist Perspectives on Family Law* (Routledge-Cavendish, 2006) 59–74

Jackson, S, 'Theorising Gender and Sexuality' in Stevi Jackson and Jackie Jones (eds), *Contemporary Feminist Theories* (Edinburgh University Press, 1998) 131–45

Kapur, R, 'The (Im)possibility of Queering International Human Rights Law' in Dianne Otto (ed), *Queering International Law: Possibilities, Alliances, Complicities, Risks* (Routledge, 2017) 131–47

Kavey, M, 'The Public Faces of Privacy: Rewriting *Lustig-Prean* and *Beckett v. United Kingdom*' in Eva Brems (ed), *Diversity and European Human Rights: Rewriting Judgments of the ECHR* (Cambridge University Press, 2012) 293–325

Kelly, R, 'Gay Marriage. Why Now? Why at All?' in Steven Seidman, Nancy Fischer and Chet Meeks (eds), *Introducing the New Sexuality Studies*, 2nd edn (Routledge, 2011) 457–62

Lau, H, 'Rewriting *Schalk and Kopf*: Shifting the Locus of Deference' in Eva Brems (ed), *Diversity and European Human Rights: Rewriting Judgments of the ECHR* (Cambridge University Press, 2012) 243–64

Lewis, ES, 'Pegging, Masculinities and Heterosexualities: How Narratives of Men Who Enjoy Being Penetrated by Women Can Contribute to Social Transformation and to Queering the Hidden Homosexual Norm in Queer Studies' in María Amelia Viteri and Manuela Lavinas Picq (eds), *Queering Paradigms V: Queering Narratives of Modernity* (Peter Lang AG, 2015) 241–63

McIntosh, M, 'Queer Theory and the War of the Sexes' in Joseph Bristow and Angelia R. Wilson (eds), *Activating Theory: Lesbian, Gay, Bisexual Politics* (Lawrence & Wishart, 1993) 30–52

Monro, S, 'Transgender: Destabilising Feminisms?' in Vanessa E Munro and Carl F Stychin (eds), *Sexuality and the Law: Feminist Engagements* (Routledge, 2007) 123–48

Morgan, W, 'Queering International Human Rights Law' in Carl Stychin and Didi Herman (eds), *Sexuality in the Legal Arena* (Athlone, 2000) 208–25

Naffine, N, 'The Body Bag' in Ngaire Naffine and Rosemary Owens (eds), *Sexing the Subject of Law* (Law Book Co, 1997) 79–93

Otto, D, 'Resisting the Heteronormative Imaginary of the Nation-State: Rethinking Kinship and Border Protection' in Dianne Otto (ed), *Queering International Law: Possibilities, Alliances, Complicities, Risks* (Routledge, 2017) 236–57

Peterson, VS and Parisi, L, 'Are Women Human? It's Not an Academic Question' in Tony Evans (ed), *Human Rights Fifty Years On: A Reappraisal* (Manchester University Press, 1998) 132–60

Pillay, N, 'What are Human Rights For?' in Daniel Moeckli, Sangeeta Shah and Sandesh Sivakumaran (eds), *International Human Rights Law* (Oxford University Press, 2010) 3–11

Przybylo, E, 'Masculine Doubt and Sexual Wonder' in Karli June Cerankowski and Megan Milks (eds), *Asexualities: Feminist and Queer Perspectives* (Routledge, 2014) 442–81

Rahman, M, 'Querying the Equation of Sexual Diversity with Modernity: Towards a Homocolonialist Test' in María Amelia Viteri, and Manuela Lavinas Picq (eds), *Queering Paradigms V: Queering Narratives of Modernity* (Peter Lang, 2015) 91–111

Robson, R, 'Compulsory Matrimony' in Martha Albertson Fineman, Jack E Jackson and Adam P Romero (eds), *Feminist and Queer Legal Theory: Intimate Encounters, Uncomfortable Conversations* (Ashgate, 2009) 313–28

Rooke, A, 'Telling Trans Stories: (Un)doing the Science of Sex' in Sally Hines and Tam Sanger (eds), *Transgender Identities: Towards a Social Analysis of Gender Identity* (Routledge, 2010) 64–83

Rubin, G, 'Thinking Sex: Notes for a Radical Theory of the Politics of Sexuality' in Carole S Vance (ed), *Pleasure and Danger: Exploring Female Sexuality* (Routledge & Kegan, 1984) 267–319

—— 'Thinking Sex: Notes for a Radical Theory of the Politics of Sexuality' in Richard Parker and Peter Aggleton (eds), *Culture, Society and Sexuality: A Reader* (Routledge, 2007) 150–87

Sanger, T, 'Beyond Gender and Sexuality Binaries in Sociological Theory: The Case for Transgender Inclusion' in Sally Hines and Tam Sanger (eds), *Transgender Identities: Towards a Social Analysis of Gender Identity* (Routledge, 2010) 259–76

Seidman, S, 'From Polluted Homosexual to the Normal Gay' in Chrys Ingraham (ed), *Thinking Straight: The Power, the Promise, and the Paradox of Heterosexuality* (Routledge, 2005) 39–61

Sharpe, A, 'From Functionality to Aesthetics: The Architecture of Transgender Jurisprudence' in Susan Stryker and Stephen Whittle (eds), *The Transgender Studies Reader* (Routledge, 2006) 621–31

Sojka, CJ, 'Partners of Transgender People' in Steven Seidman, Nancy Fischer and Chet Meeks (eds), *Introducing the New Sexuality Studies*, 2nd edn (Routledge, 2011) 236–41

Stein, E, 'The Essentials of Constructionism and the Construction of Essentialism' in Edward Stein (ed), *Forms of Desire: Sexual Orientation and the Social Constructionist Controversy* (Routledge, 1990) 325–53

Stone, S, 'The Empire Strikes Back: A Posttranssexual Manifesto' in Julia Epstein and Kristina Straub (eds), *Body Guards: The Cultural Politics of Gender Ambiguity* (Routledge, 1991) 280–304

Stychin, CF, 'Family Friendly? Rights, Responsibilities and Relationship Recognition' in Alison Diduck and Katherine O'Donovan (eds), *Feminist Perspectives on Family Law* (Routledge-Cavendish, 2006) 21–37

Threadgold, T, 'Performing Theories of Narrative: Theorizing Narrative Performance' in Joanna Thornborrow and Jennifer Coates (eds), *The Sociolinguistics of Narrative* (John Benjamins 2005) 261–278

Whittle S, 'Sex: Has It Any Place in Modern Marriage' in Robert Wintemute and Mads Andenæs (eds), *Legal Recognition of Same-Sex Partnerships: A Study of National, European and International Law* (Hart Publishing, 2001) 693–712

Wintemute, R, 'Strasbourg to the Rescue? Same-Sex Partners and Parents' in Robert Wintemute and Mads Andenæs (eds), *Legal Recognition of Same-Sex Partnerships: A Study of National, European and International Law* (Hart Publishing, 2001) 713–29

—— 'From "Sex Rights" to "Love Rights": Partnership Rights as Human Rights' in Nicholas Bamforth (ed), *Sex Rights: The Oxford Amnesty Lectures 2002* (Oxford University Press, 2005) 186–224

—— 'Sexual Orientation and Gender Identity' in Colin Harvey (ed), *Human Rights in the Community: Rights as Agents for Change* (Hart Publishing, 2005) 175–99
Wittig, M, 'The Category of Sex' in Monique Wittig, *The Straight Mind and Other Essays* (Beacon Press, 1992) 1–8

Journal Articles

Abraham, H, 'A Family Is What You Make It? Legal Recognition and Regulation of Multiple Parents' (2017) 25 *American University Journal of Gender, Social Policy and the Law* 405
Alston, P, 'The Best Interests Principle: Towards a Reconciliation of Culture and Human Rights' (1994) 8 *International Journal of Law and the Family* 1
Ashford, C, 'Barebacking and the "Cult of Violence": Queering the Criminal Law' (2010) 74 *Journal of Criminal Law* 339
Attanasio, JB, 'Rapporteur's Overview and Conclusions: Of Sovereignty, Globalization, and Courts' (1996) 28 *New York University Journal of International Law and Politics* 1
Austin, GW, 'Queering Family Law' (1999) 8 *Australasian Gay and Lesbian Law Journal* 39
Baker, A, 'The Enjoyment of Rights and Freedoms: A New Conception of the "Ambit" under Article 14 ECHR' (2006) 69 *Modern Law Review* 714
Balkin, JM, 'Deconstructive Practice and Legal Theory' (1987) 96 *Yale Law Journal* 743
Ball, CA, 'Sexual Ethics and Postmodernism in Gay Rights Philosophy' (2002) 80 *North Carolina Law Review* 371
Bamforth, N, 'Sexual Privacy and the European Convention on Human Rights' (1997) 56 *Cambridge Law Journal* 480
—— 'Sexual Orientation Discrimination After Grant v South-West Trains' (2000) 63 *Modern Law Review* 694
—— 'Families Not (Yet) Marriages? Same-Sex Partners and the Developing Convention "Margin of Appreciation"' (2011) 23 *Child and Family Law Quarterly* 128
Bauer, G, Hammond, R, Travers, R, Kaay, M, Hohenadel, K and Boyce, M, '"I Don't Think This is Theoretical; This is Our Lives": How Erasure Impacts Health Care for Transgender People' (2009) 20 *Journal of the Association of Nurses in AIDS Care* 348
Berlant, L and Warner, M, 'Sex in Public' (1998) 24 *Critical Inquiry* 547
Butler, J, 'Is Kinship Already Heterosexual' (2002) 13 *Differences: A Journal of Feminist Cultural Studies* 14
Cahn, N, 'The New Kinship' (2012) 100 *Georgetown Law Journal* 367
Chang, H, 'My Father is a Woman, Oh No! The Failure of the Courts to Uphold Individual Substantive Due Process Rights for Transgender Parents Under the Guise of the Best Interest of the Child' (2003) 43 *Santa Clara Law Review* 649
Chase, AT, 'Human Rights Contestations: Sexual Orientation and Gender Identity' (2016) 20 *International Journal of Human Rights* 703
Cobb, N, '"Gay Couple's Break Like Fawlty Towers": Dangerous Representations of Lesbian and Gay Oppression in an Era of "Progressive" Law Reform' (2009) 18 *Social and Legal Studies* 333
Currah, P, 'Defending Genders: Sex and Gender Non-Conformity in the Civil Rights Strategies of Sexual Minorities' (1997) 48 *Hastings Law Journal* 1363
De Lauretis, T, 'Queer Theory: Lesbian and Gays Sexualities: An Introduction' (1991) 3 *Differences: A Journal of Feminist Cultural Studies* iii
Doty, K, 'From *Fretté* to *E.B.*: The European Court of Human Rights on Gay and Lesbian Adoption' (2009) 18 *Law and Sexuality: A Review of Lesbian, Gay, Bisexual, and Transgender Legal Issues* 121
Douzinas, C, 'Humanity, Military Humanism and the New Moral Order' (2003) 32 *Economy and Society* 159
Duggan, L, 'Queering the State' (1994) 39 *Social Text* 1
Epstein, S, 'A Queer Encounter: Sociology and the Study of Sexuality' (1994) 12 *Sociological Theory* 188
Eskridge, WN, 'Law and the Constitution of the Closet: American Regulation of Same-Sex Intimacy, 1880–1946' (1997) 82 *Iowa Law Review* 1007

Fineman, MA, 'Why Marriage?' (2002) 9 *Virginia Journal of Social Policy and the Law* 239
Foster, S, 'Gross Indecency and the Right to Private Sexual Life' (2000) 5 *Coventry Law Journal* 77
Gartner, N, 'Lesbian (M)Otherhood: Creating an Alternative Model for Settling Child Custody Disputes' (2007) 16 *Law and Sexuality* 45
Gonzalez-Salzberg, DA, 'The Accepted Transsexual and the Absent Transgender: A Queer Reading of the Regulation of Sex/Gender by the European Court of Human Rights' (2014) 29 *American University International Law Review* 797
—— 'The Making of the Court's Homosexual: A Queer Reading of the European Court of Human Rights' Case Law on Same-Sex Sexuality' (2014) 65 *Northern Ireland Legal Quarterly* 371
—— 'Confirming (The Illusion of) Heterosexual Marriage: *Hämäläinen v Finland*' (2015) 2 *Journal of International and Comparative Law* 173
—— 'An Improved Protection for the (Mentally Ill) Trans Parent: A Queer Reading of *AP, Garçon and Nicot v France*' (2018) 81 *Modern Law Review* 526
Gotell, L, 'Queering Law: Not by Vriend' (2002) 17 *Canadian Journal of Law and Society* 89
Grabham, E, 'Governing Permanence: Trans Subjects, Time, and the Gender Recognition Act' (2010) 19 *Social and Legal Studies* 107
Green, AI, 'Queer Theory and Sociology: Locating the Subject and the Self in Sexuality Studies' (2007) 25 *Sociological Theory* 26
Greenberg, JA, 'Intersexuality and the Collision Between Law and Biology' (1999) 41 *Arizona Law Review* 270
Grigolo, M, 'Sexualities and the ECHR: Introducing the Universal Sexual Legal Subject' (2003) 14 *European Journal of International Law* 1023
Gross, A, 'Queer Theory and International Human Rights Law: Does Each Person Have a Sexual Orientation?' (2007) 101 *American Society of International Law Proceedings* 129
—— 'Sex, Love, and Marriage: Questioning Gender and Sexuality Rights in International Law' (2008) 21 *Leiden Journal of International Law* 235
—— 'Gender Outlaws Before the Law: The Courts of the Borderland' (2009) 32 *Harvard Journal of Law and Gender* 165
Halley, J, 'The Politics of the Closet: Towards Equal Protection for Gay, Lesbian, and Bisexual Identity' (1989) 36 *UCLA Law* Review 915
Halperin, DM, 'The Normalization of Queer Theory' (2003) 45 *Journal of Homosexuality* 339
Hamilton, F, 'Why the Margin of Appreciation is Not the Answer to the Gay Marriage Debate' (2013) 1 *European Human Rights Law Review* 47
Hare, I, 'Privacy and the Gay Right to Fight' (2000) 59 *Cambridge Law Journal* 6
Hart, L, 'Individual Adoption by Non-Heterosexuals and the Order of Family Life in the European Court of Human Rights' (2009) 36 *Journal of Law and Society* 536
Heinze, E, 'Sexual Orientation and International Law: A Study in the Manufacture of Cross-Cultural "Sensitivity"' (2001) 22 *Michigan Journal of International Law* 283
Herman, D, 'Are We Family Yet? Lesbian Rights and Women's Liberation' (1990) 28 *Osgoode Hall Law Journal* 789
Herring, J, 'Gay Rights Come Quietly' (2002) 118 *Law Quarterly Review* 31
Hodson, L, 'Family Values: The Recognition of Same-Sex Relationships in International Law' (2004) 22 *Netherlands Quarterly of Human Rights* 33
—— 'A Marriage by Any Other Name? *Schalk and Kopf v Austria*' (2011) 11 *Human Rights Law Review* 170
—— 'Ties that Bind: Towards a Child-Centred Approach to Lesbian, Gay, Bi-Sexual and Transgender Families under the ECHR' (2012) 20 *International Journal of Children's Rights* 501
Ingraham, C, 'The Heterosexual Imaginary: Feminist Sociology and the Theories of Gender' (1994) 12 *Sociological Theory* 203
Irvine, JM, 'A Place in the Rainbow: Theorizing Lesbian and Gay Culture' (1994) 12 *Sociological Theory* 232
Iyer, N, 'Categorical Denials: Equality Rights and the Shaping of Social Identity' (1994) 19 *Queen's Law Journal* 179

Johnson, C, 'Heteronormative Citizenship and the Politics of Passing' (2002) 5 *Sexualities* 317

Johnson, P, 'An Essentially Private Manifestation of Human Personality: Constructions of Homosexuality in the European Court of Human Rights' (2010) 10 *Human Rights Law Review* 67

—— 'Challenging the Heteronormativity of Marriage: The Role of Judicial Interpretation and Authority' (2011) 20 *Social and Legal Studies* 349

—— 'Homosexuality, Freedom of Assembly and the Margin of Appreciation Doctrine of the European Court of Human Rights: *Alekseyev v Russia*' (2011) 11 *Human Rights Law Review* 578

—— 'Adoption, Homosexuality and the European Convention on Human Rights: *Gas and Dubois v France*' (2012) 75 *Modern Law Review* 1123

—— 'Heteronormativity and the European Court of Human Rights' (2012) 23 *Law and Critique* 43

—— 'Sociology and the European Court of Human Rights' (2014) 62 *Sociological Review* 547

—— '"The Choice of Wording must be Regarded as Deliberate": Same-Sex Marriage and Article 12 of the European Convention on Human Rights' (2015) 40 *European Law Review* 207

Kennedy, D, 'The International Human Rights Movement: Part of the Problem?' (2002) 15 *Harvard Human Rights Journal* 101

Kepros, LR, 'Queer Theory: Weed or Seed in the Garden of Legal Theory' (2000) 9 *Law and Sexuality: A Review of Lesbian, Gay, Bisexual, and Transgender Legal Issues* 279

Kessler, SJ, 'The Medical Construction of Gender: Case Management of Intersexed Infants' (1990) 16 *Signs* 3

Knauer, N, 'Gender Matters: Making the Case for Trans Inclusion' (2008) 6 *Pierce Law Review* 1

Knouse, J, 'Intersexuality and the Social Construction of Anatomical Sex' (2006) 12 *Cardozo Journal of Law and Gender* 135

Langlois, AJ, 'Human Rights in Crisis? A Critical Polemic Against Polemical Critics' (2012) 11 *Journal of Human Rights* 558

Laqueur, T, 'Orgasm, Generation, and the Politics of Reproductive Biology' (1986) 14 *Representations* 1

Letsas, G, 'Two Concepts of the Margin of Appreciation' (2006) 26 *Oxford Journal of Legal Studies* 705

McGill, J and Salyzyn, A, 'Queer Insights on Women in the Legal Profession' (2014) 17 *Legal Ethics* 231

McGoldrick, D, 'The Development and Status of Sexual Orientation Discrimination Under International Human Rights Law' (2016) 16 *Human Rights Law Review* 613

McIntosh, M, 'The Homosexual Role' (1968) 16 *Social Problems* 182

Millbank, J, 'From Here to Maternity: A Review of the Research on Lesbian and Gay Families' (2003) 38 *Australian Journal of Social Issues* 541

Moran, L, '*Laskey v The United Kingdom*: Learning the Limits of Privacy' (1998) 61 *Modern Law Review* 77

Moreham, NA, 'The Right to Respect for Private Life in the European Convention on Human Rights: A Re-Examination' (2008) 1 *European Human Rights Law Review* 44

Morgan, W, 'Law & Change: Identifying Evil for What It Is: Tasmania, Sexual Perversity and the United Nations' (1994) 19 *Melbourne University Law Review* 742

—— 'Queer Law: Identity, Culture, Diversity, Law' (1995) 5 *Australasian Gay and Lesbian Law Journal* 1

Morsink, J, 'Women's Rights in the Universal Declaration' (1991) 13 *Human Rights Quarterly* 229

Namaste, K, 'The Politics of Inside/Out: Queer Theory, Poststructuralism, and a Sociological Approach to Sexuality' (1994) 12 *Sociological Theory* 220

Nye, J, 'The Gender Box' (1998) 13 *Berkeley Women's Law Journal* 226

O'Flaherty, M and Fisher, J, 'Sexual Orientation, Gender Identity and International Human Rights Law: Contextualising the Yogyakarta Principles' (2008) 8 *Human Rights Law Review* 207

Otto, D, 'Queering Gender [Identity] in International Law' (2015) 33 *Nordic Journal of Human Rights* 299

Parker, S, 'The Best Interests of the Child: Principles and Problems' (1994) 8 *International Journal of Law and the Family* 26

Pawelski, JG and others, 'The Effects of Marriage, Civil Union, and Domestic Partnership Laws on the Health and Well-Being of Children' (2006) 118 *Pediatrics* 349

Perrin, EC and others, 'Technical Report: Coparent or Second-Parent Adoption by Same-Sex Parents' (2002) 109 *Pediatrics* 341

Phelan, S, 'Queer Liberalism?' (2000) 94 *American Political Science Review* 431
Ragone, S and Volpe, V, 'An Emerging Right to a "Gay" Family Life? The Case *Oliari v. Italy* in a Comparative Perspective' (2016) 17 *German Law Journal* 451
Rich, A, 'Compulsory Heterosexuality and Lesbian Existence' (1980) 5 *Signs* 631
Richardson, D, 'Claiming Citizenship? Sexuality, Citizenship and Lesbian/Feminist Theory' (2000) 3 *Sexualities* 255
Richie, C, 'Lessons from Queer Bioethics: A Response to Timothy F. Murphy' (2016) 30 *Bioethics* 365
Romero, AP, 'Methodological Descriptions: "Feminist" and "Queer" Legal Theories' (2007) 19 *Yale Journal of Law and Feminism* 227
Roseneil, S, 'Why We Should Care About Friends: An Argument for Queering the Care Imaginary in Social Policy' (2004) 3 *Social Policy and Society* 409
Rutledge, D, 'Child Support: Discrimination Based on Sexual Orientation – Justification' (2011) 18 *Journal of Social Security Law* 15
Sabatello, M, 'Advancing Transgender Family Rights Through Science: A Proposal for an Alternative Framework' (2011) 33 *Human Rights Quarterly* 43
Sandland, R, 'Crossing and Not Crossing: Gender, Sexuality and Melancholy in the European Court of Human Rights' (2003) 11 *Feminist Legal Studies* 191
—— 'Feminism and the Gender Recognition Act 2004' (2005) 13 *Feminist Legal Studies* 43
Scott, JW, 'Deconstructing Equality-Versus-Difference: Or, the Uses of Post-Structuralist Theory for Feminism' (1988) 14 *Feminist Studies* 33
Sen, A, 'Elements of a Theory of Human Rights' (2004) 32 *Philosophy and Public Affairs* 315
Sharpe, A, 'Transgender Marriage and the Legal Obligation to Disclose Gender History' (2012) 75 *Modern Law Review* 33
—— 'The Ethicality of the Demand for (Trans)parency in Sexual Relations' (2017) 43 *Australian Feminist Law Journal* 161
Sherlock, A, 'Article 8, Privacy and the Rights of Homosexuals' (1989) 14 *European Law Review* 112
—— 'Prohibition of Homosexual Relations in Private and the Convention' (1994) 19 *European Law Review* 112
Slaughter, A, 'Judicial Globalization' (2000) 40 *Virginia Journal of International Law* 1103
Smart, C, 'Law's Power, the Sexed Body, and Feminist Discourse' (1990) 17 *Journal of Law and Society* 194
Spade, D, 'Resisting Medicine, Re/modelling Gender' (2003) 18 *Berkeley Women's Law Journal* 15
Spencer, JR, 'Incest and Article 8 of the European Convention on Human Rights' (2013) 72 *Cambridge Law Journal* 5
Stein, A and Plummer, K, '"I Can't Even Think Straight": "Queer" Theory and the Missing Sexual Revolution in Sociology' (1994) 12 *Sociological Theory* 178
Stryker, S, 'Transgender History, Homonormativity, and Disciplinarity' (2008) 100 *Radical History Review* 145
Stychin, CF, 'Essential Rights and Contested Identities: Sexual Orientation and Equality Rights Jurisprudence in Canada' (1995) 8 *Canadian Journal of Law and Jurisprudence* 49
—— 'To Take Him "At His Word": Theorizing Law, Sexuality and the US Military Exclusion Policy' (1996) 5 *Social and Legal Studies* 179
—— 'Same-Sex Sexualities and the Globalization of Human Rights Discourse' (2004) 49 *McGill Law Journal* 951
—— 'Being Gay' (2005) 40 *Government and Opposition* 90
—— 'Couplings: Civil Partnership in the United Kingdom' (2005) 8 *New York City Law Review* 543
Trispiotis, I, 'Discrimination and Civil Partnerships: Taking "Legal" Out of Legal Recognition' (2014) 14 *Human Rights Law Review* 343
Vade, D, 'Expanding Gender and Expanding the Law: Toward a Social and Legal Conceptualization of Gender that is More Inclusive of Transgender People' (2005) 11 *Michigan Journal of Gender and Law* 253
Valdes, F, 'Queers, Sissies, Dykes, and Tomboys: Deconstructing the Conflation of "Sex", "Gender", and "Sexual Orientation" in Euro-American Law and Society' (1995) 83 *California Law Review* 350

—— 'Sex and Race in Queer Legal Culture: Ruminations on Identities & Inter-connectivities' (1996) 5 *California Review of Law and Women's Studies* 25

Valocchi, S, 'Not Yet Queer Enough: The Lessons of Queer Theory for the Sociology of Gender and Sexuality' (2005) 19 *Gender and Society* 750

Van den Bogaert, S, 'ECHR Rules on Illegal Ban of Warsaw Equality Parade: The Case of Bączkowski and Others v Poland' (2007) 8 *German Law Journal* 890.

Waites, M, 'The Fixity of Sexual Identities in the Public Sphere: Biomedical Knowledge, Liberalism and the Heterosexual/Homosexual Binary in Late Modernity' (2005) 8 *Sexualities* 539

—— 'Critique of "Sexual Orientation" and "Gender Identity" in Human Rights Discourse: Global Queer Politics Beyond the Yogyakarta Principles' (2009) 15 *Contemporary Politics* 137

Warner, M, 'Normal and Normaller: Beyond Gay Marriage' (1999) 5 *GLQ: A Journal of Lesbian and Gay Studies* 119

West, C and Zimmerman, DH, 'Doing Gender' (1987) 1 *Gender and Society* 125

Wilkinson, E, 'Single People's Geographies of Home: Intimacy and Friendship Beyond "the Family"' (2014) 46 *Environment and Planning A: Economy and Space* 2452

Yoshino, K, 'The Epistemic Contract of Bisexual Erasure' (2000) 52 *Stanford Law Review* 353

Zanghellini, A, 'Scientific Positivism and the Controversy Over Research into Lesbian and Gay Parenting' (2007) 4 *Sexuality Research and Social Policy* 100

—— 'Queer, Antinormativity, Counter-normativity and Abjection' (2009) 18 *Griffith Law Review* 1

Conference Papers

Dunne, P, '"Recognizing Identities, Denying Families": Conditions for the Legal Recognition of Gender Identity in Europe' in Carlo Casonato and Alexander Schuster (eds), *Rights on the Move: Rainbow Families in Europe* (Conference Proceedings, Trento, October 2014) 295–309

Śledzińska-Simon, A, 'Transgender Rights on the Move: Towards Recognition and Gender-Neutral Definition of Parenthood' in Carlo Casonato and Alexander Schuster (eds), *Rights on the Move: Rainbow Families in Europe* (Conference Proceedings, Trento, October 2014) 311–26.

Non-Governmental Organisations' Reports and Press Releases

International Lesbian, Gay, Bisexual, Trans and Intersex Association (ILGA), *State-Sponsored Homophobia: A World Survey of Sexual Orientation Laws: Criminalisation, Protection and Recognition*, 12th edn (May 2017)

INDEX

Note: Alphabetical arrangement is word-by-word, where a group of letters followed by a space is filed before the same group of letters followed by a letter, eg 'sexual taboos' will appear before 'sexuality'. In determining alphabetical arrangement, initial articles and prepositions are ignored. Page numbers followed by the letter 'n' refer to footnotes on the quoted pages.

www.ingramcontent.com/pod-product-compliance
Ingram Content Group UK Ltd.
Pitfield, Milton Keynes, MK11 3LW, UK
UKHW020807290926
15470UKWH00003B/1009

9 781509 914937